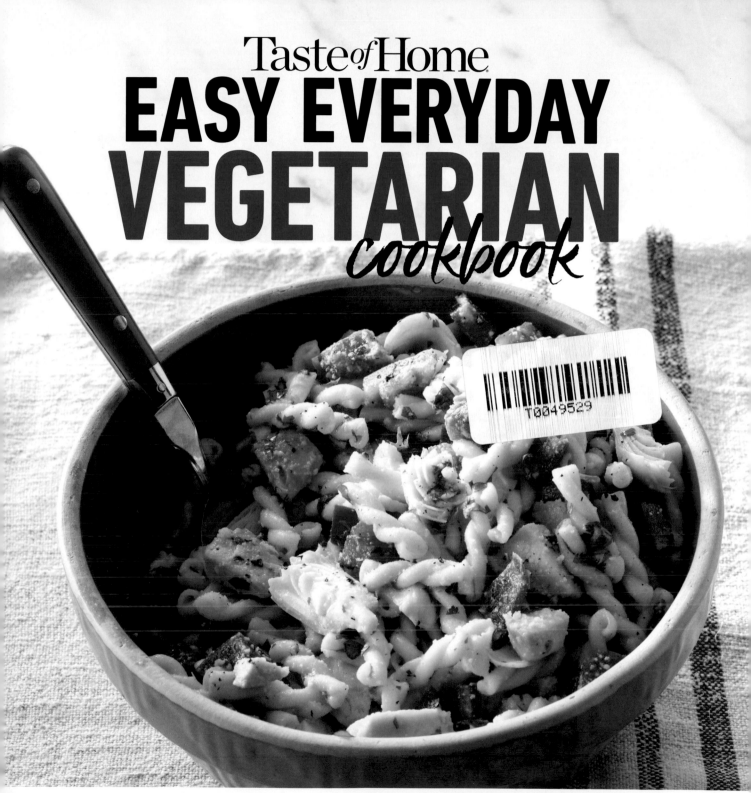

Taste of Home
EASY EVERYDAY
VEGETARIAN
cookbook

T0049529

TASTE OF HOME BOOKS • RDA ENTHUSIAST BRANDS, LLC • MILWAUKEE, WI

© 2023 RDA Enthusiast Brands, LLC.
1610 N. 2nd St., Suite 102,
Milwaukee WI 53212-3906

Visit us at tasteofhome.com for other *Taste of Home* books and products.

International Standard Book Number:
978-1-62145-980-4

Content Director: Mark Hagen
Creative Director: Raeann Thompson
Senior Editor: Christine Rukavena
Editors: Amy Glander, Hazel Wheaton
Senior Art Director: Courtney Lovetere
Art Director: Maggie Conners
Assistant Art Director: Jazmin Delgado
Designer: Sierra Schuler
Deputy Editor, Copy Desk: Dulcie Shoener
Copy Editor: Rayan Naqash

Cover Photography:
Photographer: Mark Derse
Set Stylist: Emiko Franzen
Food Stylist: Shannon Norris

Pictured on front cover:
Loaded Mexican Pizza, p. 76

Pictured on title page:
Avocado & Artichoke Pasta Salad, p. 155

Pictured on flap: Homemade Manicotti, p. 68

Printed in China
1 3 5 7 9 10 8 6 4 2

P. 94

P. 92

P. 281

P. 64

P. 205

CONTENTS

Must-Try Main Dishes 8

Pizza & Pasta Favorites.................... 46

Burgers, Sandwiches & Wraps 78

Grain Dishes & Bowls 102

Heartwarming Soups 124

Sides & Salads 152

Brunch Time 186

Small Bites & Snacks 222

Room for Dessert 256

Bonus: Vegan 292

Index 316

Meat Lover Chart 320

AT-A-GLANCE ICONS

Icons throughout the book indicate
freezer-friendly, five-ingredient,
quick-to-fix, slow-cooker,
pressure-cooker and air-fryer fare.

MORE WAYS TO CONNECT WITH US:

P. 297

WHY GO MEATLESS?

There are many reasons to choose a vegetarian (or sometimes-vegetarian) lifestyle. Here are a few of the more popular intentions.

Health: A plant-based diet is rich in antioxidants, high in fiber and low in cholesterol. Many people choose vegetarian food to reduce cholesterol and lower blood pressure; to help prevent cancers such as that of the colon, breast, stomach, esophagus, lungs and prostate; and also to help control diabetes.

Weight Loss: A well-balanced vegetarian diet can aid weight loss. However, a vegetarian diet high in calories from nuts, full-fat dairy and junk food may result in weight gain.

Budget: Meat and poultry can be a bit pricey—forgoing them for more economical staples, such as dried legumes and grains, can lower your grocery bills.

Respect for Life: Many vegans feel that all living beings have value, and oppose using animals to serve any human need—whether it's for food, clothing, everyday goods, or scientific or product testing.

Environmental Concerns: Many people refrain from consuming meat to help the environment. They believe humans should eat grains or crops rather than using farmland to grow a vast quantity of grain or grass to produce a smaller overall volume of animal protein. Animals raised for food use resources and create waste. A vegetarian diet helps reduce a person's carbon footprint.

Religious Beliefs: Dietary guidelines of various religions restrict the consumption of some or all meat.

Types of Vegetarian Diets

While all vegetarians exclude meat, some also eliminate other animal products from their diets. Here are some common guidelines.

Vegetarian
A broad term for a diet that does not include meat or fish; may or may not include other animal products, such as eggs or dairy

Lacto-Ovo Vegetarian
Meatless diet that includes dairy products and eggs

Vegan
No meat, fish, dairy or eggs; no products made by animals (such as honey)

Pescatarian
May include fish but no other type of meat

Flexitarian
A mostly vegetarian diet that occasionally includes meat or fish, with an emphasis on fresh, nutrient-dense foods

Easy Everyday Vegetarian Cookbook is appropriate for many vegetarian lifestyles. While some recipes include dairy products, eggs or honey, many do not. Further, none of the recipes in this book include gelatin, Worcestershire sauce or other ingredients made with meat products.

EASY WAYS TO EAT MEATLESS MORE OFTEN

Changing your diet overnight is an unrealistic goal; however, taking small, positive steps toward a healthier, more balanced diet is quite achievable. If you want to include more plants in your diet, here are some tips:

Swap meat-based protein for plant-based meals like those found in this book. Try going meatless on Monday to start with, and work your way from there.

Sneak in more vegetables—shoot for three types of veggies at each meal. Aim to fill at least half of your plate with vegetables.

Try a delicious new plant-based recipe every week. Get the family involved in choosing what to try for dinner success.

Enjoy a veggie-rich breakfast. This could mean greens in your smoothie, a glass of tomato juice with your toast or raiding the produce drawer to make an omelet.

Add a leafy side salad to your meals. Plan for it when grocery shopping.

Remember, it's all about making small, long-term and sustainable changes. That means lifestyle choices you feel good about, so they're easy to live with!

P. 231

MEAT LOVER OPTION PAGE 320

For some, it's just not a meal without meat. This icon highlights recipes that are easy to customize by adding a cooked protein, such as beef or poultry.

Prep one recipe and satisfy everyone with the Meat Lover Option. (See chart on p. 320 for dozens of choices.)

IMPORTANT NUTRIENTS

Be sure your meatless diet doesn't skimp on these essentials

Protein is essential for the proper growth and maintenance of body tissue. Eating a variety of foods each day—such as whole grains, legumes, soy products, seeds and vegetables—will help ensure adequate intake of essential and nonessential amino acids. So long as you eat a varied diet throughout the day, it is not necessary to eat the complementary proteins in the same meal.

Calcium is needed for building strong bones and teeth. If your diet does not include dairy, look to other sources of calcium, such as broccoli; dark green leafy vegetables like kale, collard and turnip greens; calcium-fortified soy-based products like tofu, milk and yogurt; and calcium-fortified cereal.

Vitamin D helps absorb calcium. Egg yolks and vitamin D-fortified milk are some of the best sources. If your diet excludes milk, consider vitamin D-fortified soy milk, orange juice or yogurt. If you think you need a supplement, be sure to check with your physician.

Omega-3 fatty acids are key to cardiovascular health, brain function and vision. Fish and eggs are good sources. If your diet excludes them, consult with your physician about taking a supplement.

Vitamin B-12 is crucial for red blood cells and nerve function. It is found in animal protein. If your diet does not include dairy products or eggs, look for foods fortified with B-12, such as cereals and soy-based products. Ask your physician about taking a supplement.

Iron helps form hemoglobin, which carries oxygen in the blood. Iron comes from both animal and plant foods, but the iron in plant foods is more difficult for the body to absorb. Vitamin C-rich foods like citrus fruits help with iron absorption and should be eaten in combination with iron-rich foods, such as dark green leafy vegetables, blackstrap molasses, prune juice and dried fruits.

Zinc is an essential trace mineral. It has many functions in the body, such as repairing and building immune cells. It aids digestion, and is used to make insulin to regulate blood sugar. Zinc comes from both animal and plant foods, but it is more difficult for the body to absorb zinc from plants. Like iron, zinc is best absorbed when eaten with vitamin C-rich foods like citrus. Foods that are rich in zinc include soy products, whole grains, legumes and nuts.

Getting Enough Protein on a Vegetarian Diet

A good rule of thumb for calculating your daily protein need is to multiply your body weight in pounds by 0.4 grams. For example, a 150-pound person needs about 60 grams of protein daily. Here are some popular meatless sources of protein.

PROTEIN SOURCE	GRAMS OF PROTEIN
1 cup cooked black beans	15g
1 cup cooked chickpeas	12g
1 cup cooked lentils	18g
1 cup cooked quinoa	8g
4 oz. tofu	10g
1 large egg	7g
1 cup cottage cheese	24g
1 cup flavored Greek yogurt	18g
1 cup dairy milk	8g
1 cup plain soy milk	7g
1 oz. cheddar cheese	7g
1 oz. almonds	6g
2 Tbsp. peanut butter	7g

FAVORITE WAYS TO CREATE SATISFYING VEGETARIAN DISHES

1 Go Meaty with Mushrooms. With their rich taste and meaty texture, mushrooms make vegetarian meals that are wonderfully satisfying.

AIR-FRYER PORTOBELLO MELTS, P. 81

Portobello caps make terrific vegetarian "burgers." The stems are tough and woody, though. Discard them, or use well-rinsed and coarsely chopped stems in homemade vegetable broth.

2 Get to Know Tofu. Also called soybean curd or bean curd, tofu is made from soy milk the same way cheese is made from dairy milk. Soy milk is mixed with calcium or magnesium salt to create curds. The more liquid (whey) is pressed from the curd, the firmer the tofu will be.

GREEK TOFU SCRAMBLE, P. 196

Because tofu has a pretty neutral taste, it acts as a blank flavor canvas, absorbing flavors of the surrounding ingredients. It's a natural in veggie-rich stir-fries and soups, as well as a wonderful way to add satisfying protein and fiber to breakfast smoothies.

3 Reach for Lentils & Other Legumes. Billions of people around the world rely on legumes for protein in their diets. Lentils and beans are a major food source throughout the Americas, Caribbean, Mediterranean and parts of Asia.

CURRY POMEGRANATE PROTEIN BOWL, P. 16

Lentils use few resources to grow and, calorie for calorie, produce only 2.5% as much greenhouse gas carbon dioxide as beef and 10% as much carbon dioxide as tofu. That makes lentils one of the greenest crops there is—especially when you factor in their high protein content.

4 Add an Egg. Eggs are a protein powerhouse. If your diet includes eggs, try adding one to breakfast potatoes, ramen soup, pad thai or even a vegetarian burger.

KIMCHI FRIED RICE, P.104

5 Use Smoky Spices. Ground chipotle pepper and smoked paprika add complexity to dishes. They lend sweetness, heat and smoky notes, letting you enjoy a bacony taste without the unwanted calories, fat or meat.

SMOKY VEGAN BACON, P. 306

Popular Legumes for Meatless Meals

Stock your pantry with these go-to beans and lentils in canned or dried forms. They're affordable, healthy and convenient for making hearty vegetarian dinners.

 ◀ BLACK BEANS Small and black; widely available and a staple in many Latin American dishes

 CANNELLINI BEANS ▶ Large, white Italian kidney beans; used most often in salads and soups

 ◀ CHICKPEAS Also known as garbanzo beans; medium-size, tan and acorn-shaped. Featured in Middle Eastern and Mediterranean dishes

GREAT NORTHERN BEANS ▶ Large, kidney-shaped and mild; best in stews, dips and classic French cassoulets

 ◀ KIDNEY BEANS Large, light or dark pink or red; used most often with rice and in chilis, stews and soups

 GREEN OR BROWN LENTILS ▶ Small and round; does not need soaking. Green lentils taste slightly peppery; use in salads or as a side dish. Brown lentils have an earthy flavor; fabulous in soup

 ◀ RED OR YELLOW LENTILS Small, split legume; no soaking needed. Common in Indian, Mediterranean and Middle Eastern cuisines. Soft texture; use in soups and stews

CHICKPEA & CHIPOTLE
TOSTADAS
P. 19

Must-Try Main Dishes

Whether you enjoy an occasional meatless meal or follow a vegetarian diet, you'll agree that these enticing dinners are anything but boring. From entrees featuring bold global flavors to meat-free takes on down-home classics, there's something for everyone.

AIR-FRYER SPINACH FETA TURNOVERS

These quick and easy turnovers are one of my wife's favorite entrees. The refrigerated pizza dough makes preparation a snap!
—*David Baruch, Weston, FL*

Takes: 30 min. • **Makes:** 4 servings

- 2 large eggs
- 1 pkg. (10 oz.) frozen spinach, thawed, squeezed dry and chopped
- ¾ cup crumbled feta cheese
- 2 garlic cloves, minced
- ¼ tsp. pepper
- 1 tube (13.8 oz.) refrigerated pizza crust
  Refrigerated tzatziki sauce, optional

1. Preheat air fryer to 425°. In a bowl, whisk eggs; set aside 1 Tbsp. eggs. Combine spinach, feta cheese, garlic, pepper and the remaining beaten eggs.
2. Unroll pizza crust; roll into a 12-in. square. Cut into four 6-in. squares. Top each square with about ⅓ cup spinach mixture. Fold into triangles and pinch the edges to seal. Cut slits in top; brush with 1 Tbsp. egg.
3. In batches if necessary, place triangles in a single layer on greased tray in the air-fryer basket. Cook until golden brown, 10-12 minutes. If desired, serve with tzatziki sauce.
1 TURNOVER: 361 cal., 9g fat (4g sat. fat), 104mg chol., 936mg sod., 51g carb. (7g sugars, 4g fiber), 17g pro.

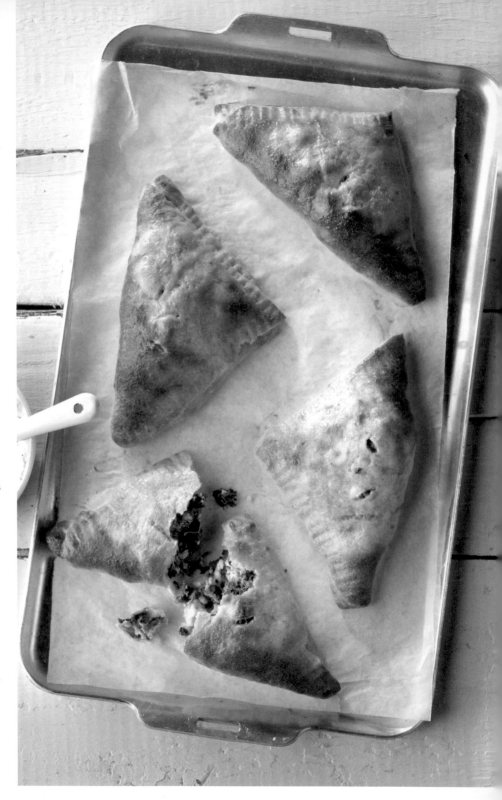

SOUTHWEST TORTILLA PIE

I found the recipe for this entree some time ago but decreased the cheese and increased the herbs. It's one of my toddler's favorite meals. She always smiles when she sees it on the table.

—*Wendy Kelly, Petersburg, NY*

Prep: 50 min. • **Bake:** 15 min.
Makes: 6 servings

1 Tbsp. olive oil
1 medium green pepper, chopped
1 medium onion, chopped
1 tsp. ground cumin
¼ tsp. pepper
3 garlic cloves, minced
2 cans (15 oz. each) black beans, rinsed and drained
1 can (14½ oz.) vegetable broth
1 pkg. (10 oz.) frozen corn, thawed
4 green onions, sliced
4 flour tortillas (8 in.)
1 cup shredded reduced-fat cheddar cheese, divided

1. Preheat oven to 400°. In a large skillet, heat oil over medium-high heat. Add green pepper, onion, cumin and pepper; cook and stir until vegetables are tender. Add garlic; cook 1 minute longer.

2. Stir in the beans and broth. Bring to a boil; cook until the liquid is reduced to about ⅓ cup, stirring occasionally. Stir in the corn and green onions; remove from the heat.

3. Place 1 tortilla in a 9-in. springform pan coated with cooking spray. Layer with 1½ cups bean mixture and ¼ cup cheese. Repeat layers twice. Top with the remaining tortilla. Place the pan on a baking sheet.

4. Bake, uncovered, for 15-20 minutes or until heated through. Sprinkle with remaining cheese. Loosen side from pan with a knife; remove rim from pan. Cut pie into 6 wedges.

1 WEDGE: 353 cal., 9g fat (3g sat. fat), 14mg chol., 842mg sod., 53g carb. (6g sugars, 8g fiber), 17g pro.

⏱ MOZZARELLA MUSHROOMS WITH GARLIC TOAST

I came up with this using ingredients I had on hand. It turned out so good, my wife and I now make it often.
—*Marc Bushee, Moorhead, MN*

- -

Takes: 30 min. • **Makes:** 6 servings

- 2   Tbsp. butter, softened
- 1   Tbsp. minced fresh basil
- 1   garlic clove, minced
- 1   French bread baguette (10½ oz.)

MUSHROOMS

- 2   Tbsp. butter, softened
- 1   lb. sliced baby portobello mushrooms
- 2   garlic cloves, minced
- 1   pkg. (3 oz.) julienned soft sun-dried tomatoes (not packed in oil)
- ¼   cup dry red wine
- 3   Tbsp. chopped fresh basil, divided
- ¼   tsp. salt
- ⅛   tsp. pepper
- 8   oz. fresh mozzarella cheese, thinly sliced

1. Preheat broiler. Mix butter, basil and garlic. Cut baguette horizontally in half; spread with butter mixture. Cut each half into 6 portions; place on a baking sheet, cut side up.

2. In a broiler-safe skillet, heat 2 Tbsp. butter over medium heat; saute the mushrooms until tender, 5-7 minutes. Add garlic; cook 1 minute. Stir in the tomatoes, wine, 2 Tbsp. basil, salt and pepper; cook, uncovered, 3 minutes, stirring occasionally. Remove from heat; top with cheese. Broil 4-5 in. from heat until cheese is melted, 2-3 minutes. Sprinkle with the remaining basil.

3. Broil baguette portions until lightly toasted. Serve with mushrooms.

2 PIECES: 366 cal., 16g fat (10g sat. fat), 50mg chol., 562mg sod., 39g carb. (9g sugars, 5g fiber), 13g pro.

PINTO BEAN ZUCCHINI BOATS

Zucchini shells take center stage when filled with vegetables, beans and sauce.
—Taste of Home *Test Kitchen*

Takes: 30 min. • **Makes:** 4 servings

- 4 large zucchini
- 8 cups water
- 1 tsp. salt
- ½ cup chopped red onion
- 1 Tbsp. olive oil
- 1 can (15 oz.) pinto beans, rinsed and drained
- 1 can (11 oz.) Mexicorn, drained
- 1 can (8 oz.) tomato sauce
- ½ cup chili sauce
- 1 tsp. dried cilantro flakes
- ½ tsp. ground cumin
- 3 oz. Gouda cheese, shredded
- ½ cup chopped tomato

1. Cut zucchini in half lengthwise. Scoop out the pulp, leaving a ⅜-in. shell. Chop the pulp and set aside. In a Dutch oven, bring water and salt to a boil. Add the zucchini shells; cook until crisp-tender, 5-8 minutes. Drain and set aside.
2. In a large skillet, saute the onion and zucchini pulp in oil until crisp-tender. Stir in the beans, corn, tomato sauce, chili sauce, cilantro and cumin. Cook over medium heat until heated through, about 5 minutes. Sprinkle with cheese; cover and cook until cheese is melted, about 1 minute. Spoon into the zucchini shells; sprinkle with tomato.
2 ZUCCHINI HALVES: 377 cal., 11g fat (4g sat. fat), 24mg chol., 1310mg sod., 55g carb. (22g sugars, 9g fiber), 17g pro.

MEAT
LOVER
OPTION
PAGE 320

ONE-POT BLACK BEAN ENCHILADA PASTA

I love this cozy pasta because it is ready in 30 minutes and is full of healthy ingredients—it has everything a busy weeknight meal calls for.
—*Nora Rushev, Reitnau, Switzerland*

- -

Takes: 30 min. • **Makes:** 6 servings

- 4 cups uncooked mini penne or other small pasta
- 4 cups vegetable broth or water
- 1 can (15 oz.) black beans, rinsed and drained
- 1 can (14½ oz.) diced tomatoes, undrained
- 1 medium sweet yellow pepper, chopped
- 1 medium sweet red pepper, chopped
- 1 cup fresh or frozen corn, thawed
- 1 can (10 oz.) enchilada sauce
- 2 Tbsp. taco seasoning
- ½ cup shredded cheddar cheese
  Optional: Fresh cilantro leaves, cherry tomatoes and lime wedges

In a Dutch oven or large skillet, combine the first 9 ingredients. Bring to a boil; reduce heat. Simmer, uncovered, until the pasta is al dente and the sauce has thickened slightly, 12-15 minutes. Add the cheese; stir until melted. Serve with desired toppings.

1¾ CUPS: 444 cal., 5g fat (2g sat. fat), 9mg chol., 1289mg sod., 84g carb. (8g sugars, 8g fiber), 18g pro.

TEST KITCHEN TIP

The best way to test if pasta is al dente is to take a bite about 2 minutes before the cooking time expires. If it's tender enough to chew but still contains a bit of a bite, you've reached al dente. If it's too firm for your liking, continue cooking the pasta until it reaches your preferred level of doneness.

LEMONY CHICKPEAS

These saucy chickpeas add a little heat to a meatless meal. They're especially good over hot brown rice.
—*April Strevell, Red Bank, NJ*

- -

Takes: 30 min. • **Makes:** 4 servings

- 2 cups uncooked instant brown rice
- 1 Tbsp. olive oil
- 1 medium onion, chopped
- 2 cans (15 oz. each) chickpeas, rinsed and drained
- 1 can (14 oz.) diced tomatoes, undrained
- 1 cup vegetable broth
- ¼ tsp. crushed red pepper flakes
- ¼ tsp. pepper
- ½ tsp. grated lemon zest
- 3 Tbsp. lemon juice

1. Cook the rice according to package directions. Meanwhile, in a large skillet, heat oil over medium heat. Add onion; cook and stir 3-4 minutes or until tender.
2. Stir in chickpeas, tomatoes, broth, pepper flakes and pepper; bring to a boil. Reduce the heat; simmer, covered, 10 minutes to allow the flavors to blend. Uncover; simmer 4-5 minutes or until the liquid is slightly reduced, stirring occasionally. Stir in lemon zest and lemon juice. Serve with rice.

FREEZE OPTION: Do not prepare rice until later. Freeze cooled chickpea mixture in freezer containers. To use, partially thaw in refrigerator overnight. Heat through, stirring occasionally; add a little broth if necessary. Serve with rice.

1 CUP CHICKPEA MIXTURE WITH 1 CUP RICE: 433 cal., 9g fat (0 sat. fat), 0 chol., 679mg sod., 76g carb. (10g sugars, 12g fiber), 13g pro.

🕐 PORTOBELLO POLENTA STACKS

My friends and I recently started growing portobello mushrooms from kits we found at a farmers market. We love to try new recipes, like this one, with our harvest. These taste delicious grilled too.
—*Breanne Heath, Chicago, IL*

- -

Takes: 30 min. • **Makes:** 4 servings

- 1 Tbsp. olive oil
- 3 garlic cloves, minced
- 2 Tbsp. balsamic vinegar
- 4 large portobello mushrooms (about 5 in.), stems removed
- ¼ tsp. salt
- ¼ tsp. pepper
- 1 tube (18 oz.) polenta, cut into 12 slices
- 4 slices tomato
- ½ cup grated Parmesan cheese
- 2 Tbsp. minced fresh basil

1. Preheat oven to 400°. In a small saucepan, heat oil over medium heat. Add garlic; cook and stir until tender, 1-2 minutes (do not allow to brown). Stir in vinegar; remove from heat.

2. Place mushrooms in a 13x9-in. baking dish, gill side up. Brush with vinegar mixture; sprinkle with salt and pepper. Top with polenta and tomato slices; sprinkle with cheese.

3. Bake, uncovered, until the mushrooms are tender, 20-25 minutes. Sprinkle with minced basil.

1 SERVING: 219 cal., 6g fat (2g sat. fat), 9mg chol., 764mg sod., 32g carb. (7g sugars, 3g fiber), 7g pro. **DIABETIC EXCHANGES:** 1½ starch, 1 vegetable, 1 lean meat, 1 fat.

CURRY POMEGRANATE PROTEIN BOWL

This simple and beautiful recipe blends together a lot of unique flavors to create a taste sensation that is out of this world. You can substitute other roasted, salted nuts for the soy nuts, and use warmed berry jam in place of the molasses.
—*Mary Baker, Wauwatosa, WI*

- -

Prep: 25 min. • **Cook:** 25 min.
Makes: 6 servings

- 3 cups cubed peeled butternut squash (½-in. cubes)
- 2 Tbsp. olive oil, divided
- ½ tsp. salt, divided
- ¼ tsp. pepper
- ½ small onion, chopped
- 1 Tbsp. curry powder
- 1 Tbsp. ground cumin
- 1 garlic clove, minced
- 1 tsp. ground coriander
- 3 cups water
- 1 cup dried red lentils, rinsed
- ½ cup salted soy nuts
- ½ cup dried cranberries
- ⅓ cup thinly sliced green onions
- ⅓ cup pomegranate molasses
- ½ cup crumbled feta cheese
- ½ cup pomegranate seeds
- ¼ cup chopped fresh cilantro

1. Preheat oven to 375°. Place squash on a greased 15x10x1-in. baking pan. Drizzle with 1 Tbsp. oil; sprinkle with ¼ tsp. salt and pepper. Roast for 25-30 minutes or until tender, turning once.

2. Meanwhile, in a skillet, heat the remaining 1 Tbsp. oil over medium-high heat. Add onion; cook and stir until crisp-tender, 4-6 minutes. Add curry powder, cumin, garlic, coriander and remaining ¼ tsp. salt; cook 1 minute longer. Add water and lentils; bring to a boil. Reduce heat; simmer, covered, until the lentils are tender and water is absorbed, about 15 minutes.

3. Gently stir in soy nuts, cranberries, green onions and roasted squash. Divide among serving bowls. Drizzle with molasses and top with feta, pomegranate seeds and cilantro.

¾ CUP: 367 cal., 9g fat (2g sat. fat), 5mg chol., 327mg sod., 60g carb. (23g sugars, 9g fiber), 14g pro.

BUTTERNUT BURRITO BOWL

Here's an easy-to-make dinner that combines fresh ingredients with wholesome convenience foods. The bowls come together in minutes and each one can be customized with everyone's favorite toppings.
—Patricia Kukuc, Clearwater, FL

- -

Takes: 30 min. • **Makes:** 4 servings

1   pkg. (10 oz.) frozen riced butternut squash
1   tsp. olive oil
1   cup frozen corn, thawed
1   can (15 oz.) black beans, rinsed and drained
⅓   cup water
½   tsp. chili powder
¼   tsp. ground cumin
¼   tsp. ground turmeric, optional
1   cup grape tomatoes, thinly sliced
1   medium ripe avocado, peeled and thinly sliced
2   green onions, thinly sliced
    Optional: Salsa, sour cream and shredded Colby-Monterey Jack cheese

1. Prepare squash according to package directions. Meanwhile, in a small skillet, heat oil over medium-high heat. Add corn; cook and stir until lightly browned, about 5 minutes. In a small saucepan, combine beans, water, chili powder, cumin and, if desired, turmeric. Cook and stir over medium heat until mixture is heated through and liquid is almost evaporated, about 5 minutes.
2. Divide the squash among 4 serving bowls. Top with the bean mixture, corn, tomatoes, avocado, green onions and toppings of your choice.
1 SERVING: 230 cal., 7g fat (1g sat. fat), 0 chol., 218mg sod., 34g carb. (6g sugars, 9g fiber), 8g pro. **DIABETIC EXCHANGES:** 2 starch, 1½ fat, 1 lean meat.

CHICKPEA & CHIPOTLE TOSTADAS

My young twins love colorful meals they can eat with their hands. In this meatless dish, they eat the chickpeas first and save the tostada for the end.
—Amber Massey, Argyle, TX

- -

Prep: 20 min. • **Cook:** 25 min.
Makes: 6 servings

¾   cup fat-free sour cream
½   cup salsa verde
1   medium sweet red pepper, chopped
1   medium onion, chopped
2   garlic cloves, minced
1   cup vegetable broth
2   cans (15 oz. each) chickpeas or garbanzo beans, rinsed and drained
2   chipotle peppers in adobo sauce, minced
1   tsp. ground cumin
½   tsp. salt
½   cup minced fresh cilantro
2   Tbsp. lime juice
12 corn tortillas (6 in.)
    Cooking spray
½   medium head iceberg lettuce, shredded
3   plum tomatoes, chopped
1   medium ripe avocado, peeled and cubed
    Shredded reduced-fat cheddar cheese

1. Preheat broiler. For sauce, mix sour cream and salsa.
2. In a large skillet coated with cooking spray, cook and stir red pepper and onion over medium heat until tender, 6-8 minutes. Add garlic; cook and stir 1 minute. Stir in the broth, chickpeas, chipotles, cumin and salt; bring to a boil. Reduce heat; simmer, covered, 5 minutes.
3. Coarsely mash mixture with a potato masher; stir in cilantro and lime juice. If desired, cook over low heat to thicken, stirring frequently.

4. In batches, spritz both sides of tortillas with cooking spray and place on a baking sheet; broil 4-5 in. from heat until crisp and lightly browned, about 1 minute per side. To serve, top tortillas with chickpea mixture, lettuce, tomatoes, avocado and sauce. Sprinkle with cheese.
NOTE: Often found canned in chili sauce in the United States, chipotles are smoked and dried jalapeno peppers that are medium to hot in heat levels and are used in a variety of Mexican and American dishes that require a hot, spicy flavor.
2 TOSTADAS: 347 cal., 9g fat (1g sat. fat), 5mg chol., 752mg sod., 59g carb. (11g sugars, 12g fiber), 12g pro.

READER RAVE

"This was a terrific healthy and family-friendly dinner recipe. My family enjoyed being able to pick their favorite toppings. I liked the tostadas with a bit of everything on them, but it was wonderful that it was easy to adapt for picky eaters."
—CURLYLIS85, TASTEOFHOME.COM

STIR-FRY RICE BOWL

My meatless version of Korean bibimbap is tasty, pretty and easy to tweak for different spice levels.
—*Devon Delaney, Westport, CT*

- -

Takes: 30 min. • **Makes:** 4 servings

- 1 Tbsp. canola oil
- 2 medium carrots, julienned
- 1 medium zucchini, julienned
- ½ cup sliced baby portobello mushrooms
- 1 cup bean sprouts
- 1 cup fresh baby spinach
- 1 Tbsp. water
- 1 Tbsp. reduced-sodium soy sauce
- 1 Tbsp. chili garlic sauce
- 4 large eggs
- 3 cups hot cooked brown rice
- 1 tsp. sesame oil

1. In a large skillet, heat the canola oil over medium-high heat. Add the carrots, zucchini and mushrooms; cook and stir for 3-5 minutes or until the carrots are crisp-tender. Add bean sprouts, spinach, water, soy sauce and chili sauce; cook and stir just until the spinach is wilted. Remove from heat; keep warm.
2. Place 2-3 in. water in a large skillet with a high side. Bring to a boil; adjust heat to maintain a gentle simmer. Break cold eggs, 1 at a time, into a small bowl; holding the bowl close to the surface of water, slip the egg into water.
3. Cook, uncovered, 3-5 minutes or until the egg whites are completely set and the yolks begin to thicken but are not hard. Using a slotted spoon, lift the eggs out of water.
4. Serve rice in bowls; top with vegetables. Drizzle with sesame oil. Top each serving with a poached egg.
1 SERVING: 305 cal., 11g fat (2g sat. fat), 186mg chol., 364mg sod., 40g carb. (4g sugars, 4g fiber), 12g pro. **DIABETIC EXCHANGES:** 2 starch,1 vegetable, 1 medium-fat meat, 1 fat.

VEGETARIAN POTATOES AU GRATIN

Fill up on veggies and load up on rich flavor with this creamy, hearty entree. You'll appreciate the homey breadcrumb topping and hands-free bake time at the end of a long day.
—Taste of Home *Test Kitchen*

Prep: 15 min. • **Bake:** 50 min. + standing
Makes: 6 servings

- 3 medium carrots, thinly sliced
- 1 medium green pepper, chopped
- 4 Tbsp. butter, divided
- 3 Tbsp. all-purpose flour
- 1 tsp. dried oregano
- ½ tsp. salt
- 2½ cups 2% milk
- 1 can (15 oz.) black beans, rinsed and drained
- 3 cups shredded Swiss cheese, divided
- 4 medium Yukon Gold potatoes, thinly sliced
- ½ cup seasoned bread crumbs

1. Preheat the oven to 400°. In a large saucepan, saute carrots and pepper in 3 Tbsp. butter until tender. Stir in flour, oregano and salt until blended; gradually add milk. Bring to a boil; cook and stir 2 minutes or until thickened. Stir in the beans and 2 cups cheese until cheese is melted.
2. Layer half the potatoes and sauce in a greased 13x9-in. baking dish; repeat layers. Sprinkle with remaining cheese. In a microwave, melt remaining butter. Stir in bread crumbs. Sprinkle over top.
3. Cover and bake 50-55 minutes. Let stand 10 minutes before serving.
1 SERVING: 557 cal., 25g fat (16g sat. fat), 77mg chol., 749mg sod., 56g carb. (12g sugars, 7g fiber), 27g pro.

MEAT LOVER OPTION PAGE 320

EASY MOROCCAN CHICKPEA STEW

When I'm invited to a potluck, I easily double or triple this healthy vegetarian recipe to treat the crowd to an exotic dish of enticing, bold flavors.
—*Heather Demeritte, Scottsdale, AZ*

Takes: 30 min. • **Makes:** 4 servings

- 1 Tbsp. olive oil
- 2 cups cubed peeled butternut squash (½-in. cubes)
- 1 large onion, chopped
- 1 large sweet red pepper, chopped
- 1 tsp. ground cinnamon
- ½ tsp. pepper
- ¼ tsp. ground ginger
- ¼ tsp. ground cumin
- ¼ tsp. salt
- 1 can (15 oz.) chickpeas or garbanzo beans, rinsed and drained
- 1 can (14½ oz.) diced tomatoes, undrained
- 1 cup water
  Chopped cilantro, optional

1. In a Dutch oven, heat the oil over medium-high heat. Add squash, onion and red pepper; cook and stir until the onion is translucent and red pepper is crisp-tender, about 5 minutes. Stir in seasonings until blended.
2. Add chickpeas, tomatoes and water; bring to a boil. Reduce heat; cover and simmer until squash is tender, about 8 minutes. If desired, top with cilantro.
1½ CUPS: 217 cal., 6g fat (1g sat. fat), 0 chol., 455mg sod., 38g carb. (11g sugars, 9g fiber), 7g pro.

TEST KITCHEN TIP

When buying butternut squash, select one with a full stem that's firm to the touch. When the stem is intact, the squash will keep longer. If the stem is missing, it may have popped out because the squash is past its prime.

✳ CHEESE ENCHILADAS

You won't bring home leftovers when you take these easy enchiladas to a potluck. With a homemade tomato sauce and cheesy filling, they always go fast. You can substitute any type of cheese that suits your taste.

—*Ashley Schackow, Defiance, OH*

Prep: 25 min. • **Bake:** 25 min.
Makes: 8 servings

- 2 cans (15 oz. each) tomato sauce
- 1⅓ cups water
- 2 Tbsp. chili powder
- 2 garlic cloves, minced
- 1 tsp. dried oregano
- ½ tsp. ground cumin
- 1 cup sour cream
- ¼ cup minced fresh parsley
- ½ tsp. salt
- ½ tsp. pepper
- 4 cups shredded Monterey Jack cheese
- 2½ cups shredded cheddar cheese, divided
- 2 medium onions, finely chopped
- 16 flour tortillas (8 in.), warmed
  Optional toppings: Shredded lettuce, sliced ripe olives, chopped tomatoes and additional sour cream

1. Preheat the oven to 350°. In a large saucepan, combine first 6 ingredients; bring to a boil. Reduce heat and simmer, uncovered, until thickened, 4-5 minutes, stirring occasionally.

2. In a large bowl, mix the sour cream, parsley, salt and pepper; stir in Monterey Jack cheese, 2 cups cheddar and onions. Spread 2 Tbsp. sauce over each tortilla; top with about ⅓ cup cheese mixture and roll up. Place in 2 greased 13x9-in. baking dishes, seam side down. Pour the remaining sauce over the top.

3. Bake, uncovered, 20 minutes. Sprinkle with remaining cheddar cheese. Bake until cheese is melted, 4-5 minutes. Serve with desired toppings.

FREEZE OPTION: Cover and freeze the enchiladas before baking. To use, partially thaw in refrigerator overnight. Remove enchiladas from the refrigerator about 30 minutes before baking. Preheat oven to 350°. Bake as directed, increasing the time as necessary to heat through and for a thermometer inserted in center to read 165°.

2 ENCHILADAS: 778 cal., 42g fat (23g sat. fat), 106mg chol., 1741mg sod., 66g carb. (4g sugars, 6g fiber), 34g pro.

VEGETARIAN SKILLET ENCHILADAS

Whether served for meatless Monday or your family's everyday vegetarian meal, these unconventional enchiladas will satisfy everyone. Garnish with the optional toppings or other favorites like tortilla chips and extra shredded cheese.
—*Susan Court, Pewaukee, WI*

- -

Takes: 25 min. • **Makes:** 4 servings

    1   Tbsp. canola oil
    1   medium onion, chopped
    1   medium sweet red pepper, chopped
    2   garlic cloves, minced
    1   can (15 oz.) black beans,
        rinsed and drained
    1   can (10 oz.) enchilada sauce
    1   cup frozen corn
    2   tsp. chili powder
    ½   tsp. ground cumin
    ⅛   tsp. pepper
    8   corn tortillas (6 in.), cut
        into ½-in. strips
    1   cup shredded Mexican cheese blend
        Optional: Chopped fresh cilantro,
        sliced avocado, sliced radishes,
        sour cream and lime wedges

1. Preheat oven to 400°. Heat oil in a 10 in. cast-iron or other ovenproof skillet over medium-high heat. Add the onion and pepper; cook and stir until tender, 2-3 minutes. Add garlic; cook 1 minute longer. Stir in beans, enchilada sauce, corn, chili powder, cumin and pepper. Stir in tortilla strips.
2. Bring to a boil. Reduce heat; simmer, uncovered, until the tortilla strips are softened, 3-5 minutes. Sprinkle with the cheese. Bake, uncovered, until the sauce is bubbly and cheese is melted, 3-5 minutes. Garnish with optional ingredients as desired.
1½ CUPS: 307 cal., 14g fat (5g sat. fat), 25mg chol., 839mg sod., 33g carb. (5g sugars, 7g fiber), 14g pro.

GARBANZO-VEGETABLE GREEN CURRY

My son loves anything with coconut milk, so I always keep some on hand for weeknight meals like this one. For a milder version, I like to use red or yellow curry paste instead of green.
—*Marie Parker, Milwaukee, WI*

- -

Takes: 20 min. • **Makes:** 6 servings

    3   cups frozen cauliflower
    2   cans (15 oz. each) garbanzo beans
          or chickpeas, rinsed and drained
    1   can (13.66 oz.) coconut milk
    ¼   cup green curry paste
    ½   tsp. salt
    2   tsp. cornstarch
    1   Tbsp. cold water
    1½   cups frozen peas
    2   pkg. (8.8 oz. each) ready-to-serve
          long grain rice
    ½   cup lightly salted cashews

1. In a large skillet, combine cauliflower, beans, coconut milk, curry paste and salt. Bring to a boil; cook, uncovered, 5-6 minutes or until cauliflower is tender.
2. Combine cornstarch and water until smooth; gradually stir into the skillet. Stir in peas. Bring to a boil. Cook and stir for 2 minutes or until thickened.
3. Meanwhile, prepare rice according to package directions. Sprinkle cauliflower mixture with cashews. Serve with rice.
NOTE: Coconut milk is a sweet milky white liquid high in oil derived from the meat of a mature coconut. It is not the naturally occurring liquid found inside a coconut. In the United States, coconut milk is usually purchased in cans and used in both savory and sweet dishes originating from tropical or Asian cuisines.
1 CUP WITH ⅔ CUP RICE: 516 cal., 24g fat (13g sat. fat), 0 chol., 646mg sod., 63g carb. (7g sugars, 10g fiber), 15g pro.

VEGGIE FAJITAS

For scrumptious and super healthy party fare, these colorful, hearty fajitas packed with crisp-tender veggies are perfect.
—*Sarah Mercer, Wichita, KS*

Takes: 25 min. • **Makes:** 8 fajitas

- 1 small zucchini, thinly sliced
- 1 medium yellow summer squash, thinly sliced
- ½ lb. sliced fresh mushrooms
- 1 small onion, halved and sliced
- 1 medium carrot, julienned
- 1 tsp. salt
- ½ tsp. pepper
- 1 Tbsp. canola oil
- 8 flour tortillas (8 in.), warmed
- 2 cups shredded cheddar cheese
- 1 cup sour cream
- 1 cup salsa

In a large cast-iron or other heavy skillet, saute the vegetables with the salt and pepper in oil until crisp-tender, 5-7 minutes. Using a slotted spoon, place about ½ cup vegetable mixture down the center of each tortilla. Sprinkle each with ¼ cup cheese; top with sour cream and salsa. Fold in sides.

1 FAJITA: 375 cal., 21g fat (10g sat. fat), 35mg chol., 853mg sod., 35g carb. (4g sugars, 3g fiber), 13g pro.

TEST KITCHEN TIP

Red, yellow and green bell peppers are among the most common veggies included in fajitas, so they'd make a fabulous addition here too. Black or pinto beans are also excellent choices for added protein.

VEGETARIAN TACOS

I wasn't all that sure about trying a vegetarian recipe, especially with a meat-and-potatoes husband. However, this meal was so tasty that he absolutely raved over it! I've made it over and over, and even my young children enjoy it.
—*Mischelle Jewell, Clermont, FL*

Prep: 20 min. • **Bake:** 20 min.
Makes: 6 servings

- 6 plum tomatoes, seeded and cut into wedges
- 2 medium green peppers, cut into ½-in. slices
- 2 medium onions, cut into ½-in. wedges
- 1 envelope taco seasoning
- 3 Tbsp. olive oil
- 1 can (16 oz.) vegetarian refried beans, warmed
- 12 taco shells, warmed
- 1 cup taco sauce

1. In a large bowl, combine the tomatoes, green peppers, onions, taco seasoning and oil. Arrange mixture in a single layer on two 15x10x1-in. baking pans. Bake, uncovered, at 475° for 20-25 minutes or until lightly browned.
2. Spread the beans over half of each taco shell. Fill with vegetable mixture; drizzle with taco sauce.
2 TACOS: 303 cal., 13g fat (2g sat. fat), 0 chol., 1252mg sod., 42g carb. (9g sugars, 8g fiber), 7g pro.

MEAT
LOVER
OPTION
PAGE 320

CURRIED TOFU WITH RICE

Go meatless and give tofu a try in this bold dish packed with curry and cilantro. You won't even miss the meat!
—*Crystal Jo Bruns, Iliff, CO*

- -

Prep: 15 min. • **Cook:** 20 min.
Makes: 4 servings

- 1 pkg. (12.3 oz.) extra-firm tofu, drained and cubed
- 1 tsp. seasoned salt
- 1 Tbsp. canola oil
- 1 small onion, chopped
- 3 garlic cloves, minced
- ½ cup light coconut milk
- ¼ cup minced fresh cilantro
- 1 tsp. curry powder
- ¼ tsp. salt
- ¼ tsp. pepper
- 2 cups cooked brown rice

1. Sprinkle tofu with seasoned salt. In a large nonstick skillet, saute the tofu in oil until lightly browned. Remove and keep warm.

2. In the same skillet, saute onion and garlic for 1-2 minutes or until crisp-tender. Stir in coconut milk, cilantro, curry, salt and pepper. Bring to a boil. Reduce heat; simmer, uncovered, for 4-5 minutes or until sauce is slightly thickened. Stir in tofu; heat through. Serve with rice.

½ CUP CURRY WITH ½ CUP RICE: 240 cal., 11g fat (3g sat. fat), 0 chol., 540mg sod., 27g carb. (2g sugars, 3g fiber), 10g pro.
DIABETIC EXCHANGES: 1½ starch, 1 medium-fat meat, 1 fat.

 SWEET POTATO LENTIL STEW

Years ago, I first experienced the spicy flavor and wonderful aroma of this hearty dish. You can serve the stew alone or as a topper for meat or poultry.
—*Heather Gray, Little Rock, AR*

- -

Prep: 15 min. • **Cook:** 5 hours
Makes: 6 servings

- 1¼ lbs. sweet potatoes (about 2 medium), peeled and cut into 1-in. pieces
- 1½ cups dried lentils, rinsed
- 3 medium carrots, cut into 1-in. pieces
- 1 medium onion, chopped
- 4 garlic cloves, minced
- ½ tsp. ground cumin
- ¼ tsp. ground ginger
- ¼ tsp. cayenne pepper
- 1 carton (32 oz.) vegetable broth
- ¼ cup minced fresh cilantro

In a 3-qt. slow cooker, combine the first 9 ingredients. Cook, covered, on low for 5-6 hours or until the vegetables and lentils are tender. Stir in cilantro.

1⅓ CUPS: 290 cal., 1g fat (0 sat. fat), 0 chol., 662mg sod., 58g carb. (16g sugars, 15g fiber), 15g pro.

READER RAVE

"Tasty, hearty, warm and just the right amount of spice."
—JMSCOKER, TASTEOFHOME.COM

MEAT LOVER OPTION
PAGE 320

🔢 GREEK SPINACH BAKE

Spanakopita is the Greek name for this traditional dish featuring spinach and feta cheese. You can serve it as a side dish or meatless main dish.
—*Sharon Olney, Galt, CA*

Prep: 10 min. • **Bake:** 1 hour
Makes: 6 servings

- 2 cups 4% cottage cheese
- 1 pkg. (10 oz.) frozen chopped spinach, thawed and squeezed dry
- 8 oz. crumbled feta cheese
- 6 Tbsp. all-purpose flour
- ½ tsp. pepper
- ¼ tsp. salt
- 4 large eggs, lightly beaten

1. Preheat oven to 350°. In a large bowl, combine the cottage cheese, spinach and feta cheese. Stir in the flour, pepper and salt. Add eggs and mix well.
2. Spoon into a greased 9-in. square baking dish. Bake, uncovered, until a thermometer reads 160°, about 1 hour.
1 SERVING: 262 cal., 13g fat (7g sat. fat), 178mg chol., 838mg sod., 14g carb. (4g sugars, 3g fiber), 21g pro.

BLACK BEAN TORTILLA CASSEROLE

My cousin gave me this recipe because she knows my family loves southwestern fare. The layers are easy to assemble too.
—*Sue Briski, Appleton, WI*

Prep: 20 min. • **Bake:** 30 min.
Makes: 9 servings

- 2 large onions, chopped
- 1½ cups chopped green peppers
- 1 can (14½ oz.) diced tomatoes, drained
- ¾ cup picante sauce
- 2 garlic cloves, minced
- 2 tsp. ground cumin
- 2 cans (15 oz. each) black beans, rinsed and drained, divided
- 8 corn tortillas (6 in.)
- 2 cups shredded reduced-fat Mexican cheese blend

TOPPINGS
- 1½ cups shredded lettuce
- 1 cup chopped fresh tomatoes
- ½ cup thinly sliced green onions
- ½ cup sliced ripe olives

1. Preheat the oven to 350°. In a large saucepan, combine the onions, peppers, tomatoes, picante sauce, garlic and cumin. Bring to a boil. Reduce heat; simmer, uncovered, for 10 minutes. Remove ½ cup black beans; set aside. Stir remaining beans into onion mixture.
2. Spread a third of the mixture in a 13x9-in. baking dish coated with cooking spray. Layer with 4 tortillas and ⅔ cup cheese. Repeat layers; top with reserved ½ cup black beans.
3. Cover and bake for 30-35 minutes or until heated through. Sprinkle with the remaining ⅔ cup cheese. Let stand until cheese is melted, about 5 minutes. Serve with toppings.
1 PIECE: 243 cal., 7g fat (3g sat. fat), 13mg chol., 638mg sod., 34g carb. (6g sugars, 8g fiber), 14g pro. **DIABETIC EXCHANGES:** 2 lean meat, 1½ starch, 1 vegetable.

🍲 CHICKPEA & POTATO CURRY

I make *chana masala*, a classic Indian dish, in my slow cooker. Browning the onion, ginger and garlic first is the key to making the curry taste amazing.
—*Anjana Devasahayam, San Antonio, TX*

Prep: 25 min. • **Cook:** 6 hours
Makes: 6 servings

- 1 Tbsp. canola oil
- 1 medium onion, chopped
- 2 garlic cloves, minced
- 2 tsp. minced fresh gingerroot
- 2 tsp. ground coriander
- 1 tsp. garam masala
- 1 tsp. chili powder
- ½ tsp. salt
- ½ tsp. ground cumin
- ¼ tsp. ground turmeric
- 1 can (15 oz.) crushed tomatoes
- 2 cans (15 oz. each) chickpeas or garbanzo beans, rinsed and drained
- 1 large baking potato, peeled and cut into ¾-in. cubes
- 2½ cups vegetable stock
- 1 Tbsp. lime juice
  Chopped fresh cilantro
  Hot cooked rice
  Optional: Sliced red onion and lime wedges

1. In a large skillet, heat the oil over medium-high heat; saute onion until tender, 2-4 minutes. Add garlic, ginger and dry seasonings; cook and stir for 1 minute. Stir in the tomatoes; transfer to a 3- or 4-qt. slow cooker.
2. Stir in chickpeas, potato and stock. Cook, covered, on low until the potato is tender and the flavors are blended, 6-8 hours.
3. Stir in lime juice; sprinkle with cilantro. Serve with rice and, if desired, red onion and lime wedges.

1¼ CUPS CHICKPEA MIXTURE: 240 cal., 6g fat (0 sat. fat), 0 chol., 767mg sod., 42g carb. (8g sugars, 9g fiber), 8g pro.

TEST KITCHEN TIP

Garam masala is a spice blend widely used in Indian cooking to enhance the aroma and flavors of curries and other dishes. In Hindi, *garam* means warm and *masala* means spice blend. This blend originated in northern India, using spices that warm up the body during cold winters. Typically, garam masala is made of roasted coriander seeds, cumin seeds, black cardamom, black peppercorns, cinnamon, green cardamom, cloves, star anise, mace, bay leaves and salt.

EGGPLANT ROLL-UPS

We love these easy Italian eggplant roll-ups stuffed with creamy ricotta and spinach. The fact that they are vegetarian is a bonus!

—*Laura Haugen, Portland, OR*

- -

Prep: 50 min. • **Bake:** 20 min.
Makes: 6 servings

- 2 medium eggplants (about 2½ lbs.), divided
  Cooking spray
- ½ tsp. salt
- 3 cups fresh spinach leaves

SAUCE
- 1 Tbsp. olive oil
- 2 garlic cloves, minced
- 1 can (14½ oz.) diced tomatoes
- 1 can (15 oz.) tomato puree
- 3 Tbsp. minced fresh basil or 3 tsp. dried basil
- 2 tsp. sugar
- 1 tsp. dried oregano
- ¼ tsp. salt
- ¼ tsp. pepper

FILLING
- 1 carton (15 oz.) reduced-fat ricotta cheese
- ¼ cup grated Parmesan cheese
- ½ tsp. dried oregano
- ¼ tsp. pepper
  Dash ground nutmeg

TOPPING
- ¼ cup grated Parmesan cheese
- 3 Tbsp. panko bread crumbs
  Minced fresh parsley, optional

1. Preheat oven to 400°. Cut eggplants lengthwise into eighteen ¼-in.-thick slices; reserve the leftover pieces. Line 2 baking sheets with foil. Coat both sides of eggplant slices with cooking spray; place in a single layer on prepared pans. Sprinkle with ½ tsp. salt. Bake until just pliable (do not let soften completely), 10-12 minutes; cool slightly.

2. Meanwhile, in a large saucepan, bring ½ in. water to a boil. Add spinach; cover and boil 2-3 minutes or until wilted. Drain spinach and squeeze dry. Chop spinach and set aside.

3. For sauce, finely chop leftover eggplant pieces to measure 1 cup (discard remaining or save for another use). In a large saucepan, heat oil over medium heat. Add chopped eggplant; cook and stir until tender. Add garlic; cook 1 minute longer. Stir in tomatoes, tomato puree, basil, sugar, oregano, salt and pepper. Bring to a boil. Reduce heat; simmer, uncovered, 8-10 minutes or until the flavors are blended.

4. Spread 1 cup sauce into a 13x9-in. baking dish coated with cooking spray. In a small bowl, combine filling ingredients and spinach. Place 1 rounded Tbsp. filling on the wide end of each eggplant slice; carefully roll up. Place roll-ups in baking dish over sauce, seam side down. Top with 1½ cups sauce. In a small bowl, mix Parmesan cheese and bread crumbs; sprinkle over top. Bake for 20-25 minutes or until heated through and bubbly. Serve with remaining sauce. If desired, sprinkle with parsley.

3 ROLL-UPS: 257 cal., 10g fat (3g sat. fat), 23mg chol., 652mg sod., 28g carb. (14g sugars, 8g fiber), 12g pro. **DIABETIC EXCHANGES:** 2 starch, 2 medium-fat meat, ½ fat.

CRISPY TOFU WITH BLACK PEPPER SAUCE

Sometimes tofu can be boring and tasteless, but not in this recipe! The crispy vegetarian bean curd is so loaded with flavor, you'll never shy away from tofu again.
—*Nick Iverson, Denver, CO*

Takes: 30 min. • **Makes:** 4 servings

- 2 Tbsp. reduced-sodium soy sauce
- 2 Tbsp. chili garlic sauce
- 1 Tbsp. packed brown sugar
- 1 Tbsp. rice vinegar
- 4 green onions
- 8 oz. extra-firm tofu, drained
- 3 Tbsp. cornstarch
- 6 Tbsp. canola oil, divided
- 8 oz. fresh sugar snap peas (about 2 cups), trimmed and thinly sliced
- 1 tsp. freshly ground pepper
- 3 garlic cloves, minced
- 2 tsp. grated fresh gingerroot

1. Mix the first 4 ingredients. Mince the white parts of green onions; thinly slice the green parts.
2. Cut tofu into ½-in. cubes; pat dry with paper towels. Toss tofu with cornstarch. In a large skillet, heat 4 Tbsp. oil over medium-high heat. Add tofu; cook until crisp and golden brown, 5-7 minutes, stirring occasionally. Remove from pan; drain on paper towels.
3. In same pan, heat 1 Tbsp. oil over medium-high heat. Add peas; stir-fry until crisp-tender, 2-3 minutes. Remove from pan.
4. In same pan, heat the remaining 1 Tbsp. oil over medium-high heat. Add pepper; cook 30 seconds. Add garlic, ginger and minced green onions; stir-fry for 30-45 seconds. Stir in the soy sauce mixture; cook and stir until slightly thickened. Remove from heat; stir in the tofu and peas. Sprinkle with sliced green onions.
1 CUP: 316 cal., 24g fat (2g sat. fat), 0 chol., 583mg sod., 20g carb. (8g sugars, 2g fiber), 7g pro.

COCONUT-GINGER CHICKPEAS & TOMATOES

This is my go-to quick dish. When you add tomatoes, you can also toss in some chopped green peppers to make it even more colorful.
—*Mala Udayamurthy, San Jose, CA*

Takes: 30 min. • **Makes:** 6 servings

- 2 Tbsp. canola oil
- 2 medium onions, chopped (about 1⅓ cups)
- 3 large tomatoes, seeded and chopped (about 2 cups)
- 1 jalapeno pepper, seeded and chopped
- 1 Tbsp. minced fresh gingerroot
- 2 cans (15 oz. each) chickpeas or garbanzo beans, rinsed and drained
- ¼ cup water
- 1 tsp. salt
- 1 cup light coconut milk
- 3 Tbsp. minced fresh cilantro
- 4½ cups hot cooked brown rice Additional minced fresh cilantro, optional

1. In a large skillet, heat oil over medium-high heat. Add onions; cook and stir until crisp-tender. Add tomatoes, jalapeno and ginger; cook and stir 2-3 minutes longer or until tender.
2. Stir in the chickpeas, water and salt; bring to a boil. Reduce heat; simmer, uncovered, 4-5 minutes or until liquid is almost evaporated. Remove from heat; stir in coconut milk and cilantro.
3. Serve with rice; sprinkle with additional cilantro if desired.
NOTE: Wear disposable gloves when cutting hot peppers; the oils can burn skin. Avoid touching your face.
⅔ CUP CHICKPEA MIXTURE WITH ¾ CUP RICE: 402 cal., 12g fat (3g sat. fat), 0 chol., 590mg sod., 65g carb. (10g sugars, 10g fiber), 11g pro.

MEAT LOVER OPTION
PAGE 320

SOUTHERN OKRA BEAN STEW

When this spicy stew's simmering on the stove, my family has a hard time waiting for dinner. It's much like a thick tomato-based soup with a hearty mix of okra, brown rice and beans. Everyone leaves the table feeling satisfied—and eager to have it again soon.
—*Beverly McDowell, Athens, GA*

Takes: 30 min.
Makes: 11 servings (about 4 qt.)

- 4 cups water
- 1 can (28 oz.) diced tomatoes, undrained
- 1½ cups chopped green peppers
- 1 large onion, chopped
- 3 garlic cloves, minced
- 1 tsp. Italian seasoning
- 1 tsp. chili powder
- ½ to 1 tsp. hot pepper sauce
- ½ tsp. salt
- 1 bay leaf
- 4 cups cooked brown rice
- 2 cans (16 oz. each) kidney beans, rinsed and drained
- 3 cans (8 oz. each) tomato sauce
- 1 pkg. (16 oz.) frozen sliced okra

1. In a large Dutch oven, combine the first 10 ingredients. Bring to a boil. Reduce heat; simmer, uncovered, for 5 minutes.
2. Add the rice, beans, tomato sauce and okra. Simmer, uncovered, until the vegetables are tender, 8-10 minutes. Discard bay leaf.
1½ CUPS: 217 cal., 1g fat (0 sat. fat), 0 chol., 661mg sod., 44g carb. (7g sugars, 9g fiber), 10g pro.

MUSHROOM BROCCOLI PIZZA

I wouldn't say I'm a vegetarian, but I do like meatless entrees. I enjoy gardening and often cook with my own homegrown veggies, finding creative ways to use them up, like in this fresh, filling pizza.
—*Kathleen Kelley, Roseburg, OR*

Prep: 30 min. + rising
Bake: 15 min. • **Makes:** 6 servings

- 1   pkg. (¼ oz.) active dry yeast
- ¾ cup warm water (110° to 115°)
- 1   tsp. olive oil
- ½ tsp. sugar
- ½ cup whole wheat flour
- ½ tsp. salt
- 1½ cups all-purpose flour

TOPPINGS
- 1   Tbsp. olive oil
- 1   cup sliced fresh mushrooms
- ¼ cup chopped onion
- 4   garlic cloves, minced
- 3   cups broccoli florets
- 2   Tbsp. water
- ½ cup pizza sauce
- 4   plum tomatoes, sliced
- ¼ cup chopped fresh basil
- 1½ cups shredded part-skim mozzarella cheese
- ⅓ cup shredded Parmesan cheese

1. In a bowl, dissolve the yeast in warm water. Add the oil and sugar; mix well. Combine whole wheat flour and salt; stir into the yeast mixture until smooth. Stir in enough all-purpose flour to form a soft dough.
2. Turn dough onto a floured surface; knead for 6-8 minutes or until smooth and elastic. Place in a bowl coated with cooking spray, turning once to coat top. Cover and let rise in a warm place until doubled, about 1½ hours. Preheat oven to 425°.
3. Punch down dough; press onto a 12-in. pizza pan coated with cooking spray. Prick dough several times with a fork. Bake until edge is light golden brown, 10-12 minutes.

4. In a nonstick skillet, heat the oil over medium-high heat; saute mushrooms, onion and garlic until tender. Place the broccoli and water in a microwave-safe bowl; microwave, covered, on high until broccoli is crisp-tender, about 2 minutes. Drain well.
5. Spread pizza sauce over the crust. Top with the mushroom mixture, tomatoes, broccoli, basil and cheeses. Bake until crust is golden brown and the cheese is melted, 12-14 minutes.

1 PIECE: 317 cal., 11g fat (5g sat. fat), 21mg chol., 558mg sod., 40g carb. (4g sugars, 4g fiber), 16g pro. **DIABETIC EXCHANGES:** 2 starch, 2 medium-fat meat, 1 vegetable, ½ fat.

AIR-FRYER GENERAL TSO'S CAULIFLOWER

Cauliflower florets are fried to a crispy golden brown, then coated in a sauce with just the right amount of kick. This General Tso's cauliflower is a fun alternative to the classic chicken dish.
—*Nick Iverson, Denver, CO*

Prep: 25 min. • **Cook:** 20 min.
Makes: 4 servings

- ½ cup all-purpose flour
- ½ cup cornstarch
- 1   tsp. salt
- 1   tsp. baking powder
- ¾ cup club soda
- 1   medium head cauliflower, cut into 1-in. florets (about 6 cups)

SAUCE
- ¼ cup orange juice
- 3   Tbsp. sugar
- 3   Tbsp. soy sauce
- 3   Tbsp. vegetable broth
- 2   Tbsp. rice vinegar
- 2   tsp. sesame oil
- 2   tsp. cornstarch
- 2   Tbsp. canola oil
- 2   to 6 dried pasilla or other hot chiles, chopped
- 3   green onions, white part minced, green part thinly sliced
- 3   garlic cloves, minced

- 1   tsp. grated fresh gingerroot
- ½ tsp. grated orange zest
- 4   cups hot cooked rice

1. Preheat air fryer to 400°. Combine the flour, cornstarch, salt and baking powder. Stir in the club soda just until blended (batter will be thin). Toss florets in batter; transfer to a wire rack set over a baking sheet. Let stand 5 minutes. In batches, place cauliflower on greased tray in air-fryer basket. Cook until golden brown and tender, 10-12 minutes.
2. Meanwhile, whisk together the first 6 sauce ingredients; whisk in cornstarch until smooth.
3. In a large saucepan, heat canola oil over medium-high heat. Add chiles; cook and stir until fragrant, 1-2 minutes. Add white part of onions, garlic, ginger and orange zest; cook until fragrant, about 1 minute. Stir orange juice mixture; add to saucepan. Bring to a boil; cook and stir until thickened, 2-4 minutes.
4. Add cauliflower to sauce; toss to coat. Serve with rice; sprinkle with thinly sliced green onions.

1 CUP WITH 1 CUP RICE: 528 cal., 11g fat (1g sat. fat), 0 chol., 1614mg sod., 97g carb. (17g sugars, 5g fiber), 11g pro.

TEST KITCHEN TIP

It's easy to adjust the spice-heat level in this dish. Just use more or fewer hot chiles. If you're highly sensitive to spiciness, omit them entirely.

MEAT
LOVER
OPTION
PAGE 320

FIERY STUFFED POBLANOS

As a dietitian, I come up with nutritious twists on recipes, which is how this stuffed pepper dish was born.
—Amber Massey, Argyle, TX

- -

Prep: 50 min. + standing • **Bake:** 20 min.
Makes: 8 servings

- 8 poblano peppers
- 1 can (15 oz.) black beans, rinsed and drained
- 1 medium zucchini, chopped
- 1 small red onion, chopped
- 4 garlic cloves, minced
- 1 can (15¼ oz.) whole kernel corn, drained
- 1 can (14½ oz.) fire-roasted diced tomatoes, undrained
- 1 cup cooked brown rice
- 1 Tbsp. ground cumin
- 1 to 1½ tsp. ground ancho chile pepper
- ¼ tsp. salt
- ¼ tsp. pepper
- 1 cup shredded reduced-fat Mexican cheese blend, divided
- 3 green onions, chopped
- ½ cup reduced-fat sour cream

1. Broil peppers 3 in. from heat until skins blister, about 5 minutes. With tongs, rotate peppers a quarter turn. Broil and rotate until all sides are blistered and blackened. Immediately place peppers in a large bowl; cover and let stand for 20 minutes.

2. Meanwhile, in a small bowl, coarsely mash black beans; set aside. In a large nonstick skillet, cook and stir zucchini and onion until tender. Add garlic; cook 1 minute longer. Add corn, tomatoes, rice, seasonings and beans. Remove from heat; stir in ½ cup cheese. Set aside.

3. Preheat oven to 375°. Peel charred skins from poblanos and discard. Cut a lengthwise slit through each pepper, leaving stem intact; discard membranes and seeds. Spoon about ⅔ cup filling into each pepper.

4. Place peppers in a 13x9-in. baking dish coated with cooking spray. Bake until heated through, 18-22 minutes, sprinkling with green onions and the remaining cheese during last 5 minutes of baking. Serve with sour cream.

NOTE: Wear disposable gloves when cutting hot peppers; the oils can burn skin. Avoid touching your face.

1 STUFFED PEPPER: 223 cal., 5g fat (2g sat. fat), 15mg chol., 579mg sod., 32g carb. (9g sugars, 7g fiber), 11g pro. **DIABETIC EXCHANGES:** 2 vegetable, 1 starch, 1 lean meat, 1 fat.

READER RAVE

"Wow! Love this dish. Have made it several times, as it is very popular with my family. Extra filling makes a great wrap."
—JDOEPEL, TASTEOFHOME.COM

MEAT
LOVER
OPTION
PAGE 320

VEGETARIAN BEAN TACOS

I love Mexican food but was looking for a healthier option to share. My family devours these tasty tacos whenever I make them.
—*Amanda Petrucelli, Plymouth, IN*

Takes: 25 min. • **Makes:** 4 servings

- 1 Tbsp. canola oil
- 1 medium onion, chopped
- 1 jalapeno pepper, seeded and finely chopped
- 2 garlic cloves, minced
- 1 Tbsp. chili powder
- 2 tsp. ground cumin
- 1 tsp. ground coriander
- 1 can (16 oz.) refried beans
- 1 can (15 oz.) black beans, rinsed and drained
- 1 can (14½ oz.) no-salt-added diced tomatoes, drained
- 4 whole wheat tortillas (8 in.), warmed
  Optional toppings: Shredded lettuce, shredded cheddar cheese, cubed avocado, sour cream and salsa

1. In a large nonstick skillet, heat oil over medium heat. Add onion and jalapeno; cook and stir until tender. Add garlic and seasonings; cook 1 minute longer. Stir in beans and tomatoes; heat through.
2. Serve bean mixture in tortillas with toppings as desired.
NOTE: Wear disposable gloves when cutting hot peppers; the oils can burn skin. Avoid touching your face.
1 TACO: 413 cal., 9g fat (1g sat. fat), 9mg chol., 774mg sod., 66g carb. (8g sugars, 16g fiber), 17g pro.

SPINACH & BROCCOLI ENCHILADAS

I top this wonderful meatless meal with lettuce and serve it with extra picante sauce. It's quick, easy, filled with fresh flavor and definitely satisfying!
—*Lesley Tragesser, Charleston, MO*

Prep: 25 min. • **Bake:** 25 min.
Makes: 8 servings

- 1 medium onion, chopped
- 2 tsp. olive oil
- 1 pkg. (10 oz.) frozen chopped spinach, thawed and squeezed dry
- 1 cup finely chopped fresh broccoli
- 1 cup picante sauce, divided
- ½ tsp. garlic powder
- ½ tsp. ground cumin
- 1 cup 1% cottage cheese
- 1 cup shredded reduced-fat cheddar cheese, divided
- 8 flour tortillas (8 in.), warmed

1. Preheat the oven to 350°. In a large nonstick skillet over medium heat, cook and stir onion in oil until tender. Add spinach, broccoli, ⅓ cup picante sauce, garlic powder and cumin; heat through.
2. Remove from heat; stir in the cottage cheese and ½ cup cheddar cheese. Spoon about ⅓ cup spinach mixture down center of each tortilla. Roll up and place seam side down in a 13x9-in. baking dish coated with cooking spray. Spoon remaining picante sauce over top.
3. Cover and bake for 20-25 minutes or until heated through. Uncover; sprinkle with remaining cheese. Bake 5 minutes longer or until cheese is melted.
1 ENCHILADA: 246 cal., 8g fat (3g sat. fat), 11mg chol., 614mg sod., 32g carb. (4g sugars, 2g fiber), 13g pro.**DIABETIC EXCHANGES:** 1½ starch, 1 vegetable, 1 lean meat, ½ fat.

CORN, RICE & BEAN BURRITOS

No one will miss the meat when you dish up these satisfying burritos bursting with fresh filling. Fast to fix, they won't put a dent in your wallet.
—*Sharon Bickett, Chester, SC*

Takes: 30 min. • **Makes:** 8 servings

1 Tbsp. canola oil
1⅓ cups fresh or frozen corn, thawed
1 medium onion, chopped
1 medium green pepper, sliced
2 garlic cloves, minced
1½ tsp. chili powder
½ tsp. ground cumin
1 can (15 oz.) black beans, rinsed and drained
1½ cups cooked brown rice
8 flour tortillas (8 in.), warmed
¾ cup shredded reduced-fat cheddar cheese
½ cup reduced-fat plain yogurt
2 green onions, sliced
½ cup salsa

1. In a large skillet, heat oil over medium-high heat. Add corn, onion and pepper; cook and stir until tender. Add garlic, chili powder and cumin; cook 1 minute longer. Add beans and rice; heat through.
2. Spoon ½ cup filling across center of each tortilla; top with cheese, yogurt and green onions. Fold bottom and sides of tortilla over filling and roll up. Serve the burritos with salsa.

1 BURRITO WITH 1 TBSP. SALSA: 326 cal., 8g fat (2g sat. fat), 8mg chol., 500mg sod., 52g carb. (5g sugars, 4g fiber), 13g pro.

LENTIL BURRITOS

I incorporate healthy but tasty meals into our menus. Everyone loves these mildly spiced burritos that combine filling lentils with zucchini. They're healthy, satisfying, fast and tasty!
—*Pam Masters, Wickenburg, AZ*

Takes: 30 min. • **Makes:** 8 burritos

- 2   cups water
- 1   cup dried brown lentils
- 2   Tbsp. dried minced onion
- ½   tsp. dried minced garlic
- ½   tsp. ground cumin
- ⅛   tsp. hot pepper sauce
- 1   small zucchini, chopped
- 1   cup taco sauce
- 1   cup shredded part-skim mozzarella cheese
- 8   flour tortillas (8 in.), warmed

1. Place the first 6 ingredients in a large saucepan; bring to a boil. Reduce heat; simmer, covered, until lentils are tender, 15-20 minutes. Drain if necessary.

2. Stir zucchini, taco sauce and cheese into lentils. To serve, place about ½ cup lentil mixture on each tortilla and roll up.
1 BURRITO: 313 cal., 7g fat (3g sat. fat), 9mg chol., 452mg sod., 47g carb. (4g sugars, 5g fiber), 14g pro. **DIABETIC EXCHANGES:** 3 starch, 2 lean meat, 1 fat.

CRISPY RICE PATTIES WITH VEGETABLES & EGGS

Serve these patties any time of day. The recipe features protein, grains and fresh vegetables all in one dish. It's also a great way to use leftover rice.
—*Megumi Garcia, Milwaukee, WI*

Takes: 30 min. • **Makes:** 4 servings

- 2   pkg. (7.4 oz. each) ready-to-serve white sticky rice
- 1   Tbsp. plus 2 tsp. canola oil, divided
- 1   tsp. reduced-sodium soy sauce
- 2   cups thinly sliced Brussels sprouts
- 1   cup julienned carrots
- 1   medium sweet red pepper, julienned
- ½   tsp. sesame oil
- ½   tsp. salt
- ⅛   tsp. freshly ground pepper
- 1   Tbsp. water
- 4   large eggs
      Minced fresh chives
      Additional pepper

1. Cook the rice according to the package directions; cool slightly. Press a fourth of the rice into a ½-cup measuring cup that has been moistened lightly with water; invert onto a large sheet of plastic wrap. Fold plastic around rice; shape rice into a ½-in.-thick patty. Repeat 3 times.
2. In a large nonstick skillet, heat 1 Tbsp. canola oil over medium-high heat. Cook patties until crisp, 3-5 minutes per side; brush tops with soy sauce after turning. Remove from pan; keep warm.
3. In same pan, cook and stir vegetables over medium-high heat until lightly browned. Stir in sesame oil, salt and pepper. Add water; reduce the heat to medium. Cook, covered, until vegetables are crisp-tender, 1-2 minutes. Remove from pan; keep warm.
4. In same pan, heat remaining canola oil over medium heat. Break eggs, 1 at a time, into pan; immediately reduce heat to low. Cook, uncovered, until whites are completely set and yolks just begin to thicken, about 5 minutes. To serve, top the rice patties with vegetables and fried eggs. Sprinkle with minced chives and additional pepper.
1 SERVING: 320 cal., 11g fat (2g sat. fat), 186mg chol., 447mg sod., 43g carb. (4g sugars, 3g fiber), 11g pro. **DIABETIC EXCHANGES:** 3 starch, 1 medium-fat meat, 1 fat.

THE BEST EGGPLANT PARMESAN

I love eggplant and have many recipes that include it, but this one is my favorite. The cheeses and seasonings make the dish unforgettable.

—*Dorothy Kilpatrick, Wilmington, NC*

- -

Prep: 1¼ hours • **Bake:** 35 min. + standing
Makes: 2 casseroles (8 servings each)

- 3 garlic cloves, minced
- ⅓ cup olive oil
- 2 cans (28 oz. each) crushed tomatoes
- 1 cup pitted ripe olives, chopped
- ¼ cup thinly sliced fresh basil leaves or 1 Tbsp. dried basil
- 3 Tbsp. capers, drained
- 1 tsp. crushed red pepper flakes
- ¼ tsp. pepper

EGGPLANT

- 1 cup all-purpose flour
- 4 large eggs, beaten
- 3 cups dry bread crumbs
- 1 Tbsp. garlic powder

- 1 Tbsp. minced fresh oregano or 1 tsp. dried oregano
- 4 small eggplants (about 1 lb. each), peeled and cut lengthwise into ½-in. slices
- 1 cup olive oil

CHEESE

- 2 large eggs, beaten
- 2 cartons (15 oz. each) ricotta cheese
- 1¼ cups shredded Parmesan cheese, divided
- ½ cup thinly sliced fresh basil leaves or 2 Tbsp. dried basil
- ½ tsp. pepper
- 8 cups shredded part-skim mozzarella cheese

1. In a Dutch oven over medium heat, cook garlic in oil 1 minute. Stir in the tomatoes, olives, basil, capers, pepper flakes and pepper. Bring to a boil. Reduce heat; simmer, uncovered, 45-60 minutes or until thickened.

2. Meanwhile, for eggplant, place flour and eggs in separate shallow bowls. In another bowl, combine bread crumbs, garlic powder and oregano. Dip eggplant in flour, eggs, then bread crumb mixture.

3. In a large skillet, cook the eggplant in batches in oil for 5 minutes on each side or until tender. Drain on paper towels. In a large bowl, combine the eggs, ricotta cheese, ½ cup Parmesan cheese, basil and pepper.

4. Preheat the oven to 350°. In each of 2 greased 13x9-in. baking dishes, layer 1½ cups tomato sauce, 4 eggplant slices, 1 cup ricotta mixture and 2 cups mozzarella cheese. Repeat layers. Sprinkle each with remaining Parmesan cheese. Bake, uncovered, 35-40 minutes or until bubbly. Let stand 10 minutes before cutting. If desired, sprinkle with additional fresh basil.

1 PIECE: 585 cal., 40g fat (14g sat. fat), 132mg chol., 935mg sod., 32g carb. (11g sugars, 7g fiber), 29g pro.

SWEET POTATO CURRY

Here's one of my favorite vegetarian dishes that packs a lot of flavor and nutrition. Serve the curry over rice or on its own.
—*Aubrei Weigand, Harrisburg, PA*

- -

Prep: 15 min. • **Cook:** 30 min.
Makes: 6 servings

  2 Tbsp. olive oil
  4 celery ribs (including tops), chopped
  2 medium onions, chopped
  2 large sweet potatoes (about 1½ lbs.), cut into 1-in. cubes
  3 garlic cloves, minced
  3 tsp. curry powder
1½ tsp. chili powder
 ¾ tsp. ground cumin
 ½ tsp. salt
 ⅛ tsp. crushed red pepper flakes
  1 can (13.66 oz.) light coconut milk
  1 cup vegetable broth
  2 cups cut fresh green beans
  1 can (15 oz.) garbanzo beans or chickpeas, rinsed and drained
     Hot cooked rice

1. In a 6-qt. stockpot, heat oil over medium-high heat; saute celery and onions until tender, 3-5 minutes. Stir in sweet potatoes, garlic, seasonings, coconut milk and broth; bring to a boil. Reduce heat; simmer, uncovered, just until potatoes are tender, 15-20 minutes, stirring occasionally.
2. Stir in green beans and garbanzo beans; cook, uncovered, until green beans are tender, about 5 minutes, stirring occasionally. Serve with rice.
1⅓ CUPS CURRY MIXTURE: 314 cal., 11g fat (4g sat. fat), 0 chol., 502mg sod., 48g carb. (18g sugars, 9g fiber), 6g pro. **DIABETIC EXCHANGES:** 3 starch, 2 fat, 1 lean meat.

MAMA RACHEL'S
MEDITERRANEAN PIZZA
P. 54

Pizza & Pasta Favorites

Mama mia! From meatless takes on old-world classics to fresh new favorites, these pizza and pasta recipes prove tempting Italian dishes can be just as delicious without the meat!

❄ EASY VEGETABLE LASAGNA

Bursting with garden favorites, this lasagna is a vegetable lover's dream. The pasta layers are generously stuffed with roasted zucchini, mushrooms, peppers and onion in homemade tomato sauce.
—*Susanne Ebersol, Bird-in-Hand, PA*

Prep: 45 min. • **Bake:** 20 min. + standing
Makes: 12 servings

- 1   large onion, chopped
- 1   Tbsp. olive oil
- 6   garlic cloves, minced
- 1   can (28 oz.) tomato puree
- 1   can (8 oz.) tomato sauce
- 3   Tbsp. minced fresh basil
- 3   Tbsp. minced fresh oregano
- 1   tsp. sugar
- ½   tsp. crushed red pepper flakes

ROASTED VEGETABLES
- 4   cups sliced zucchini
- 3   cups sliced fresh mushrooms
- 2   medium green peppers, cut into 1-in. pieces
- 1   medium onion, cut into 1-in. pieces
- ½   tsp. salt
- ¼   tsp. pepper
- 6   lasagna noodles, cooked, rinsed and drained
- 4   cups shredded part-skim mozzarella cheese
- 1   cup shredded Parmesan cheese

1. Preheat the oven to 450°. In a large saucepan, saute onion in oil until tender over medium heat; add garlic and cook 1 minute longer. Stir in next 6 ingredients. Bring to a boil. Reduce heat; simmer, uncovered, for 20-25 minutes or until slightly thickened.

2. Meanwhile, in a large bowl, combine vegetables, salt and pepper. Transfer to two 15x10x1-in. baking pans coated with cooking spray. Bake until golden brown, 15-18 minutes. Reduce oven temperature to 400°.

3. Spread ½ cup sauce into a 13x9-in. baking dish coated with cooking spray. Layer with 3 noodles, 1¾ cups sauce, and half of the roasted vegetables and cheeses. Repeat layers.

4. Cover and bake 10 minutes. Uncover; bake until bubbly and golden brown, 10-15 minutes longer. Let stand for 10 minutes before serving. If desired, garnish with additional fresh oregano.

1 PIECE: 258 cal., 11g fat (6g sat. fat), 29mg chol., 571mg sod., 23g carb. (6g sugars, 3g fiber), 16g pro. **DIABETIC EXCHANGES:** 2 vegetable, 2 medium-fat meat, ½ starch.

TEST KITCHEN TIP

If you want to make this ahead of time, assemble the lasagna as directed, wrap tightly, and store in the refrigerator for up to 2 days or freeze for up to 3 months. If cooking from frozen, thaw overnight before baking.

SPINACH PIZZA

Looking for a fun twist on a traditional favorite? Veggies and Alfredo sauce add dimension to simple pizza.
—*Dawn Bartholomew, Raleigh, NC*

Takes: 25 min. • **Makes:** 4 servings

- 1 pkg. (6½ oz.) pizza crust mix
- ½ cup Alfredo sauce
- 2 medium tomatoes
- 4 cups chopped fresh spinach
- 2 cups shredded Italian cheese blend

1. Prepare pizza dough according to package directions. With floured hands, press the dough onto a greased 12-in. pizza pan.
2. Spread Alfredo sauce over dough to within 1 in. of the edge. Thinly slice or chop tomatoes; top pizza with spinach, tomatoes and cheese.
3. Bake at 450° for 10-15 minutes or until the cheese is melted and the crust is golden brown.
2 PIECES: 403 cal., 16g fat (10g sat. fat), 49mg chol., 822mg sod., 40g carb. (4g sugars, 3g fiber), 20g pro.

STUFFED VEGETARIAN SHELLS

When my aunt first told me about these shells, they sounded like a lot of work—but the recipe whips up in no time. Sometimes I add a little cooked bacon to the ricotta filling.
—*Amelia Hopkin, Salt Lake City, UT*

Prep: 20 min. • **Bake:** 30 min.
Makes: 8 servings

- 24 uncooked jumbo pasta shells
- 1 carton (15 oz.) part-skim ricotta cheese
- 3 cups frozen chopped broccoli, thawed and drained
- 1 cup shredded part-skim mozzarella cheese
- 2 large egg whites
- 1 Tbsp. minced fresh basil or 1 tsp. dried basil
- ½ tsp. garlic salt
- ¼ tsp. pepper
- 1 jar (26 oz.) meatless spaghetti sauce
- 2 Tbsp. shredded Parmesan cheese

1. Cook the pasta according to package directions. In a large bowl, combine the ricotta, broccoli, mozzarella, egg whites and seasonings. Drain pasta and rinse in cold water.

2. Spread half the spaghetti sauce into a 13x9-in. baking dish coated with cooking spray. Stuff pasta shells with the ricotta mixture; arrange over spaghetti sauce. Pour remaining sauce over pasta shells.

3. Cover and bake at 375° for 25 minutes. Uncover; sprinkle with the Parmesan cheese. Bake until heated through, about 5 minutes longer.

3 STUFFED SHELLS: 279 cal., 8g fat (5g sat. fat), 26mg chol., 725mg sod., 36g carb. (8g sugars, 4g fiber), 18g pro. **DIABETIC EXCHANGES:** 2½ starch, 2 lean meat.

MEAT LOVER OPTION
PAGE 320

🕐 EGGPLANT FLATBREAD PIZZAS

I loved to make these back in the day. Now I'm a chef and still enjoy them.
—*Christine Wendland, Browns Mills, NJ*

Takes: 30 min. • **Makes:** 4 servings

3 Tbsp. olive oil, divided
2½ cups cubed eggplant (½ in.)
1 small onion, halved and thinly sliced
½ tsp. salt
⅛ tsp. pepper
1 garlic clove, minced
2 naan flatbreads
½ cup part-skim ricotta cheese
1 tsp. dried oregano
½ cup roasted garlic tomato sauce
½ cup loosely packed basil leaves
1 cup shredded part-skim mozzarella cheese
2 Tbsp. grated Parmesan cheese
 Sliced fresh basil, optional

1. Preheat oven to 400°. In a large skillet, heat 1 Tbsp. oil over medium-high heat; saute eggplant and onion with salt and pepper until eggplant begins to soften, 4-5 minutes. Stir in the garlic; remove from heat.

2. Place naans on a baking sheet. Spread with ricotta cheese; sprinkle with the oregano. Spread with tomato sauce. Top with eggplant mixture and whole basil leaves. Sprinkle with mozzarella and Parmesan cheeses; drizzle with the remaining oil.

3. Bake until the crust is golden brown and cheese is melted, 12-15 minutes. If desired, top with sliced basil. Cut each naan in half.

NOTE: A meatless pasta sauce or any flavored tomato sauce may be substituted for the roasted garlic tomato sauce.

½ PIZZA: 340 cal., 21g fat (7g sat. fat), 32mg chol., 996mg sod., 25g carb. (5g sugars, 3g fiber), 14g pro.

MEAT
LOVER
OPTION
PAGE 320

ZUCCHINI CRUST PIZZA

My mother-in-law shared the recipe for this unique pizza with me. It's just right for brunch, lunch or a light supper. Use a metal spatula to loosen the nutritious zucchini crust from the pan.
—*Ruth Denomme, Englehart, ON*

Prep: 20 min. • **Bake:** 25 min.
Makes: 6 servings

    2 cups shredded zucchini
       (1 to 1½ medium), squeezed dry
    ½ cup egg substitute
       or 2 large eggs, lightly beaten
    ¼ cup all-purpose flour
    ¼ tsp. salt
    2 cups shredded part-skim
       mozzarella cheese, divided
    ½ cup grated Parmesan cheese,
       divided
    2 small tomatoes, halved and sliced
    ½ cup chopped red onion
    ½ cup julienned bell pepper
    1 tsp. dried oregano
    ½ tsp. dried basil
       Chopped fresh basil, optional

1. Preheat oven to 450°. In a large bowl, combine the first 4 ingredients; stir in ½ cup mozzarella cheese and ¼ cup Parmesan cheese. Transfer to a 12-in. pizza pan coated generously with cooking spray; spread to an 11-in. circle.
2. Bake until crust is golden brown, 13-16 minutes. Reduce the oven setting to 400°. Sprinkle with the remaining mozzarella cheese; top with tomatoes, onion, pepper, herbs and remaining Parmesan cheese. Bake until edge is golden brown and cheese is melted, 10-15 minutes. Sprinkle with chopped basil if desired.
1 PIECE: 188 cal., 10g fat (5g sat. fat), 30mg chol., 514mg sod., 12g carb. (4g sugars, 1g fiber), 14g pro. **DIABETIC EXCHANGES:** 2 vegetable, 2 lean meat, ½ fat.

WHITE BEANS & BOW TIES

When we have fresh veggies, we toss them with pasta shapes like penne or bow ties. What a tasty way to enjoy a meatless meal!
—*Angela Buchanan, Longmont, CO*

Takes: 25 min. • **Makes:** 4 servings

    2½ cups uncooked whole wheat
        bow tie pasta (about 6 oz.)
    1   Tbsp. olive oil
    1   medium zucchini, sliced
    2   garlic cloves, minced
    2   large tomatoes, chopped
        (about 2½ cups)
    1   can (15 oz.) cannellini beans,
        rinsed and drained
    1   can (2¼ oz.) sliced ripe olives,
        drained
    ¾   tsp. freshly ground pepper
    ½   cup crumbled feta cheese

1. Cook pasta according to package directions. Drain, reserving ½ cup pasta water.
2. Meanwhile, in a large skillet, heat oil over medium-high heat; saute zucchini until crisp-tender, 2-4 minutes. Add the garlic; cook and stir 30 seconds. Stir in tomatoes, beans, olives and pepper; bring to a boil. Reduce heat; simmer, uncovered, until tomatoes are softened, 3-5 minutes, stirring occasionally.
3. Stir in pasta and enough pasta water to moisten as desired. Stir in cheese.
1½ CUPS: 348 cal., 9g fat (2g sat. fat), 8mg chol., 394mg sod., 52g carb. (4g sugars, 11g fiber), 15g pro.

READER RAVE

"This is a tried-and-true weeknight meal in our house! Easy and tasty! We've been making it for a couple of years at least."
—ERIN962, TASTEOFHOME.COM

MAMA RACHEL'S MEDITERRANEAN PIZZA

Pizza has been a regular weekend dinner at our house since my pizza-crazy boys, now 21 and 25, were just little guys. We laughingly call pizza an art form around here. Every one is an original!
—*Rachel Barton, Austin, TX*

Prep: 35 min. + rising • **Bake:** 20 min.
Makes: 2 pizzas (6 servings each)

- 1 Tbsp. active dry yeast
- 1 cup warm water (110° to 115°)
- 1 Tbsp. sugar
- 1 Tbsp. olive oil
- ½ tsp. salt
- 2½ to 3 cups all-purpose flour
- 2 Tbsp. cornmeal
    TOPPINGS
- 2 Tbsp. olive oil
- 3 garlic cloves, peeled and thinly sliced
- 2 cups shredded part-skim mozzarella cheese
- 2 large tomatoes, thinly sliced
- ⅓ cup pitted kalamata olives, thinly sliced
- ½ cup shredded Parmesan cheese
- ¼ tsp. crushed red pepper flakes
- 6 fresh basil leaves, thinly sliced

1. In a large bowl, dissolve yeast in warm water. Add the sugar, oil, salt and 1 cup flour; beat until smooth. Stir in enough remaining flour to form a stiff dough.
2. Turn dough onto a floured surface; knead for 6-8 minutes or until smooth and elastic. Place in a greased bowl, turning once to grease the top. Cover and let rise in a warm place until doubled, about 45 minutes.
3. Preheat oven to 400°. Grease two 12-in. pizza pans; sprinkle with cornmeal. Punch down dough; divide in half. Press to fit pans. Pinch edges to form a rim. Cover; let rest 10 minutes. Bake for 8-10 minutes or until the edges are lightly browned.
4. Increase oven setting to 450°. Brush the crusts with oil; top with the garlic, mozzarella cheese, tomatoes, olives and Parmesan cheese. Bake 10-12 minutes or until the crust is golden and cheese is melted. Sprinkle pizza with pepper flakes and basil.
1 PIECE: 216 cal., 9g fat (3g sat. fat), 13mg chol., 307mg sod., 25g carb. (3g sugars, 1g fiber), 9g pro. **DIABETIC EXCHANGES:** 1½ starch, 1 medium-fat meat, 1 fat.

PENNE WITH VEGGIES & BLACK BEANS

Chock-full of zucchini, tomato, sweet pepper and carrot, this hearty pasta dish puts your garden harvest to good use.
—*Vickie Spoerle, Carmel, IN*

Takes: 25 min. • **Makes:** 2 servings

- ¾ cup uncooked penne pasta
- ⅓ cup sliced zucchini
- ⅓ cup sliced fresh carrot
- 4 medium fresh mushrooms, sliced
- ½ small green pepper, thinly sliced
- ½ small onion, thinly sliced
- 1 small garlic clove, minced
- ¼ tsp. each dried basil, oregano and thyme
- ¼ tsp. salt
- ⅛ tsp. pepper
- 2 tsp. olive oil, divided
- 1 cup canned black beans, rinsed and drained
- ¼ cup chopped seeded tomato
- 2 Tbsp. shredded Parmesan cheese
- 2 tsp. minced fresh parsley

1. Cook pasta according to package directions. Meanwhile, in a large nonstick skillet, saute the zucchini, carrot, mushrooms, green pepper, onion, garlic and seasonings in 1 tsp. oil until crisp-tender. Stir in the beans.
2. Drain pasta; add to vegetable mixture. Add tomato and remaining olive oil; toss gently. Sprinkle with Parmesan cheese and parsley.
1⅓ CUPS: 300 cal., 7g fat (2g sat. fat), 4mg chol., 643mg sod., 47g carb. (6g sugars, 8g fiber), 14g pro.

MEAT
LOVER
OPTION

PAGE 320

CHEESE TORTELLINI WITH TOMATOES & CORN

Fresh corn and basil make this dish taste like summer. I think it's delightful to take to picnics or gatherings, but it's also wonderful for weeknight dinners.
—*Sally Maloney, Dallas, GA*

Takes: 25 min. • **Makes:** 4 servings

- 1 pkg. (9 oz.) refrigerated cheese tortellini
- 3⅓ cups fresh or frozen corn (about 16 oz.)
- 2 cups cherry tomatoes, quartered
- 2 green onions, thinly sliced
- ¼ cup minced fresh basil
- 2 Tbsp. grated Parmesan cheese
- 4 tsp. olive oil
- ¼ tsp. garlic powder
- ⅛ tsp. pepper

In a 6-qt. stockpot, cook the tortellini according to package directions, adding the corn during the last 5 minutes of cooking. Drain; transfer to a large bowl. Add remaining ingredients; toss to coat.

1¾ CUPS: 366 cal., 12g fat (4g sat. fat), 30mg chol., 286mg sod., 57g carb. (6g sugars, 5g fiber), 14g pro.

GREEK ISLE PIZZA

I visited the Greek island of Corfu more than 20 years ago and wanted to create a pizza inspired by the delicious salads I enjoyed there. This recipe is loaded with many of those same ingredients and is so easy to prepare.
—Amanda Cooke, Los Angeles, CA

- -

Prep: 20 min. • **Bake:** 10 min. + standing
Makes: 6 servings

- 1 prebaked 12-in. thin pizza crust
- 1 jar (7 oz.) oil-packed sun-dried tomatoes, divided
- 1 small red onion, thinly sliced
- 1 tsp. olive oil
- 2 garlic cloves, minced
- 1 tsp. dried rosemary, crushed
- ¼ tsp. pepper
  Grated lemon zest, optional
- 2 cups fresh baby spinach, chopped
- 1¼ cups crumbled feta cheese
- ¼ cup Greek olives, pitted and chopped
- 4 slices part-skim mozzarella cheese

1. Place the crust on an ungreased 12-in. pizza pan; brush with 1 Tbsp. oil from the sun-dried tomatoes. Set aside.
2. In a small skillet, saute onion in olive oil until tender. Add garlic; cook 1 minute longer. Remove from the heat; stir in the rosemary, pepper and, if desired, lemon zest. Spread over crust. Top with spinach and ½ cup sun-dried tomatoes (save the remaining tomatoes and oil for a future use).
3. Sprinkle with feta cheese and olives; top with mozzarella cheese. Bake at 425° for 10-12 minutes or until cheese is melted. Let pizza stand for 10 minutes before cutting.
1 PIECE: 328 cal., 16g fat (6g sat. fat), 23mg chol., 725mg sod., 30g carb. (1g sugars, 3g fiber), 15g pro. **DIABETIC EXCHANGES:** 2 starch, 1 high-fat meat, 1 fat.

VEGETARIAN BLACK BEAN PASTA

This hearty vegetarian dish is loaded with flavor. I use fresh rosemary when I have it on hand.
—Ashlynn Azar, Beaverton, OR

- -

Takes: 25 min. • **Makes:** 6 servings

- 9 oz. uncooked whole wheat fettuccine
- 1 Tbsp. olive oil
- 1¾ cups sliced baby portobello mushrooms
- 1 garlic clove, minced
- 1 can (15 oz.) black beans, rinsed and drained
- 1 can (14½ oz.) diced tomatoes, undrained
- 1 tsp. dried rosemary, crushed
- ½ tsp. dried oregano
- 2 cups fresh baby spinach

1. Cook fettuccine according to package directions. Meanwhile, in a large skillet, heat oil over medium-high heat. Add mushrooms; cook and stir 4-6 minutes or until tender. Add the garlic; cook 1 minute longer.
2. Stir in the black beans, tomatoes, rosemary and oregano; heat through. Stir in spinach until wilted. Drain the fettuccine; add to bean mixture and toss to combine.
1¼ CUPS: 255 cal., 3g fat (0 sat. fat), 0 chol., 230mg sod., 45g carb. (4g sugars, 9g fiber), 12g pro. **DIABETIC EXCHANGES:** 3 starch, 1 lean meat, ½ fat.

ALL VEGGIE LASAGNA

People often tell me you can't call something lasagna if it doesn't have meat. But then they try this dish and ask for the recipe. Bring a pan to your next party or potluck.
—*Kim Bender, Aurora, CO*

Prep: 20 min. • **Bake:** 1 hour + standing
Makes: 12 servings

- 2 cups 1% cottage cheese
- 1 carton (15 oz.) reduced-fat ricotta cheese
- 2 Tbsp. minced fresh parsley
- 1 jar (26 oz.) meatless spaghetti sauce
- 9 uncooked lasagna noodles
- 2 medium carrots, shredded
- 1½ cups broccoli florets
- 4 oz. fresh mushrooms, sliced
- 1 small zucchini, thinly sliced
- 1 small yellow summer squash, thinly sliced
- 2 cups fresh spinach
- 2 cups shredded part-skim mozzarella cheese

1. Preheat the oven to 350°. In a bowl, combine the cottage cheese, ricotta and parsley. Spread ½ cup spaghetti sauce in a 13x9-in. baking dish coated with cooking spray. Top with 3 noodles and a third of the cheese mixture. Sprinkle with half each of the carrots, broccoli, mushrooms, zucchini and squash. Top with a third of the remaining sauce.

2. Arrange half the spinach over the spaghetti sauce; sprinkle with a third of the mozzarella cheese. Repeat the layers of noodles, cheese mixture, vegetables, sauce, spinach and mozzarella. Top with the remaining noodles, cheese mixture, sauce and mozzarella.

3. Cover tightly and bake 45 minutes. Uncover; bake until noodles are tender, about 15 minutes longer. Let stand for 15 minutes before cutting.

1 PIECE: 252 cal., 6g fat (4g sat. fat), 24mg chol., 759mg sod., 27g carb. (10g sugars, 2g fiber), 21g pro..

HERBED ARTICHOKE CHEESE TORTELLINI

Both vegetarians and meat-and-potato lovers rave about this flavor-packed meatless recipe with tomatoes, black olives and artichoke hearts tossed with tender cheese tortellini.
—*Karen Anzelc, Peoria, AZ*

Takes: 30 min. • **Makes:** 8 servings

- 2 cans (14½ oz. each) Italian diced tomatoes
- 2 jars (6½ oz. each) marinated quartered artichoke hearts
- ½ cup olive oil
- 2 medium onions, chopped
- ½ cup minced fresh parsley
- 2 to 4 Tbsp. minced fresh basil or 2 to 4 tsp. dried basil
- ½ tsp. dried oregano
- 2 garlic cloves, minced
- ⅛ tsp. crushed red pepper flakes
- 2 pkg. (9 oz. each) refrigerated cheese tortellini
- 1 can (2¼ oz.) sliced ripe olives, drained
- ½ tsp. salt
- ¼ cup shredded Parmesan cheese

1. Drain tomatoes, reserving ⅔ cup juice. Drain artichoke hearts, reserving ¾ cup marinade; chop artichokes.
2. In a Dutch oven, heat oil over medium-high heat. Add onions, herbs, garlic and pepper flakes; cook and stir until onions are tender, 4-5 minutes. Stir in tomatoes and reserved tomato juice and artichoke marinade; bring to a boil. Reduce the heat; simmer, uncovered, until slightly thickened, 10-12 minutes. Meanwhile, cook the tortellini according to the package directions.
3. Drain the tortellini; add to the tomato mixture. Gently stir in the olives, salt and artichoke hearts; heat through. Sprinkle with cheese.
1¼ CUPS: 474 cal., 28g fat (7g sat. fat), 29mg chol., 975mg sod., 45g carb. (12g sugars, 3g fiber), 11g pro.

HOMEMADE MEATLESS SPAGHETTI SAUCE

When my tomatoes ripen, the first things I make are BLTs and this homemade spaghetti sauce.
—*Sondra Bergy, Lowell, MI*

Prep: 20 min. • **Cook:** 3¼ hours
Makes: 2 qt.

- 4 medium onions, chopped
- ½ cup canola oil
- 12 cups chopped peeled fresh tomatoes
- 4 garlic cloves, minced
- 3 bay leaves
- 4 tsp. salt
- 2 tsp. dried oregano
- 1¼ tsp. pepper
- ½ tsp. dried basil
- 2 cans (6 oz. each) tomato paste
- ⅓ cup packed brown sugar
  Hot cooked pasta
  Minced fresh basil, optional

1. In a Dutch oven, saute the onions in oil until tender. Add the tomatoes, garlic, bay leaves, salt, oregano, pepper and dried basil. Bring to a boil. Reduce the heat; cover and simmer for 2 hours, stirring occasionally.
2. Add tomato paste and brown sugar; simmer, uncovered, for 1 hour. Discard bay leaves. Serve with pasta and, if desired, minced fresh basil.
½ CUP: 133 cal., 7g fat (1g sat. fat), 0 chol., 614mg sod., 17g carb. (12g sugars, 3g fiber), 2g pro.

LACTOSE-FREE SPINACH LASAGNA

Even if you don't think you'll like tofu, you have to give it a try in this lasagna. The tofu in it tastes like ricotta cheese.
—*Peggy Kern, Tucson, AZ*

Prep: 45 min. • **Bake:** 35 min. + standing
Makes: 12 servings

- 1¾ cups sliced fresh mushrooms
- ¼ cup chopped onion
- 1 Tbsp. olive oil
- 1 pkg. (10 oz.) frozen chopped spinach, thawed and squeezed dry
- 2 garlic cloves, minced
- 2 cans (14½ oz. each) diced tomatoes, undrained
- 1 can (8 oz.) tomato sauce
- 1 can (6 oz.) tomato paste
- 2 Tbsp. minced fresh basil or 2 tsp. dried basil
- 1 tsp. dried marjoram
- 9 uncooked lasagna noodles
- 1 pkg. (14 oz.) firm tofu, drained and cubed
- 2 large eggs, lightly beaten
- 2 Tbsp. dried parsley flakes
- ½ tsp. salt
- ¼ tsp. pepper
- 1½ cups shredded mozzarella-flavored soy cheese
- 1 cup shredded cheddar-flavored soy cheese

1. In a large nonstick skillet, saute the mushrooms and onion in oil until tender. Add spinach and garlic; cook 2 minutes longer. Stir in the tomatoes, tomato sauce, tomato paste, basil and dried marjoram. Bring to a boil. Reduce the heat; cover and simmer for 15 minutes, stirring occasionally.
2. Meanwhile, cook lasagna noodles according to package directions; drain.
3. In a small bowl, combine the tofu, eggs, parsley, salt and pepper. Place 3 noodles in the bottom of a 13x9-in. baking dish coated with cooking spray. Layer with half the tofu mixture, 1½ cups spinach mixture, ½ cup mozzarella-flavored soy cheese and ⅓ cup cheddar-flavored soy cheese. Repeat layers. Top with remaining noodles and spinach mixture; sprinkle with remaining cheeses.
4. Cover and bake at 375° until heated through, 35-40 minutes. Let stand for 10 minutes before cutting.
1 PIECE: 216 cal., 7g fat (1g sat. fat), 35mg chol., 531mg sod., 24g carb. (5g sugars, 3g fiber), 14g pro. **DIABETIC EXCHANGES:** 2 vegetable, 1 starch, 1 medium-fat meat.

51 STUFFED PASTA SHELLS

These savory shells never fail to make a big impression, even though the recipe is easy. One or two of the shells makes a perfect individual serving at a potluck, so a single batch goes a long way.
—*Jena Coffey, St. Louis, MO*

Prep: 15 min. • **Bake:** 30 min.
Makes: 12 servings

- 4   cups shredded mozzarella cheese
- 1   carton (15 oz.) ricotta cheese
- 1   pkg. (10 oz.) frozen chopped spinach, thawed and squeezed dry
- 1   pkg. (12 oz.) jumbo pasta shells, cooked and drained
- 3½ cups spaghetti sauce
     Grated Parmesan cheese, optional

Preheat oven to 350°. Combine cheeses and spinach; stuff into shells. Arrange in a greased 13x9-in. baking dish. Pour spaghetti sauce over the shells. Cover and bake until heated through, about 30 minutes. If desired, sprinkle with Parmesan cheese after baking.

1 SERVING: 314 cal., 13g fat (7g sat. fat), 44mg chol., 576mg sod., 32g carb. (9g sugars, 3g fiber), 18g pro.

READER RAVE

"I have been making this for years and everyone, including all the grandchildren, loves this recipe. It's so easy but it looks as if you worked for hours."
—JETCAROLINET, TASTEOFHOME.COM

PESTO VEGETABLE PIZZA

My family loves pizza, but we rarely have it delivered since I created this fresh and flavorful version. Always a winner in my house, it's a fast and delicious meal.
—*Kate Selner, Lino Lakes, MN*

Takes: 30 min. • **Makes:** 6 servings

1 prebaked 12-in. thin pizza crust
2 garlic cloves, halved
½ cup pesto sauce
¾ cup packed fresh spinach, chopped
2 large portobello mushrooms, thinly sliced
1 medium sweet yellow pepper, julienned
2 plum tomatoes, seeded and sliced
⅓ cup packed fresh basil, chopped
1 cup shredded part-skim mozzarella cheese
¼ cup grated Parmesan cheese
½ tsp. fresh or dried oregano

1. Preheat oven to 450°. Place crust on an ungreased 12-in. pizza pan. Rub cut side of garlic cloves over crust; discard garlic. Spread pesto sauce over crust. Top with spinach, mushrooms, yellow pepper, tomatoes and basil. Sprinkle with cheeses and oregano.

2. Bake until pizza is heated through and cheese is melted, 10-15 minutes.

1 PIECE: 310 cal., 15g fat (4g sat. fat), 15mg chol., 707mg sod., 31g carb. (4g sugars, 2g fiber), 13g pro. **DIABETIC EXCHANGES:** 2 starch, 2 fat, 1 lean meat, 1 medium-fat meat.

MEAT LOVER OPTION
PAGE 320

OVER-THE-TOP BAKED ZITI

I adapted a ziti recipe to remove ingredients my kids did not like, such as ground beef. The revised recipe was a success not only with my family but at potlucks too. It's so versatile: You can use jarred sauce, double or triple the recipe, and even freeze it.
—*Kimberley Pitman, Smyrna, DE*

Prep: 20 min.
Bake: 4 hours 20 min. • **Makes:** 8 servings

- 2 cans (29 oz. each) tomato puree
- 1 can (12 oz.) tomato paste
- 1 medium onion, chopped
- ¼ cup minced fresh parsley
- 2 Tbsp. dried oregano
- 4 tsp. sugar
- 3 garlic cloves, minced
- 1 Tbsp. dried basil
- 1 tsp. salt
- ½ tsp. pepper

ZITI

- 1 pkg. (16 oz.) ziti
- 1 large egg, beaten
- 1 carton (15 oz.) reduced-fat ricotta cheese
- 2 cups shredded part-skim mozzarella cheese, divided
- ¾ cup grated Parmesan cheese
- ¼ cup minced fresh parsley
- ½ tsp. salt
- ¼ tsp. pepper
  Additional minced fresh parsley, optional

1. In a 3- or 4-qt. slow cooker, combine the first 10 ingredients. Cover and cook on low for 4 hours.

2. Cook ziti according to the package directions. In a large bowl, combine the egg, ricotta cheese, 1 cup mozzarella, Parmesan, parsley, salt, pepper and 5 cups slow-cooked sauce. Drain ziti; stir into cheese mixture.

3. Transfer to a 13x9-in. baking dish coated with cooking spray. Pour the remaining sauce over top; sprinkle with remaining mozzarella cheese. Bake at 350° for 20-25 minutes or until bubbly. If desired, garnish with additional parsley.

1 SERVING: 499 cal., 10g fat (6g sat. fat), 62mg chol., 826mg sod., 72g carb. (16g sugars, 6g fiber), 29g pro.

SAUCY MAC & CHEESE

I love the curly noodles in this creamy recipe. Cavatappi, also sold under the name cellentani, is a corkscrew pasta, but any type of spiral pasta will work. The dish is fun to make and looks so pretty topped with extra cheese and crunchy, golden crumbs. I add ground pepper to my serving.
—*Sara Martin, Brookfield, WI*

Takes: 25 min. • **Makes:** 4 servings

- 2 cups cavatappi or spiral pasta
- 3 Tbsp. butter, divided
- ⅓ cup panko bread crumbs
- 2 Tbsp. all-purpose flour
- 1½ cups 2% milk
- ¾ lb. Velveeta, cubed
- ¼ cup shredded cheddar cheese

1. Cook pasta according to package directions. Meanwhile, in a large nonstick skillet, melt 1 Tbsp. butter over medium-high heat. Add bread crumbs; cook and stir until golden brown. Remove to a small bowl and set aside.
2. In the same skillet, melt remaining butter. Stir in the flour until smooth. Gradually add milk; bring to a boil. Cook and stir until thickened, about 2 minutes. Reduce the heat. Stir in the Velveeta until melted.
3. Drain pasta; add to the cheese mixture. Cook and stir until heated through, 3-4 minutes. Sprinkle with cheddar cheese and bread crumbs.
1¼ CUPS: 661 cal., 36g fat (21g sat. fat), 121mg chol., 1267mg sod., 58g carb. (11g sugars, 2g fiber), 27g pro.

MEAT LOVER OPTION
PAGE 320

TOMATO MAC & CHEESE

White cheddar cheese and tomatoes add a new dimension to the classic mac and cheese dish.
—Taste of Home *Test Kitchen*

Takes: 30 min. • **Makes:** 6 servings

- 12 oz. uncooked penne pasta
- 3 Tbsp. butter
- 3 Tbsp. all-purpose flour
- 3 cups whole milk
- 1 lb. white cheddar cheese, shredded
- ½ tsp. salt
- ½ tsp. ground mustard
- ¼ tsp. white pepper
- 1 cup chopped seeded tomatoes
  Fresh basil leaves, thinly sliced

1. Cook pasta according to package directions. Meanwhile, in a Dutch oven, melt butter over medium heat. Stir in flour until smooth; gradually add the milk. Bring to a boil; cook and stir until thickened, about 2 minutes.
2. Reduce heat to medium. Stir in cheese, salt, mustard and pepper. Cook and stir until cheese is melted, 1-2 minutes. Drain pasta; stir into cheese sauce. Cook and stir 3 minutes or until heated through. Stir in tomatoes just until combined. Garnish with fresh basil.

1½ CUPS: 655 cal., 36g fat (22g sat. fat), 111mg chol., 789mg sod., 52g carb. (9g sugars, 2g fiber), 31g pro.

TEST KITCHEN TIP

For a variation on this mac, swap in a different type of cheese, such as mozzarella or pepper jack, for the white cheddar. You could also try adding homemade herbed bread crumbs on top for extra flavor and crunch.

SLOW-COOKER VEGGIE LASAGNA

This veggie-licious alternative to traditional lasagna makes use of slow-cooker convenience. I suggest using chunky spaghetti sauce.
—Laura Davister, Little Suamico, WI

Prep: 25 min. • **Cook:** 3½ hours
Makes: 2 servings

- ½ cup shredded part-skim mozzarella cheese
- 3 Tbsp. 1% cottage cheese
- 2 Tbsp. grated Parmesan cheese
- 2 Tbsp. egg substitute
- ½ tsp. Italian seasoning
- ⅛ tsp. garlic powder
- ¾ cup meatless spaghetti sauce, divided
- ½ cup sliced zucchini, divided
- 2 no-cook lasagna noodles
- 4 cups fresh baby spinach
- ½ cup sliced fresh mushrooms

1. Cut two 18x3-in. strips of heavy-duty foil; crisscross so they resemble an "X". Place strips on bottom and up side of a 1½-qt. slow cooker. Coat strips with cooking spray.
2. In a small bowl, combine the first 6 ingredients. Spread 1 Tbsp. spaghetti sauce on bottom of the prepared slow cooker. Top with half of the zucchini and a third of the cheese mixture.
3. Break the noodles into 1-in. pieces; sprinkle half of the noodles over cheese mixture. Spread with 1 Tbsp. sauce. Top with half of the spinach and half of the mushrooms. Repeat layers. Top with the remaining cheese mixture and the remaining spaghetti sauce.
4. Cover and cook on low for 3½-4 hours or until noodles are tender.

1 SERVING: 259 cal., 8g fat (4g sat. fat), 23mg chol., 859mg sod., 29g carb. (9g sugars, 4g fiber), 19g pro. **DIABETIC EXCHANGES:** 2 lean meat, 2 medium-fat meat, 1½ starch, 1 vegetable, ½ fat.

ZITI BAKE

My kids frown on some of my casserole recipes, but they give a cheer when they hear we're having this dish for supper. They even devour the leftovers!
—*Charity Burkholder, Pittsboro, IN*

Prep: 20 min. • **Bake:** 50 min.
Makes: 6 servings

   3   cups uncooked ziti or
        small tube pasta
1¾   cups meatless spaghetti sauce,
        divided
   1   cup 4% cottage cheese
1½   cups shredded part-skim
        mozzarella cheese, divided
   1   large egg, lightly beaten
   2   tsp. dried parsley flakes
  ½   tsp. dried oregano
  ¼   tsp. garlic powder
  ⅛   tsp. pepper

1. Cook pasta according to package directions. Meanwhile, in a large bowl, combine ¾ cup spaghetti sauce, cottage cheese, 1 cup mozzarella cheese, egg, parsley, oregano, garlic powder and pepper. Drain the pasta; stir into the cheese mixture.
2. In a greased 8-in. square baking dish, spread ¼ cup spaghetti sauce. Top with pasta mixture and the remaining sauce and mozzarella cheese.
3. Cover and bake at 375° for 45 minutes. Uncover; bake until a thermometer reads 160°, 5-10 minutes longer.
1½ CUPS: 297 cal., 9g fat (5g sat. fat), 52mg chol., 639mg sod., 37g carb. (8g sugars, 3g fiber), 18g pro.

HOMEMADE MANICOTTI

These tender manicotti are easier to stuff than the purchased variety. People are always amazed when I tell them I make my own noodles. My son fixed the dish for his friends, and they were impressed.
—*Richard Bunt, Painted Post, NY*

Prep: 70 min. • **Bake:** 40 min.
Makes: 6 servings

CREPE NOODLES
1½   cups all-purpose flour
   1   cup whole milk
   3   large eggs
  ½   tsp. salt
FILLING
1½   lbs. ricotta cheese
  ¼   cup grated Romano cheese
   1   large egg
   1   Tbsp. minced fresh parsley or
        1 tsp. dried parsley flakes
   1   jar (26 oz.) meatless spaghetti sauce
        Grated Romano cheese, optional

1. Place flour in a bowl; whisk in milk, eggs and salt until smooth. Heat a lightly greased 8-in. skillet; pour about 2 Tbsp. batter into center of skillet. Spread into a 5-in. circle. Cook over medium heat until set; do not brown or turn. Repeat with the remaining batter, making 18 crepes. Stack the crepes with waxed paper in between; set aside.
2. For filling, combine cheeses, egg and parsley. Spoon 3-4 Tbsp. down the center of each crepe; roll up. Pour half of the spaghetti sauce into an ungreased 13x9-in. baking dish. Place crepes, seam side down, over sauce; pour remaining sauce over top.
3. Cover and bake at 350° for 20 minutes. Uncover and bake 20 minutes longer or until heated through. Sprinkle with Romano cheese if desired.
3 MANICOTTI: 480 cal., 22g fat (11g sat. fat), 201mg chol., 1128mg sod., 44g carb. (17g sugars, 3g fiber), 27g pro.

EASY PESTO PIZZA

Knead basil, oregano and Parmesan cheese into packaged bread dough for a full-flavored crust. Prepared pesto keeps this pizza big on taste and convenience.
—Taste of Home *Test Kitchen*

Prep: 20 min. • **Bake:** 20 min.
Makes: 8 servings

- 1   loaf (1 lb.) frozen bread dough, thawed
- ½   cup shredded Parmesan cheese, divided
- ½   tsp. dried basil
- ½   tsp. dried oregano
- ¼   cup prepared pesto
- 1   cup sliced fresh mushrooms
- 1   cup shredded part-skim mozzarella cheese

1. Preheat oven to 425°. Place dough on a lightly floured surface; let rest for 10 minutes. Knead in ¼ cup cheese, basil and the oregano. Roll into a 12-in. circle; place on a greased 14-in. pizza pan. Prick with a fork. Bake 10 minutes.
2. Spread pesto sauce over the crust. Sprinkle with mushrooms, mozzarella cheese and the remaining Parmesan cheese. Bake pizza until golden brown, 8-10 minutes longer.
1 PIECE: 259 cal., 11g fat (4g sat. fat), 17mg chol., 513mg sod., 31g carb. (3g sugars, 2g fiber), 12g pro.

MEAT LOVER OPTION PAGE 320

CREAMY PASTA PRIMAVERA

This pasta dish is a wonderful blend of crisp, colorful vegetables and a creamy Parmesan cheese sauce.
—Darlene Brenden, Salem, OR

Takes: 30 min. • Makes: 6 servings

- 2 cups uncooked gemelli or spiral pasta
- 1 lb. fresh asparagus, trimmed and cut into 2-in. pieces
- 3 medium carrots, shredded
- 2 tsp. canola oil
- 2 cups cherry tomatoes, halved
- 1 garlic clove, minced
- ½ cup grated Parmesan cheese
- ½ cup heavy whipping cream
- ¼ tsp. pepper

1. Cook pasta according to package directions. In a large skillet over medium-high heat, saute asparagus and carrots in oil until crisp-tender. Add the tomatoes and garlic; cook 1 minute longer.
2. Stir in Parmesan cheese, cream and pepper. Drain the pasta; toss with the asparagus mixture.

1⅓ CUPS: 275 cal., 12g fat (6g sat. fat), 33mg chol., 141mg sod., 35g carb. (5g sugars, 3g fiber), 10g pro. **DIABETIC EXCHANGES:** 2 starch, 2 fat, 1 vegetable.
HEALTH TIP: Using just a small amount of a rich ingredient, like heavy cream, is a smart way keep a dish tasting indulgent while cutting calories.

TORTELLINI WITH TOMATO SPINACH CREAM SAUCE

I enjoy all things pasta, and tortellini is my favorite. The flavor of this dish is amazing. Even my husband, who hates pasta of any kind, loves it! It's a great recipe for non-spinach fans to try too.
—Jenny Dubinsky, Inwood, WV

Takes: 30 min. • Makes: 6 servings

- 1 Tbsp. olive oil
- 1 small onion, chopped
- 3 garlic cloves, minced
- 1 can (14½ oz.) petite diced tomatoes, undrained
- 5 oz. frozen chopped spinach, thawed and squeezed dry (about ½ cup)
- 1 tsp. dried basil
- ¾ tsp. salt
- ½ tsp. pepper
- 1 cup heavy whipping cream
- 1 pkg. (19 oz.) frozen cheese tortellini
- ½ cup grated Parmesan cheese

1. In a large skillet, heat oil over medium-high heat. Add onion; cook and stir until tender, 2-3 minutes. Add garlic; cook 1 minute longer. Add tomatoes, spinach and seasonings. Cook and stir over medium heat until liquid is absorbed, about 3 minutes.
2. Stir in the cream; bring to a boil. Reduce heat; simmer, uncovered, until thickened, about 10 minutes. Meanwhile, cook tortellini according to the package directions; drain. Stir into sauce. Sprinkle with cheese.

1 CUP: 404 cal., 22g fat (13g sat. fat), 80mg chol., 810mg sod., 38g carb. (6g sugars, 4g fiber), 13g pro.

SPINACH LASAGNA ROLL-UPS

One night, some friends on a tight schedule stopped by. I invited them to stay for dinner, so I needed something I could fix quickly. I created these savory roll-ups featuring a creamy three-cheese filling. They taste like lasagna but bake in a fraction of the time.
—*Julia Trachsel, Victoria, BC*

Prep: 30 min. • **Bake:** 25 min.
Makes: 6 servings

- 12   uncooked lasagna noodles
- 2   large eggs, lightly beaten
- 1   pkg. (10 oz.) frozen chopped spinach, thawed and squeezed dry
- 2½   cups whole-milk ricotta cheese
- 2½   cups shredded part-skim mozzarella cheese
- ½   cup grated Parmesan cheese
- ¼   tsp. salt
- ¼   tsp. pepper
- ¼   tsp. ground nutmeg
- 1   jar (24 oz.) meatless pasta sauce

1. Preheat oven to 375°. Cook noodles according to package directions; drain. Meanwhile, mix eggs, spinach, cheeses and seasonings.

2. Pour 1 cup meatless pasta sauce into an ungreased 13x9-in. baking dish. Spread ⅓ cup cheese mixture over each noodle; roll up and place over sauce, seam side down. Top with the remaining sauce. Bake, covered, for 20 minutes. Uncover; bake until heated through, 5-10 minutes longer.

2 ROLL-UPS: 569 cal., 22g fat (13g sat. fat), 145mg chol., 1165mg sod., 57g carb. (17g sugars, 5g fiber), 38g pro.

PIZZA MARGHERITA

This classic pie starts with a chewy homemade crust, then is topped with tomatoes, mozzarella, oregano and fresh basil. It's so scrumptious!
—*Loretta Lawrence, Myrtle Beach, SC*

Prep: 30 min. + rising • **Bake:** 15 min.
Makes: 2 pizzas (8 servings each)

- 3   tsp. active dry yeast
- 1   cup warm water (110° to 115°)
- 2   Tbsp. olive oil
- 1   tsp. sugar
- 1   tsp. salt
- 3   cups bread flour

TOPPINGS
- 2   cans (14½ oz. each) diced tomatoes, drained
- 8   cups shredded part-skim mozzarella cheese
- 2   Tbsp. minced fresh oregano or 2 tsp. dried oregano
- 20   fresh basil leaves, roughly torn
- ½   tsp. crushed red pepper flakes
- ⅛   tsp. salt
- ⅛   tsp. pepper
- 2   Tbsp. olive oil

1. In a small bowl, dissolve the yeast in warm water. In a large bowl, combine the oil, sugar, salt and 1 cup flour; beat until smooth. Stir in enough remaining flour to form a soft dough.

2. Turn dough onto a floured surface; knead for 6-8 minutes or until smooth and elastic. Place in a greased bowl, turning once to grease the top. Cover and let rise in a warm place until doubled, about 1 hour.

3. Punch dough down; divide in half. Roll each portion into a 13-in. circle. Transfer to 2 greased 14-in. pizza pans; build up edges slightly. Cover with a clean kitchen towel; let rest for 10 minutes.

4. Spoon tomatoes over dough. Top with cheese, oregano, basil, pepper flakes, salt and pepper. Drizzle with oil. Bake at 450° for 15-20 minutes or until crust is golden brown.

1 PIECE: 304 cal., 15g fat (7g sat. fat), 36mg chol., 625mg sod., 25g carb. (3g sugars, 2g fiber), 17g pro.

❄ SWEET POTATO TORTELLINI WITH HAZELNUT SAUCE

Using wonton wrappers instead of fresh pasta dough makes homemade tortellini easier to prepare. This vegetarian entree is delicious anytime but also impressive enough for formal occasions.

—*Charlene Chambers, Ormond Beach, FL*

Prep: 1 hour • **Cook:** 15 min.
Makes: 8 servings

- 3 large sweet potatoes (about 2½ lbs.), peeled and cubed
- ¼ cup olive oil, divided
- 1½ tsp. herbes de Provence
- ¾ tsp. salt, divided
- ½ tsp. pepper, divided
- 2 shallots, chopped
- 2 garlic cloves, minced
- 1 cup whole-milk ricotta cheese
- 1 Tbsp. hazelnut liqueur
- ¼ tsp. ground nutmeg
- 72 wonton wrappers
- 3 qt. water
- ¾ cup unsalted butter, cubed
- 3 Tbsp. minced fresh sage
- ½ cup dried cherries, chopped
- ¼ cup chopped hazelnuts, toasted
- 1 cup shaved Asiago cheese

1. Preheat the oven to 400°. Place sweet potatoes in a greased 15x10x1-in. baking pan; toss with 2 Tbsp. oil, herbes de Provence, ½ tsp. salt and ¼ tsp. pepper. Roast for 25-30 minutes or until tender, stirring once. Cool slightly.

2. In a small skillet, heat remaining oil over medium-high heat. Add shallots and garlic; cook and stir until tender. Transfer to a food processor. Add sweet potatoes, ricotta cheese, hazelnut liqueur, nutmeg and remaining salt and pepper; process until blended.

3. Place 1 Tbsp. filling in center of each wonton wrapper. (Cover remaining wrappers with a damp paper towel until ready to use.) Moisten wrapper edges with water. Fold 1 corner diagonally over filling to form a triangle; press edges to seal. Pull opposite corners together, forming a boat; moisten with water and pinch to seal.

4. In a Dutch oven, bring water to a boil. Reduce heat to a gentle boil. Cook the tortellini in batches 30-60 seconds or until they float. Remove with a slotted spoon; keep warm.

5. In a small heavy saucepan, melt butter over medium heat. Add the sage; heat for 5-7 minutes or until butter is golden brown, stirring constantly. Remove from heat; stir in cherries and hazelnuts. Serve with tortellini. Top with cheese.

FREEZE OPTION: Freeze the uncooked tortellini between waxed paper-lined baking sheets in an airtight container. To use, cook the tortellini as directed, increasing time to 1½-2 minutes or until they float. Serve as directed.

NOTE: Look for herbes de Provence in the spice aisle.

9 TORTELLINI WITH 2 TBSP. SAUCE:
662 cal., 34g fat (17g sat. fat), 77mg chol., 718mg sod., 73g carb. (16g sugars, 4g fiber), 17g pro.

TEST KITCHEN TIP

Sweet potato puree can be made and refrigerated the day before the wontons are filled.

⏱ LOADED MEXICAN PIZZA
(PICTURED ON COVER)

My husband is a picky eater, but this healthy pizza has such amazing flavor that he looks forward to it. Leftovers taste even better the next day.
—*Mary Barker, Knoxville, TN*

Takes: 30 min. • **Makes:** 6 servings

- 1 can (15 oz.) black beans, rinsed and drained
- 1 medium red onion, chopped
- 1 small sweet yellow pepper, chopped
- 3 tsp. chili powder
- ¾ tsp. ground cumin
- 3 medium tomatoes, chopped
- 1 jalapeno pepper, seeded and finely chopped
- 1 garlic clove, minced
- 1 prebaked 12-in. thin pizza crust
- 2 cups chopped fresh spinach
- 2 Tbsp. minced fresh cilantro
   Hot pepper sauce to taste
- ½ cup shredded reduced-fat cheddar cheese
- ½ cup shredded pepper jack cheese

1. In a small bowl, mash black beans. Stir in the onion, yellow pepper, chili powder and cumin. In another bowl, combine the tomatoes, jalapeno and garlic.

2. Place the crust on an ungreased 12-in. pizza pan; spread with bean mixture. Top with tomato mixture and spinach. Sprinkle with cilantro, pepper sauce and cheeses.

3. Bake at 400° for 12-15 minutes or until the cheese is melted.

NOTE: Wear disposable gloves when cutting hot peppers; the oils can burn skin. Avoid touching your face.

1 PIECE: 295 cal., 8g fat (3g sat. fat), 17mg chol., 581mg sod., 40g carb. (5g sugars, 6g fiber), 15g pro. **DIABETIC EXCHANGES:** 2½ starch, 1 vegetable, 1 lean meat.

❄ FOUR-CHEESE STUFFED SHELLS

More cheese, please! You'll get your fill from saucy jumbo pasta shells loaded with four kinds—mozzarella, Asiago, ricotta and cottage cheese. Do the prep work, and then freeze according to the recipe directions to have a ready-to-bake meal for a future busy night.
—Taste of Home *Test Kitchen*

- -

Prep: 20 min. • **Bake:** 25 min.
Makes: 2 servings

- 6 uncooked jumbo pasta shells
- ½ cup shredded part-skim mozzarella cheese, divided
- ¼ cup shredded Asiago cheese
- ¼ cup ricotta cheese
- ¼ cup 4% cottage cheese
- 1 Tbsp. minced chives
- 1 pkg. (10 oz.) frozen chopped spinach, thawed and squeezed dry
- 1 cup meatless spaghetti sauce

1. Preheat oven to 350°. Cook pasta according to the package directions. Meanwhile, in a small bowl, combine ¼ cup mozzarella cheese, Asiago cheese, ricotta cheese, cottage cheese, chives and ½ cup spinach (save the remaining spinach for another use).
2. Spread ½ cup spaghetti sauce into a shallow 1½-qt. baking dish coated with cooking spray. Drain pasta; stuff with cheese mixture. Arrange in prepared dish. Top with remaining spaghetti sauce and mozzarella.
3. Cover and bake until heated through, 25-30 minutes.
FREEZE OPTION: Cover and freeze the unbaked casserole. To use, partially thaw in refrigerator overnight. Remove from refrigerator 30 minutes before baking. Preheat oven to 350°. Bake as directed, increasing time as necessary to heat through and for a thermometer inserted in the center of 2 or 3 shells to read 165°.
3 STUFFED SHELLS: 376 cal., 14g fat (9g sat. fat), 49mg chol., 959mg sod., 39g carb. (13g sugars, 4g fiber), 25g pro.

GRILLED EGGPLANT PANINI
WITH BASIL AIOLI
P. 98

Burgers,
Sandwiches
& Wraps

Who says you need meat to make a rich and
hearty sandwich? Whether you're planning a picnic
or packing your lunch, these delicious vegetarian
handhelds are guaranteed to satisfy.

FESTIVE FALL FALAFEL

Falafel is the ultimate Israeli street food. Pumpkin adds a light sweetness and keeps the patties moist while baking. Top these beauties with maple tahini sauce. You can serve them sandwich-style, as an appetizer over a bed of greens, or with soup and salad.
—*Julie Peterson, Crofton, MD*

Prep: 20 min. • **Bake:** 30 min.
Makes: 4 servings

- 1   cup canned garbanzo beans or chickpeas, rinsed and drained
- ½   cup canned pumpkin
- ½   cup fresh cilantro leaves
- ¼   cup chopped onion
- 1   garlic clove, halved
- ¾   tsp. salt
- ½   tsp. ground ginger
- ½   tsp. ground cumin
- ¼   tsp. ground coriander
- ¼   tsp. cayenne pepper

MAPLE TAHINI SAUCE
- ½   cup tahini
- ¼   cup water
- 2   Tbsp. maple syrup
- 1   Tbsp. cider vinegar
- ½   tsp. salt
- 8   pita pocket halves
       Optional: Sliced cucumber, onions and tomatoes

1. Preheat oven to 400°. Place the first 10 ingredients in a food processor; pulse until combined. Drop by tablespoonfuls onto a greased baking sheet. Bake until firm and golden brown, 30-35 minutes.
2. Meanwhile, in a small bowl, combine the tahini, water, syrup, vinegar and salt. Serve falafel in pita pocket halves with maple tahini sauce and optional toppings as desired.

2 FILLED PITA HALVES: 469 cal., 21g fat (3g sat. fat), 0 chol., 1132mg sod., 57g carb. (10g sugars, 8g fiber), 14g pro.

🍴⏱ AIR-FRYER PORTOBELLO MELTS

We're always looking for satisfying vegetarian meals, and this one tops the list. The open-face melts are especially delicious in the summer when we have lots of homegrown tomatoes.
—*Amy Smalley, Morehead, KY*

Takes: 25 min. • **Makes:** 2 servings

- 2   large portobello mushrooms (4 oz. each), stems removed
- ¼   cup olive oil
- 2   Tbsp. balsamic vinegar
- ½   tsp. salt
- ½   tsp. dried basil
- 4   tomato slices
- 2   slices mozzarella cheese
- 2   slices Italian bread (1 in. thick)
  Chopped fresh basil

1. Place mushrooms in a shallow bowl. Mix oil, vinegar, salt and dried basil; brush onto both sides of mushrooms. Let stand 5 minutes. Reserve remaining marinade. Preheat air fryer to 400°.
2. Place mushrooms on greased tray in air-fryer basket, stem side down. Cook until tender, 3-4 minutes per side. Remove from basket. Top stem sides with tomato and cheese; secure with toothpicks. Cook until cheese is melted, about 1 minute. Remove and keep warm; discard toothpicks.
3. Place bread on tray in the air-fryer basket; brush with reserved marinade. Cook until lightly toasted, 2-3 minutes. Top with mushrooms. Sprinkle sandwiches with chopped basil.
1 OPEN-FACED SANDWICH: 427 cal., 30g fat (4g sat. fat), 4mg chol., 864mg sod., 33g carb. (8g sugars, 4g fiber), 8g pro.

CORN & SQUASH QUESADILLAS

Grilled vegetables give these quesadillas their distinctive flair, while cumin and jalapeno peppers add a little zip.
—*Mildred Sherrer, Fort Worth, TX*

Prep: 40 min. • **Cook:** 10 min.
Makes: 6 servings

- 2 medium ears sweet corn, husked
- 2 medium yellow summer squash, halved lengthwise
- ½ small sweet onion, cut into ¼-in. slices
- 1 to 2 jalapeno peppers
- 1 Tbsp. minced fresh basil
- 1½ tsp. minced fresh oregano
- 1 garlic clove, minced
- ¼ tsp. salt
- ¼ tsp. ground cumin
- 6 flour tortillas (8 in.), warmed
- 1 cup shredded Monterey Jack cheese
- 1 Tbsp. canola oil

1. Grill corn, covered, over medium heat for 10 minutes; turn. Place the squash, onion and jalapenos on grill; cover and cook for 5-6 minutes on each side. When vegetables are cool enough to handle, remove corn from the cobs, chop the squash and onion, and seed and chop the jalapenos. Place in a large bowl.
2. Stir in the basil, oregano, garlic, salt and cumin. Place ½ cup filling on 1 side of each tortilla; sprinkle with cheese. Fold the tortillas over filling. In a large cast-iron skillet or griddle, cook the quesadillas in oil over medium heat until heated through, 1-2 minutes on each side. Cut into wedges.
NOTE: Wear disposable gloves when cutting hot peppers; the oils can burn skin. Avoid touching your face.
1 QUESADILLA: 301 cal., 12g fat (5g sat. fat), 17mg chol., 454mg sod., 38g carb. (5g sugars, 3g fiber), 11g pro. **DIABETIC EXCHANGES:** 2 starch, 1 vegetable, 1 medium-fat meat, ½ fat.

SAUCY TEMPEH SLOPPY JOES

I grew up eating sloppy joe sandwiches and couldn't get enough of the messy deliciousness. Now I eat meatless once or twice a week, so I decided to create a meatless twist on the classic sandwich. I use tempeh here, a fermented soy product that's high in protein and has a savory, nutty, earthy flavor. Its taste and texture work well in dishes that usually feature ground beef.
—*Trisha Kruse, Eagle, ID*

Prep: 15 min. • **Cook:** 25 min.
Makes: 10 servings

- 2 Tbsp. olive oil
- 1 medium onion, chopped
- ½ medium green pepper, chopped
- 2 garlic cloves, minced
- 2 pkg. (8 oz. each) tempeh
- 2 cans (15 oz. and 8 oz.) tomato sauce
- 3 Tbsp. brown sugar
- 1 Tbsp. soy sauce
- ½ tsp. dried oregano
- ½ tsp. dried thyme
- ¼ tsp. salt
- ⅛ tsp. cayenne pepper
- 10 hamburger buns, split

In a large skillet, heat oil over medium-high heat. Add onion and green pepper; cook and stir until tender, 6-8 minutes. Add garlic; cook 1 minute longer. Crumble tempeh into skillet; cook and stir for 5 minutes. Add tomato sauce, brown sugar, soy sauce and seasonings; cook and stir over medium heat until thickened, 10-15 minutes. Serve on buns.
1 SANDWICH: 273 cal., 10g fat (2g sat. fat), 0 chol., 674mg sod., 34g carb. (9g sugars, 2g fiber), 15g pro.

TEST KITCHEN TIP

Tempeh is high in protein and is a rich source of calcium, iron and manganese.

MEAT
LOVER
OPTION
PAGE 320

SPINACH QUESADILLAS

My family gave these cheesy quesadillas a big thumbs-up. Remove the spinach from the heat as soon as it wilts so it keeps a little bit of crunch.
—*Pam Kaiser, Mansfield, MO*

Takes: 25 min. • **Makes:** 4 servings

- 3 oz. fresh baby spinach (about 4 cups)
- 4 green onions, chopped
- 1 small tomato, chopped
- 2 Tbsp. lemon juice
- 1 tsp. ground cumin
- ¼ tsp. garlic powder
- 1 cup shredded reduced-fat Monterey Jack cheese or Mexican cheese blend
- ¼ cup reduced-fat ricotta cheese
- 6 flour tortillas (6 in.), warmed Reduced-fat sour cream, optional

1. In a large nonstick skillet, cook and stir first 6 ingredients until spinach is wilted. Remove from heat; stir in cheeses.
2. Top half of each tortilla with spinach mixture; fold the other half over filling. Place on a griddle coated with cooking spray; cook over medium heat until golden brown, 1-2 minutes per side. Cut the quesadillas in half. If desired, serve with sour cream.

3 WEDGES: 281 cal., 12g fat (6g sat. fat), 24mg chol., 585mg sod., 30g carb. (3g sugars, 4g fiber), 14g pro. **DIABETIC EXCHANGES:** 2 starch, 1 vegetable, 1 medium-fat meat.

HEALTH TIP: Use whole wheat tortillas to get almost twice the fiber per serving.

GREEN CHILE GRILLED CHEESE MELT

My daughter created a masterpiece with her ultimate grilled cheese and chilies. Want more heat? Use a 4-ounce can of diced jalapenos instead.
—*Julia Huntington, Cheyenne, WY*

Takes: 30 min. • **Makes:** 6 servings

- 4 oz. cream cheese, softened
- 1 cup shredded Colby-Monterey Jack cheese
- 1 cup shredded part-skim mozzarella cheese
- 1 can (4 oz.) chopped green chiles, drained
- 2 Tbsp. mayonnaise
- ¼ tsp. garlic powder Dash seasoned salt
- 12 slices white bread
- 6 slices tomato
- ¼ cup butter, melted

1. In a small bowl, mix first 7 ingredients until blended. Spread mixture over half the bread slices. Top with tomato and remaining bread.
2. Brush outsides of sandwiches with melted butter. In a large cast-iron or other heavy skillet, toast sandwiches in batches over medium-low heat until golden brown and heated through, 3-4 minutes on each side.

1 SANDWICH: 431 cal., 29g fat (15g sat. fat), 70mg chol., 730mg sod., 29g carb. (4g sugars, 2g fiber), 15g pro.

GRILLED CHICKPEA SALAD SANDWICH

When my mother comes to visit, she enjoys a good old-fashioned chicken salad sandwich. As a vegetarian, I make chickpea salad sandwiches all the time and finally decided to make one for her. After some hesitation, she tasted it and was instantly hooked!
—*Dannika Stevenson, Akron, OH*

- -

Takes: 30 min. • **Makes:** 4 servings

1 can (16 oz.) chickpeas or garbanzo beans, rinsed and drained
1 celery rib, finely chopped
2 sweet pickles, finely chopped
2 Tbsp. dried cranberries
2 Tbsp. finely chopped red onion
2 Tbsp. reduced-fat mayonnaise
2 tsp. sweet pickle juice
½ tsp. minced fresh parsley
¼ tsp. salt
¼ tsp. pepper
4 slices provolone cheese
8 slices multigrain bread

In a small bowl, mix first 10 ingredients. Place cheese slices on 4 bread slices; top with chickpea mixture and remaining bread. Preheat panini maker or indoor electric grill. Cook sandwiches, covered, until the bread is browned and cheese is melted, 3-5 minutes.

1 SANDWICH: 370 cal., 13g fat (4g sat. fat), 18mg chol., 753mg sod., 49g carb. (13g sugars, 9g fiber), 17g pro.

BUFFALO TOFU WRAP

My family loves the tofu filling in these wraps. For parties, we often serve it as a dip with tortilla chips or pita bread. It's easy to double the recipe if needed.
—*Deanna Wolfe, Muskegon, MI*

Takes: 20 min. • **Makes:** 6 servings

- 1 cup shredded dairy-free cheddar-flavored cheese
- ½ cup vegan mayonnaise
- ¼ cup finely chopped onion
- ¼ cup finely chopped celery
- 3 Tbsp. Louisiana-style hot sauce
- 1 Tbsp. lemon juice
- ½ tsp. garlic powder
- ¼ tsp. salt
- ¼ tsp. pepper
- 1 pkg. (16 oz.) extra-firm tofu, drained
- 1½ cups fresh baby spinach
- 6 spinach tortillas (8 in.), room temperature

In a large bowl, combine the first 9 ingredients. Crumble tofu into the bowl; mix well. Spoon about ½ cup tofu mixture down center of each tortilla; top with spinach. Fold bottom and sides of tortilla over filling and roll up.

1 WRAP: 452 cal., 29g fat (7g sat. fat), 0 chol., 1066mg sod., 38g carb. (1g sugars, 2g fiber), 11g pro.

TEST KITCHEN TIP

The tofu portion can be prepared ahead and chilled for a few hours or overnight.

SUPER GRILLED CHEESE SANDWICHES

Heat up your indoor grill to make this ooey-gooey grilled cheese sandwich. These are delicious served with soup.
—*Debbie Murray, Fort Worth, TX*

- -

Takes: 15 min. • **Makes:** 2 servings

- 4   slices Italian bread
- 2   slices (¾ oz. each) Muenster cheese
- 2   slices (¾ oz. each) Swiss cheese
- 2   slices (¾ oz. each) American cheese
- 2   slices (¾ oz. each) part-skim mozzarella cheese
- 1   Tbsp. butter, softened
- ¼   tsp. garlic salt with parsley

1. On 2 slices of bread, layer the cheeses; top with remaining bread. Butter the outsides of sandwiches; sprinkle with garlic salt.
2. Cook on an indoor grill or panini maker for 1-2 minutes or until bread is browned and cheese is melted.
1 SANDWICH: 430 cal., 20g fat (11g sat. fat), 57mg chol., 1094mg sod., 34g carb. (4g sugars, 2g fiber), 29g pro.

GRILLED GOAT CHEESE & ARUGULA SANDWICHES

To create a more grown-up grilled cheese, I threw in tangy goat cheese and peppery arugula. I enjoy a similar combination on pizza.
—*Jess Apfe, Berkeley, CA*

- -

Takes: 30 min. • **Makes:** 4 servings

- ½   cup sun-dried tomato pesto
- 8   slices sourdough bread
- 1½   cups roasted sweet red peppers, drained and patted dry
- 8   slices part-skim mozzarella cheese
- ½   cup crumbled goat cheese
- 1   cup fresh arugula
- ¼   cup butter, softened

1. Spread pesto over 4 slices of bread. Layer with peppers, mozzarella cheese, goat cheese and arugula; top with remaining bread. Spread outsides of sandwiches with butter.
2. In a large skillet, toast sandwiches over medium heat for 3-4 minutes on each side or until golden brown and the cheese is melted.
1 SANDWICH: 499 cal., 30g fat (17g sat. fat), 84mg chol., 1438mg sod., 33g carb. (9g sugars, 2g fiber), 22g pro.

PHILLY CHEESE FAKES

Mushrooms are the key to this twist on popular Philly steak sandwiches.
—*Veronica Vichit-Vadakan, Portland, OR*

Prep: 30 min. • **Broil:** 5 min.
Makes: 4 servings

- ¼ cup lemon juice
- 3 garlic cloves, minced
- 1 Tbsp. olive oil
- ½ tsp. smoked paprika
- ¼ tsp. salt
- ¼ tsp. pepper
- 1 lb. sliced fresh shiitake mushrooms
- 2 medium green peppers, sliced
- 1 small onion, thinly sliced
- 4 hoagie buns, split
- 4 slices reduced-fat provolone cheese

1. Preheat oven to 450°. In a small bowl, whisk the first 6 ingredients. In a large bowl, combine the mushrooms, green peppers and onion. Pour dressing over vegetables; toss to coat.

2. Transfer to two 15x10x1-in. baking pans coated with cooking spray. Bake for 15-20 minutes or until crisp-tender, stirring once.

3. Divide mushroom mixture among buns and top with cheese. Arrange on an ungreased baking sheet. Add bun tops to baking sheet, cut side up. Broil 3-4 in. from heat 2-3 minutes or until cheese is melted and bun tops are lightly browned. Replace tops.

1 SANDWICH: 344 cal., 12g fat (4g sat. fat), 10mg chol., 681mg sod., 47g carb. (9g sugars, 4g fiber), 17g pro.

CUMIN-SPICED LENTIL BURGERS

I adapted my Turkish daughter-in-law's traditional recipe for lentil logs—typically wrapped in a lettuce leaf and served with a lemon wedge—into vegan burgers. If you prefer a spicier version, add hot chili powder or crushed red chili peppers.
—*Sheila Joan Suhan, Scottdale, PA*

Prep: 30 min. + standing
Cook: 10 min./batch • **Makes:** 8 servings

2¼ cups water, divided
1 cup dried red lentils, rinsed
1 cup bulgur (fine grind)
1½ tsp. salt, divided
6 Tbsp. canola oil, divided
1 large onion, chopped
1 Tbsp. ground cumin
1 Tbsp. chili powder
1 large egg, lightly beaten
6 green onions, sliced
3 Tbsp. chopped fresh parsley
8 flatbread wraps
8 Tbsp. Sriracha mayonnaise
   Optional toppings: Lettuce leaves, sliced tomato and sliced onions

1. Place 2 cups water and lentils in a large saucepan. Bring to a boil. Reduce the heat; simmer, uncovered, until the lentils are tender, 15-20 minutes, stirring occasionally. Remove from heat; stir in bulgur and 1 tsp. salt. Cover and let stand until bulgur is tender and the liquid is absorbed, 15-20 minutes.
2. Meanwhile, in a large nonstick skillet, heat 2 Tbsp. oil over medium-high heat. Add onion; cook and stir until tender, 5-7 minutes. Add cumin and chili powder; cook 1 minute longer. Remove from heat. Add onion mixture to lentil mixture. Stir in the egg, green onions, parsley and remaining ½ tsp. salt, mixing lightly but thoroughly. If needed, add remaining ¼ cup water, 1 Tbsp. at a time, to help mixture stay together when squeezed; shape into eight ½-in.-thick patties.
3. In the same skillet, heat remaining 4 Tbsp. oil over medium heat. Add burgers in batches; cook until golden brown, 3-5 minutes on each side. Serve in wraps with Sriracha mayonnaise and, if desired, toppings of your choice.
1 BURGER: 434 cal., 23g fat (2g sat. fat), 1mg chol., 780mg sod., 54g carb. (2g sugars, 16g fiber), 16g pro.

EGGPLANT MUFFULETTA

I often prepare this recipe when I'm hosting a casual party. It's a marvelous meatless sandwich, with subtle olive flavors and melted cheese in every bite, that makes each gathering special.
—*Elizabeth Dumont, Madison, MS*

Prep: 35 min. • **Broil:** 5 min.
Makes: 3 sandwiches (6 servings each)

1 jar (8 oz.) roasted sweet red peppers, drained
1 cup pimiento-stuffed olives
1 cup pitted ripe olives
1 cup giardiniera
¾ cup olive oil, divided
¼ cup packed fresh parsley sprigs
3 Tbsp. white wine vinegar
4 garlic cloves, halved
1½ tsp. salt, divided
½ tsp. pepper, divided
1 lb. sliced fresh mushrooms
1 large onion, thinly sliced
2 Tbsp. butter
1 cup all-purpose flour
1 medium eggplant, cut into 9 slices
3 loaves (10 oz. each) focaccia bread
2 large tomatoes, sliced
9 slices provolone cheese
9 slices part-skim mozzarella cheese

1. In a food processor, combine the red peppers, olives, giardiniera, ¼ cup oil, parsley, vinegar, garlic, 1 tsp. salt and ¼ tsp. pepper. Cover and process until blended; set aside.
2. In a large skillet, saute mushrooms and onion in butter and ¼ cup oil. Remove and keep warm.
3. In a bowl or shallow dish, combine flour and remaining salt and pepper. Add eggplant, a few slices at a time, and turn to coat. In the same skillet, cook eggplant in remaining oil for 2-3 minutes on each side or until golden brown.
4. Split each loaf of focaccia in half. Spread the reserved olive mixture over each focaccia bottom; top with the eggplant, mushroom mixture, tomatoes and cheeses.
5. Place on a baking sheet. Broil 2-3 in from the heat for 2-4 minutes or until cheese is melted. Replace focaccia tops. Cut each loaf into 6 wedges.
1 PIECE: 372 cal., 20g fat (6g sat. fat), 18mg chol., 881mg sod., 39g carb. (5g sugars, 3g fiber), 12g pro.

BLACK BEAN RICE BURGERS

A salsa and sour cream sauce helps dress up these hearty vegetarian burgers. My fiance, who's a confirmed meat-and-potatoes man, loves the sandwiches and asks for them often.
—Laura Wimbrow, Ocean City, MD

Takes: 20 min. • **Makes:** 4 servings

- 1 small onion, very finely chopped
- 2 Tbsp. canola oil, divided
- 1 can (15 oz.) black beans, rinsed and drained
- 1 cup cooked brown rice
- ¼ cup dry bread crumbs
- 2 large egg yolks, lightly beaten
- 2 Tbsp. plus ¼ cup salsa, divided
- ½ tsp. salt
- ¼ tsp. pepper
- ¼ cup reduced-fat sour cream
- 4 lettuce leaves
- 4 slices reduced-fat cheddar cheese (1 oz. each)
- 4 hamburger buns, split
   Optional: Sliced tomato and sliced red onion

1. In a large nonstick skillet, cook the onion in 1 Tbsp. oil over medium heat until translucent but not browned, 2-4 minutes; remove from heat and set aside. In bowl of a food processor fitted with blade attachment, pulse half the beans and ½ cup rice until mixture forms a thick paste. In a large bowl, add processed bean mixture, remaining black beans and rice, cooked onion, bread crumbs, egg yolks, 2 Tbsp. salsa, salt, and pepper; mix well with hands, squeezing until mixture holds together. Form bean mixture into 4 patties. Cook the burgers over medium heat in remaining 1 Tbsp. oil until firm and browned, 4-5 minutes on each side.

2. In a small bowl, combine sour cream and remaining ¼ cup salsa. Layer a lettuce leaf, burger, cheese and sour cream mixture on each bun bottom, adding tomato and red onion as desired. Replace bun tops.

1 BURGER: 482 cal., 18g fat (6g sat. fat), 101mg chol., 1070mg sod., 55g carb. (7g sugars, 6g fiber), 21g pro.

CURRIED EGG SALAD

A curry kick gives this egg salad big appeal. We love these sandwiches when the weather gets warm.
—Joyce McDowell, West Union, OH

Takes: 15 min. • **Makes:** 6 servings

- ½ cup mayonnaise
- ½ tsp. ground curry
- ½ tsp. honey
   Dash ground ginger
- 6 hard-boiled large eggs, coarsely chopped
- 3 green onions, sliced
- 6 slices whole wheat bread
   Optional: Tomato slices and cracked pepper

Mix the first 4 ingredients; stir in eggs and green onions. Spread on bread. If desired, top with tomato and sprinkle with pepper.

1 OPEN-FACED SANDWICH: 273 cal., 20g fat (4g sat. fat), 188mg chol., 284mg sod., 14g carb. (2g sugars, 2g fiber), 10g pro.

TEST KITCHEN TIP

For easiest peeling, use eggs that aren't super fresh. Add eggs to a pot with enough water to submerge them 1 inch and bring to a boil. Turn off the heat and cover for 14 minutes. Remove eggs and put in an ice bath to cool completely.

BASIL-TOMATO GRILLED CHEESE

Keep the taste of summer going all year long with this easy Italian-style grilled cheese sandwich. It tastes fresh and comforting all in one bite, and is fast to make on busy days.
—*Sylvia Schmitt, Sun City, AZ*

Takes: 20 min. • **Makes:** 4 servings

- 8   slices Italian bread (¾ in. thick)
- 8   slices part-skim mozzarella cheese
- 2   large plum tomatoes, sliced
- 2   Tbsp. minced fresh basil
- 2   tsp. balsamic vinegar
      Salt and pepper to taste
- ¼   cup olive oil
- 3   Tbsp. grated Parmesan cheese
- ¼   tsp. garlic powder

1. On 4 slices of bread, layer mozzarella cheese and tomatoes; sprinkle with the basil, vinegar, salt and pepper. Top with remaining bread.

2. In a small bowl, combine the oil, Parmesan cheese and garlic powder; brush mixture over the outsides of each sandwich.

3. In a skillet over medium heat, toast sandwiches until golden brown on both sides and cheese is melted.

1 SANDWICH: 467 cal., 27g fat (9g sat. fat), 34mg chol., 723mg sod., 34g carb. (4g sugars, 2g fiber), 23g pro.

GRILLED VEGGIE SANDWICHES WITH CILANTRO PESTO

I first ate this sandwich while vacationing in Sedona, Arizona, and fell in love with it. When I returned home, I developed this one that tastes just like the original.
—*Carolyn Phenicie, Titusville, PA*

Prep: 20 min. • **Grill:** 20 min. + standing
Makes: 4 servings

- ⅔ cup packed fresh cilantro sprigs
- ¼ cup packed fresh parsley sprigs
- 2 Tbsp. grated Parmesan cheese
- 2 garlic cloves, peeled
- 2 Tbsp. water
- 1 Tbsp. pine nuts
- 1 Tbsp. olive oil

SANDWICHES

- 2 large sweet red peppers
- 4 slices eggplant (½ in. thick)
  Cooking spray
- ½ tsp. salt
- ¼ tsp. pepper
- ½ cup shredded part-skim mozzarella cheese
- 4 kaiser rolls, split

1. For pesto, place cilantro, parsley, Parmesan cheese and garlic in a small food processor; pulse until chopped. Add water and pine nuts; process until blended. While processing, slowly add olive oil.

2. Grill peppers, covered, over medium heat until the skins are blistered and blackened, turning occasionally, 10-15 minutes. Immediately place peppers in a large bowl; let stand, covered, for 20 minutes. Peel off and discard charred skin. Cut peppers in half; remove stems and seeds.

3. Lightly spritz both sides of eggplant slices with cooking spray; sprinkle with salt and pepper. Grill, covered, over medium heat until tender, 3-5 minutes on each side. Top with peppers; sprinkle with mozzarella cheese. Grill, covered, until the cheese is melted, 2-3 minutes; remove from grill.

4. Spread roll bottoms with pesto. Top with eggplant stacks and roll tops.

1 SANDWICH: 310 cal., 12g fat (3g sat. fat), 11mg chol., 755mg sod., 40g carb. (6g sugars, 4g fiber), 12g pro.
DIABETIC EXCHANGES: 2 starch, 1 vegetable, 1 lean meat, 1 fat.

TEST KITCHEN TIP

Also known as pignolia or pinon, the pine nut is a small seed from one of the several pine tree varieties. They are small, elongated ivory-colored nuts measuring about ⅜ in. and having a soft texture and a buttery flavor. Frequently used in Italian dishes and sauces such as pesto, pine nuts are often toasted to enhance their flavor.

GRILLED BLACK BEAN & PINEAPPLE BURGERS

Sometimes you need a break from the beef, and this recipe offers a new option. The pineapple slices are a flavorful topper for this tasty bean burger loaded with the goodness of veggies.
—Carole Resnick, Cleveland, OH

Prep: 30 min. + chilling • **Grill:** 10 min.
Makes: 6 servings

- 2 cans (15 oz. each) black beans, rinsed and drained
- 1 medium red onion, finely chopped
- 2 large eggs, beaten
- ½ cup panko bread crumbs
- ½ cup crushed baked tortilla chip scoops
- ⅓ cup chopped green pepper
- 1 Tbsp. minced fresh cilantro
- 1 tsp. ground cumin
- 1 tsp. chili powder
- ½ tsp. hot pepper sauce
- ½ cup fat-free mayonnaise
- 4 tsp. chopped green onion
- 4 tsp. Dijon mustard
- 2 tsp. honey
- 1½ tsp. orange juice
- ½ tsp. reduced-sodium soy sauce
- 6 slices unsweetened pineapple
- 6 whole wheat hamburger buns, split

1. In a large bowl, mash beans. Add the red onion, eggs, bread crumbs, chips, green pepper, cilantro, cumin, chili powder and pepper sauce. Shape into 6 patties. Refrigerate for 1 hour.
2. In a bowl, combine the mayonnaise, green onion, mustard, honey, orange juice and soy sauce; refrigerate sauce until serving.
3. On a lightly oiled rack, grill burgers, covered, over medium heat or broil 4 in. from the heat for 3-5 minutes on each side or until a thermometer reads 160°.
4. Grill or broil the pineapple slices until heated through, 2-3 minutes on each side. Place burgers and pineapple on bun bottoms; top each with 1 rounded Tbsp. sauce.

1 BURGER: 357 cal., 5g fat (1g sat. fat), 73mg chol., 807mg sod., 65g carb. (16g sugars, 11g fiber), 14g pro.

DILLY CHICKPEA SALAD SANDWICHES

This chickpea salad is flavorful and contains less fat and cholesterol than chicken salad. These make delightful picnic sandwiches.
—Deanna Wolfe, Muskegon, MI

Takes: 15 min. • **Makes:** 6 servings

- 1 can (15 oz.) chickpeas or garbanzo beans, rinsed and drained
- ½ cup finely chopped onion
- ½ cup finely chopped celery
- ½ cup reduced-fat mayonnaise or vegan mayonnaise
- 3 Tbsp. honey mustard or Dijon mustard
- 2 Tbsp. snipped fresh dill
- 1 Tbsp. red wine vinegar
- ¼ tsp. salt
- ¼ tsp. paprika
- ¼ tsp. pepper
- 12 slices multigrain bread
  Optional toppings: Romaine leaves, tomato slices, dill pickle slices and sweet red pepper rings

Place chickpeas in a large bowl; mash to desired consistency. Stir in onion, celery, mayonnaise, mustard, dill, vinegar, salt, paprika and pepper. Spread over 6 bread slices; layer with toppings of your choice and remaining bread.
1 SANDWICH: 295 cal., 11g fat (2g sat. fat), 7mg chol., 586mg sod., 41g carb. (9g sugars, 7g fiber), 10g pro.

GRILLED EGGPLANT PANINI WITH BASIL AIOLI

I love using the bounty of fresh veggies and herbs from my garden for meals. This sandwich is loaded with veggies and has such a satisfying crunch. The melty provolone finishes things off perfectly.
—*Joseph Sciascia, San Mateo, CA*

Prep: 25 min. • **Grill:** 5 min./batch
Makes: 4 servings

¾ cup mayonnaise
⅓ cup chopped fresh basil
3 Tbsp. grated Parmesan cheese
2 Tbsp. minced fresh chives
1 Tbsp. lemon juice
2 garlic cloves, minced
½ tsp. salt
½ tsp. pepper
1 large eggplant, cut into 8 slices
2 large sweet red peppers, cut into large pieces
2 Tbsp. olive oil
4 ciabatta rolls, split
8 slices provolone cheese

1. For aioli, place the first 8 ingredients in a blender; cover and process until mixture is smooth.

2. Brush the vegetables with oil. Place in broiling pan in oven and broil 3-4 in. from heat, or grill, covered, over medium heat until tender, 4-5 minutes per side. Chop the peppers when cool enough to handle.

3. Spread the cut sides of each roll with 1 Tbsp. aioli. Layer bottoms with 1 slice cheese, 2 slices eggplant, peppers and remaining cheese. Replace tops.

4. In a panini maker, grill sandwiches until the cheese is melted, 5-7 minutes. Serve remaining aioli with sandwiches or save for another use.

1 SANDWICH: 732 cal., 38g fat (11g sat. fat), 33mg chol., 1116mg sod., 83g carb. (12g sugars, 9g fiber), 23g pro.

🕐 VEGGIE BROWN RICE WRAPS

Salsa gives a bit of zip to the brown rice and bean filling in these tasty meatless tortilla wraps.

—*Lisa Sullivan, St. Marys, OH*

Takes: 20 min. • **Makes:** 6 servings

- 1 medium sweet red or green pepper, diced
- 1 cup sliced fresh mushrooms
- 1 Tbsp. olive oil
- 2 garlic cloves, minced
- 2 cups cooked brown rice
- 1 can (16 oz.) kidney beans, rinsed and drained
- 1 cup frozen corn, thawed
- ¼ cup chopped green onions
- ½ tsp. ground cumin
- ½ tsp. pepper
- ¼ tsp. salt
- 6 flour tortillas (8 in.), warmed
- ½ cup shredded reduced-fat cheddar cheese
- ¾ cup salsa

1. In a large cast-iron or other heavy skillet, saute red pepper and mushrooms in oil until tender. Add the garlic; cook 1 minute. Add the rice, beans, corn, green onions, cumin, pepper and salt. Cook and stir until heated through, 4-6 minutes.

2. Spoon ¾ cup rice mixture onto each tortilla. Sprinkle with cheese; drizzle with salsa. Fold sides of tortilla over the filling; roll up. Serve immediately.

1 WRAP: 377 cal., 8g fat (2g sat. fat), 7mg chol., 675mg sod., 62g carb. (4g sugars, 7g fiber), 15g pro.

MEAT LOVER OPTION
PAGE 320

MEAT LOVER OPTION PAGE 320

1 jalapeno pepper, seeded
 and finely chopped
1 large egg
1 tsp. minced fresh cilantro
1 garlic clove, minced
4 whole wheat hamburger buns, split
 Optional: Reduced-fat sour cream
 and guacamole

1. Preheat air fryer to 375°. Place beans in a food processor; cover and process until blended. Transfer to a large bowl. Add bread crumbs, tomato, jalapeno, egg, cilantro and garlic. Mix until combined. Shape into 4 patties.
2. In batches, place patties on greased tray in air-fryer basket. Cook until lightly browned, 3-4 minutes. Turn; cook until lightly browned, 3-4 minutes longer. Serve on buns. If desired, top with sour cream and guacamole.
1 BURGER: 323 cal., 8g fat (1g sat. fat), 47mg chol., 576mg sod., 51g carb. (6g sugars, 9g fiber), 13g pro.

TEST KITCHEN TIP

If you want to make these burgers ahead of time, simply assemble the uncooked veggie patties and store them in an airtight container in the fridge for up to 1 week. Use a piece of parchment to keep the patties from sticking together. When you're craving veggie burgers, cook patties in an air fryer.

MONTEREY ARTICHOKE PANINI

Looking for a new sandwich idea? This melty combination of cheese, tomatoes, artichokes and spinach tastes farmers market fresh and is special enough for a laid-back date night.
—Jean Ecos, Hartland, WI

- -

Takes: 25 min. • **Makes:** 2 servings

    4 slices sourdough or multigrain
       bread
    4 slices Monterey Jack cheese
       (¾ oz. each)
    ½ cup water-packed artichoke hearts,
       rinsed, drained and halved
    ½ cup fresh baby spinach
    4 slices tomato
    1 Tbsp. butter, softened

1. Top 2 slices of bread with a slice of cheese each; layer each with ¼ cup artichokes, ¼ cup spinach, 2 tomato slices and remaining cheese. Top with the remaining bread. Spread the butter over outside of sandwiches.
2. Cook on a panini maker or indoor grill until the bread is toasted and the cheese is melted.
1 SANDWICH: 416 cal., 20g fat (12g sat. fat), 56mg chol., 855mg sod., 38g carb. (2g sugars, 3g fiber), 18g pro.

AIR-FRYER SALSA BLACK BEAN BURGERS

Meatless meals will be so tasty when these hearty bean burgers are on the menu. Guacamole and sour cream make them seem decadent.
—Jill Reichardt, St. Louis, MO

- -

Takes: 30 min. • **Makes:** 4 servings

    1 can (15 oz.) black beans,
       rinsed and drained
    ⅔ cup dry bread crumbs
    1 small tomato, seeded
       and finely chopped

MEDITERRANEAN
BULGUR SALAD
P. 111

Grain Dishes & Bowls

If you find yourself aimlessly snacking by mid-afternoon, then these grain recipes are for you. Chock-full of fresh veggies, meatless protein and good-for-you grains, they're guaranteed to help you power through your day.

KIMCHI FRIED RICE

Forget ordinary fried rice! Kimchi fried rice is just as easy, but it packs a flavorful punch. This is a fantastic use for leftovers, too. You can freeze the fried rice for up to three months. When cooking your thawed rice, add a little extra soy sauce so it doesn't dry out.
—Taste of Home *Test Kitchen*

Takes: 20 min. • **Makes:** 4 servings

- 2 Tbsp. canola oil, divided
- 1 small onion, chopped
- 1 cup kimchi, coarsely chopped
- ½ cup matchstick carrots
- ¼ cup kimchi juice
- 1 garlic cloves, minced
- 1 tsp. minced fresh gingerroot
- 3 cups leftover short grain rice
- 2 green onions, thinly sliced
- 3 tsp. soy sauce
- 1 tsp. sesame oil
- 4 large eggs
  Optional: Sliced nori, green onions and black sesame seeds

1. In large skillet, heat 1 Tbsp. canola oil over medium-high heat. Add onion; cook and stir until tender, 2-4 minutes. Add kimchi, carrots, kimchi juice, garlic and ginger; cook 2 minutes longer. Add rice, green onions, soy sauce and sesame oil; heat through, stirring frequently.
2. In another large skillet, heat the remaining 1 Tbsp. canola oil over medium-high heat. Break eggs, 1 at a time, into pan; reduce heat to low. Cook to desired doneness, turning after whites are set if desired. Serve over rice. If desired, sprinkle with nori, green onions and sesame seeds.
1 CUP FRIED RICE WITH 1 EGG: 331 cal., 14g fat (2g sat. fat), 186mg chol., 546mg sod., 41g carb. (4g sugars, 2g fiber), 11g pro.

COUSCOUS TABBOULEH WITH FRESH MINT & FETA

Using couscous instead of bulgur for tabbouleh speeds up the cook time of this colorful salad. Other quick-cooking grains, such as barley or quinoa, also work well.

—*Elodie Rosinovsky, Brighton, MA*

Takes: 20 min. • **Makes:** 3 servings

¾ cup water
½ cup uncooked couscous
1 can (15 oz.) garbanzo beans or chickpeas, rinsed and drained
1 large tomato, chopped
½ English cucumber, halved and thinly sliced
3 Tbsp. lemon juice
2 tsp. grated lemon zest
2 tsp. olive oil
2 tsp. minced fresh mint
2 tsp. minced fresh parsley
¼ tsp. salt
⅛ tsp. pepper
¾ cup crumbled feta cheese
Lemon wedges, optional

1. In a saucepan, bring water to a boil. Stir in couscous. Remove from the heat; cover and let stand for 5-8 minutes or until water is absorbed. Fluff with a fork.

2. In a large bowl, combine the beans, tomato and cucumber. In a small bowl, whisk the lemon juice, lemon zest, oil, herbs and seasonings. Drizzle over bean mixture. Add couscous; toss to combine. Serve immediately or refrigerate until chilled. Sprinkle with cheese. If desired, serve with lemon wedges.

1⅔ CUPS: 362 cal., 11g fat (3g sat. fat), 15mg chol., 657mg sod., 52g carb. (7g sugars, 9g fiber), 15g pro.

HEALTH TIP: Make this salad gluten-free by replacing the couscous with about 1½ cups cooked quinoa.

GREEK COUSCOUS SALAD

I love the fresh taste of crisp veggies in this satisfying salad, hearty enough for a full meal.
—*Teri Rasey, Cadillac, MI*

Prep: 15 min. • **Cook:** 5 min. + cooling
Makes: 12 servings

    1   can (14½ oz.) vegetable broth
    1¾ cups uncooked whole wheat
        couscous (about 11 oz.)
DRESSING
    ½   cup olive oil
    1½ tsp. grated lemon zest
    ¼   cup lemon juice
    1   tsp. adobo seasoning
    ¼   tsp. salt
SALAD
    1   English cucumber, halved
        lengthwise and sliced
    2   cups grape tomatoes, halved
    1   cup coarsely chopped fresh parsley
    1   can (6½ oz.) sliced ripe olives,
        drained
    4   green onions, chopped
    ½   cup crumbled feta cheese

1. In a large saucepan, bring broth to a boil. Stir in couscous. Remove from heat; let stand, covered, until broth is absorbed, about 5 minutes. Transfer to a large bowl; cool completely.
2. Whisk together dressing ingredients. Add cucumber, tomatoes, parsley, olives and green onions to couscous; stir in dressing. Gently stir in cheese. Serve salad immediately or refrigerate and serve cold.
¾ CUP: 335 cal., 18g fat (3g sat. fat), 4mg chol., 637mg sod., 39g carb. (3g sugars, 7g fiber), 9g pro.

LEMON RICE SALAD

This refreshing salad is wonderful year-round. The people I serve it to like the combination of flavors—I like that it can be prepared ahead.
—*Margery Richmond, Lacombe, AB*

Prep: 25 min. + chilling
Makes: 16 servings (¾ cup each)

    1   cup olive oil
    ⅓   cup white wine vinegar
    1   garlic clove, minced
    1   to 2 tsp. grated lemon zest
    2   tsp. sugar
    1   tsp. Dijon mustard
    ½   tsp. salt
    6   cups cooked long grain rice
    2   cup cooked wild rice
    2   cups diced seeded cucumbers
    ⅔   cup thinly sliced green onions
    ¼   cup minced fresh parsley
    ¼   cup minced fresh basil or
         1 Tbsp. dried basil
    ½   tsp. pepper
    ½   cup chopped pecans, toasted

1. For dressing, place the oil, vinegar, garlic, lemon zest, sugar, Dijon and salt in a jar with a tight-fitting lid; shake well. In a large bowl, toss long grain rice and wild rice with dressing. Refrigerate, covered, overnight.
2. Stir cucumbers, green onions, parsley, basil and pepper into the rice mixture. Refrigerate, covered, 2 hours. Stir in the pecans just before serving.
NOTE: To toast nuts, bake in a shallow pan in a 350°; oven for 5-10 minutes or cook in a skillet over low heat until lightly browned, stirring occasionally.

MINTED RICE WITH GARBANZO CURRY

Fluffy flavored rice and tender beans in a well-seasoned, aromatic sauce make this easy, meatless main dish a fitting introduction to Indian cooking.

—*Jemima Madhavan, Lincoln, NE*

- -

Prep: 20 min. • **Cook:** 20 min.
Makes: 3 servings

- 1 cinnamon stick (3 in.)
- 2 whole cloves
- ⅛ tsp. cumin seeds
- 2 tsp. canola oil
- 1 cup uncooked long grain rice
- 2 cups water
- ½ cup minced fresh mint

GARBANZO CURRY

- 1 medium onion, chopped
- 1 cinnamon stick (3 in.)
- 1 Tbsp. canola oil
- 1 tsp. curry powder
- 1 garlic clove, minced
- ¼ tsp. minced fresh gingerroot
- 1 can (15 oz.) garbanzo beans or chickpeas, rinsed and drained
- 1 cup water
- 1 can (8 oz.) tomato sauce
- 2 Tbsp. lemon juice
- ½ tsp. salt
- ½ cup minced fresh cilantro

1. In a large saucepan over medium heat, saute the cinnamon, cloves and cumin seeds in oil until aromatic, 1-2 minutes. Add rice; cook and stir until lightly browned. Add water and mint. Bring to a boil. Reduce heat; cover and simmer for 15-20 minutes or until rice is tender.

2. Meanwhile, in a large skillet, saute onion and cinnamon in oil until onion is tender. Add the curry, garlic and ginger; cook 1 minute longer. Add the garbanzo beans, water, tomato sauce, lemon juice and salt; bring to a boil. Reduce heat; simmer, uncovered, for 4-6 minutes or until slightly thickened. Discard the cinnamon; stir in cilantro.

3. Fluff rice with a fork. Discard cinnamon and cloves. Serve with garbanzo curry.

1 SERVING: 475 cal., 11g fat (1g sat. fat), 0 chol., 932mg sod., 82g carb. (8g sugars, 9g fiber), 12g pro.

TABBOULEH

Tabbouleh, also known as tabouleh, is a classic Middle Eastern salad. The fresh veggies and mint leaves make it light and refreshing on a hot day.
—*Michael & Mathil Chebat, Lake Ridge, VA*

Takes: 30 min. • **Makes:** 8 servings

- ¼ cup bulgur
- 3 bunches fresh parsley, minced (about 2 cups)
- 3 large tomatoes, finely chopped
- 1 small onion, finely chopped
- ¼ cup lemon juice
- ¼ cup olive oil
- 5 fresh mint leaves, minced
- ½ tsp. salt
- ½ tsp. pepper
- ¼ tsp. cayenne pepper

Prepare bulgur according to package directions; cool. Transfer to a large bowl. Stir in remaining ingredients. If desired, chill before serving.

⅔ CUP: 100 cal., 7g fat (1g sat. fat), 0 chol., 164mg sod., 9g carb. (3g sugars, 2g fiber), 2g pro. **DIABETIC EXCHANGES:** 1½ fat, ½ starch.

DID YOU KNOW?

Bulgur is a type of whole grain wheat. It has more fiber than quinoa, oats and corn. Since it's precooked then dried, it only needs to boil for about 10 minute to be ready to eat.

MEDITERRANEAN BULGUR SALAD

Whether it's nutrition or taste you're after, it doesn't get any better than this. Bulgur, beans, tomatoes, pine nuts and olive oil team up in this vegetarian main dish salad.
—Taste of Home *Test Kitchen*

Prep: 15 min. • **Cook:** 20 min. + cooling
Makes: 9 servings

3	cups vegetable broth
1½	cups uncooked bulgur
6	Tbsp. olive oil
2	Tbsp. lemon juice
2	Tbsp. minced fresh parsley
½	tsp. salt
¼	tsp. pepper
1	can (15 oz.) garbanzo beans or chickpeas, rinsed and drained
2	cups halved cherry tomatoes
1	cup chopped cucumber
8	green onions, sliced
1	pkg. (4 oz.) crumbled feta cheese
½	cup pine nuts, toasted

1. In a large saucepan, bring broth and bulgur to a boil over high heat. Reduce heat; cover and simmer for 20 minutes or until tender and broth is almost absorbed. Remove from the heat; let stand at room temperature, uncovered, until broth is absorbed.
2. In a small bowl, whisk the oil, lemon juice, parsley, salt and pepper.
3. In a large serving bowl, combine the bulgur, beans, tomatoes, cucumber and onions. Drizzle with dressing; toss to coat. Sprinkle with cheese and pine nuts.
1 CUP: 298 cal., 17g fat (3g sat. fat), 7mg chol., 657mg sod., 31g carb. (4g sugars, 8g fiber), 10g pro.

GREAT GRAIN SALAD

I can't think of a better dish to round out a meal. My grain salad features all my favorite nuts, seeds and fruits. Feel free to toss in some grilled chicken to make it a light meal.
—*Rachel Dueker, Gervais, OR*

Prep: 15 min. • **Cook:** 1 hour + chilling
Makes: 12 servings (¾ cup each)

3	cups water
½	cup medium pearl barley
½	cup uncooked wild rice
⅔	cup uncooked basmati rice
½	cup slivered almonds
½	cup sunflower kernels
½	cup salted pumpkin seeds or pepitas
½	cup each golden raisins, chopped dried apricots and dried cranberries
⅓	cup minced fresh parsley
4	tsp. grated orange zest

VINAIGRETTE

⅔	cup walnut oil
⅔	cup raspberry vinegar
2	tsp. orange juice
2	tsp. pepper
1	tsp. salt

1. In a large saucepan, bring water to a boil. Add the barley and wild rice. Reduce the heat; cover and simmer until tender, 55-65 minutes. Meanwhile, cook basmati rice according to package directions. Cool barley and rices to room temperature.
2. In a large bowl, combine the almonds, sunflower kernels, pumpkin seeds, dried fruit, parsley and orange zest; add barley and rices.
3. In a small bowl, whisk the vinaigrette ingredients. Pour over salad and toss to coat. Cover and refrigerate for at least 2 hours.
¾ CUP: 368 cal., 22g fat (3g sat. fat), 0 chol., 281mg sod., 39g carb. (11g sugars, 4g fiber), 8g pro.

BLACK BEAN QUINOA BOWLS

Did you know that quinoa is a seed? This recipe tastes so good, you'd never guess it was the healthy main-dish equivalent of eating straight spinach!
—*Laura Lewis, Boulder, CO*

Prep: 15 min. • **Cook:** 30 min.
Makes: 4 servings

- 1 Tbsp. olive oil
- 2 cups sliced baby portobello mushrooms
- 1 medium onion, chopped
- 3 garlic cloves, minced
- ¾ cup quinoa, rinsed
- 1 tsp. ground cumin
- ⅛ tsp. cayenne pepper
- ⅛ tsp. pepper
- 1½ cups vegetable broth
- 1 medium zucchini, halved and thinly sliced
- 1 can (15 oz.) black beans, rinsed and drained
- 1 cup frozen corn (about 5 oz.)
- ½ cup crumbled feta cheese
  Minced fresh cilantro

1. In a large saucepan, heat oil over medium-high heat; saute mushrooms and onion until tender and lightly browned, 4-6 minutes. Add the garlic; cook and stir 1 minute. Stir in the quinoa, seasonings and broth; bring to a boil. Reduce the heat; simmer, covered, 15 minutes. Stir in the zucchini; cook, covered, 5 minutes or until crisp-tender.
2. Stir in beans and corn; heat through. Top with cheese and cilantro.
1½ CUPS: 333 cal., 8g fat (2g sat. fat), 8mg chol., 699mg sod., 50g carb. (5g sugars, 9g fiber), 15g pro. **DIABETIC EXCHANGES:** 3 starch, 1 lean meat, 1 fat.

ORZO-LENTIL RICE

A versatile medley of small orzo pasta, lentils, rice and more makes a perfect partner for grilled beef, pork—just about any main course you choose.
—*Misty Scondras, Dalton, PA*

Prep: 15 min. • **Cook:** 40 min.
Makes: 8 servings

- 1 small onion, chopped
- 1 celery rib, chopped
- ¼ cup finely chopped carrot
- ¼ cup finely chopped sweet red pepper
- 4 tsp. butter
- 5 cups water
- ½ cup dried lentils, rinsed
- 1 tsp. salt
- ½ tsp. ground cumin
- ¼ tsp. dried rosemary, crushed
- ¼ tsp. dried thyme
- ¼ tsp. rubbed sage
- ¼ tsp. pepper
- 1 cup uncooked orzo pasta
- 1 cup uncooked long grain rice

1. In a large saucepan, saute the onion, celery, carrot and red pepper in butter until tender. Stir in the water, lentils and seasonings. Bring to a boil. Reduce heat; cover and simmer for 15 minutes.
2. Stir in pasta and rice. Bring to a boil; cover and cook 15-20 minutes longer or until pasta and rice are tender.
¾ CUP: 244 cal., 3g fat (1g sat. fat), 5mg chol., 320mg sod., 46g carb. (2g sugars, 5g fiber), 8g pro.

TEST KITCHEN TIP

Many people think orzo is rice but it's actually a rice-shaped pasta that gets its name from the Italian word for barley. This tiny pasta (a kind of pastina) is often used in soups and pasta salads.

PESTO QUINOA SALAD

My daughter-in-law got me hooked on quinoa, and I'm so glad she did! I've been using quinoa in place of pasta in some of my favorite recipes, and this dish is the happy result of one of those experiments. I love adding my own garden tomatoes and peppers to this salad; however, sun-dried tomatoes and roasted red peppers are equally delicious.
—*Sue Gronholz, Beaver Dam, WI*

- -

Prep: 25 min. + chilling
Makes: 4 servings

⅔ cup water
⅓ cup quinoa, rinsed
2 Tbsp. prepared pesto
1 Tbsp. finely chopped sweet onion
1 Tbsp. olive oil
1 tsp. balsamic vinegar
¼ tsp. salt
1 medium sweet red pepper, chopped
1 cup cherry tomatoes, quartered
⅔ cup fresh mozzarella cheese pearls (about 4 oz.)
2 Tbsp. minced fresh basil, optional

1. In a small saucepan, bring water to a boil; stir in quinoa. Reduce the heat; simmer, covered, until liquid is absorbed, 10-12 minutes. Cool slightly.

2. Mix pesto, onion, oil, vinegar and salt; stir in pepper, tomatoes, cheese and quinoa. Refrigerate, covered, to allow flavors to blend, 1-2 hours. If desired, stir in basil.

¾ CUP: 183 cal., 11g fat (4g sat. fat), 15mg chol., 268mg sod., 14g carb. (3g sugars, 2g fiber), 6g pro. **DIABETIC EXCHANGES:** 1 starch, 1 medium-fat meat, ½ fat.

PEPPERED CILANTRO RICE

This colorful confetti rice is a traditional dish in Puerto Rico. We enjoy it in the summer alongside grilled shrimp kabobs, but it's good with almost any main entree.

—*Laura Lunardi, West Chester, PA*

- -

Takes: 30 min. • **Makes:** 6 servings

1 small onion, finely chopped
1 small sweet yellow pepper, finely chopped
1 small sweet red pepper, finely chopped
2 garlic cloves, minced
1 Tbsp. olive oil
2 cups water
1 cup uncooked long grain rice
¾ tsp. salt
¼ tsp. pepper
2 Tbsp. minced fresh cilantro

1. In a large saucepan, saute the onion, peppers and garlic in oil until crisp-tender. Add the water, rice, salt and pepper. Bring to a boil. Reduce heat; cover and simmer until rice is tender, 18-22 minutes.

2. Remove from the heat; fluff with a fork. Stir in cilantro.

⅔ CUP: 156 cal., 3g fat (0 sat. fat), 0 chol., 298mg sod., 30g carb. (1g sugars, 1g fiber), 3g pro. **DIABETIC EXCHANGES:** 2 starch, ½ fat.

VEGETABLE BARLEY BAKE

Forget the potatoes and rice, and consider this change-of-pace dinner accompaniment. Wholesome barley makes for a heart-smart dish that complements just about any main course and other sides too.

—*Shirley Doyle, Mount Prospect, IL*

Prep: 25 min. • **Bake:** 55 min.
Makes: 10 servings

- 3 medium sweet red or green peppers, chopped
- 4 cups sliced fresh mushrooms
- 2 medium onions, chopped
- 2 Tbsp. butter
- 2 cups vegetable broth
- 1½ cups medium pearl barley
- ⅛ tsp. pepper

1. Preheat oven to 350°. In a large nonstick skillet, saute the peppers, mushrooms and onions in butter until tender, 8-10 minutes. Transfer to a 13x9-in. baking dish coated with cooking spray. Stir in broth, barley and pepper.
2. Cover and bake 50 minutes. Uncover; bake 5-10 minutes longer or until barley is tender and liquid is absorbed.
¾ CUP: 157 cal., 3g fat (2g sat. fat), 6mg chol., 153mg sod., 30g carb. (4g sugars, 6g fiber), 5g pro. **DIABETIC EXCHANGES:** 1½ starch, 1 vegetable, ½ fat.

KALE QUINOA SALAD

Here's a holiday side dish you can feel good about serving. Kale packs a mighty punch of vitamins, while quinoa delivers a hearty serving of protein. Best of all, the flavor can't be beat!
—*Lisa Warren, Washington D.C.*

Prep: 15 min. • **Cook:** 25 min.
Makes: 6 servings

- 1½ cups water
- ½ cup tomato juice
- 1 cup quinoa, rinsed
- 1 small onion, chopped
- 1 Tbsp. olive oil
- 1 garlic clove, minced
- ½ tsp. crushed red pepper flakes
- 6 cups coarsely chopped fresh kale
- ¼ cup pine nuts
- ¼ cup dried currants
- 1 Tbsp. balsamic vinegar
- 1 tsp. lemon juice
- 1 tsp. grated lemon zest
- ¼ tsp. salt
- ⅛ tsp. pepper

1. In a large saucepan, bring water and tomato juice to a boil. Add quinoa. Reduce heat; cover and simmer until liquid is absorbed, 18-22 minutes. Remove from the heat; fluff with a fork.
2. In a large skillet, saute onion in oil until tender. Add the garlic and pepper flakes; cook 1 minute longer. Stir in kale and cook until wilted, 3-4 minutes.
3. Stir in pine nuts and currants; cook until kale is tender, about 2 minutes. Stir in the vinegar, lemon juice, zest, salt and pepper; cook 1-2 minutes longer. Remove from the heat and stir in quinoa. Serve at room temperature.

⅔ CUP: 190 cal., 7g fat (1g sat. fat), 0 chol., 164mg sod., 28g carb. (6g sugars, 3g fiber), 6g pro. **DIABETIC EXCHANGES:** 2 starch, 1 fat.

TEST KITCHEN TIP

Go for freshly squeezed lemon juice when preparing this salad. Bottled lemon juice, which is from concentrate, won't provide the same bright, fresh flavor.

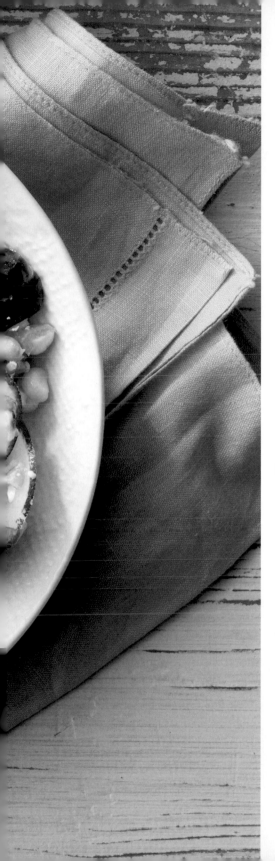

FARRO SALAD WITH CHARRED SHISHITO PEPPERS & CORN

I'm lucky my mom has a great garden and gives me all kinds of vegetables to try. I've found most shishito peppers to be mild in heat. After discarding the stems, I add the remaining chopped pepper, including the seeds, to this dish. The salad can be enjoyed warm or refrigerated and served cold.
—*Tracy Kaifesh, Laguna Niguel, CA*

- -

Prep: 25 min. • **Cook:** 25 min.
Makes: 8 servings

- 1 cup farro, rinsed
- ¼ cup plus 2 tsp. olive oil, divided
- ¼ cup lime juice
- 1 tsp. garlic powder
- ½ tsp. ground cumin
- ½ tsp. kosher salt
- 4 oz. shishito peppers (about 20 peppers)
- 2 medium ears sweet corn, husked
- 1 cup chopped fresh tomatoes
- ½ cup crumbled Cotija cheese
- ½ cup sliced radishes
- ½ cup chopped green onions

1. Place farro in a large saucepan; add water to cover. Bring to a boil. Reduce the heat; cook, covered, until tender, 25-30 minutes.

2. Meanwhile, for dressing, whisk together ¼ cup oil, lime juice, garlic powder, cumin and salt; set aside. Preheat a grill pan over medium-high heat. Toss the peppers with 1 tsp. oil. Cook until all sides are blistered and blackened, 6-8 minutes, turning occasionally with tongs. Transfer to a cutting board. Chop peppers; discard stems. Transfer to a large bowl.

3. Brush the corn with remaining 1 tsp. oil. Cook until lightly browned and tender, 10-12 minutes, turning occasionally. Cool slightly. Cut corn from cobs; add to the chopped peppers. Drain farro; add to corn mixture. Stir in tomatoes, cheese, radishes, green onions and dressing; toss to coat. Serve warm or chilled.

¾ CUP: 233 cal., 11g fat (2g sat. fat), 8mg chol., 240mg sod., 27g carb. (3g sugars, 5g fiber), 7g pro. **DIABETIC EXCHANGES:** 2 starch, 2 fat.

DID YOU KNOW?

Farro, also called emmer, is a whole wheat grain and a close cousin of durum wheat. Farro is in semolina flour, which is used to make many pastas. It's high in protein (and that includes gluten!), as well as iron and fiber. Farro is a tasty grain to add to salads, soups and risottos.

COCONUT LENTILS WITH RICE

Years ago, I made this recipe for my kids and they loved it. One of my daughter's friends always requested this dish when she came over to visit. I suggest using basmati rice for the best results.
—*Diane Donato, Columbus, OH*

Prep: 20 min. • **Cook:** 35 min.
Makes: 6 servings

- 1 Tbsp. canola oil
- 6 green onions, chopped
- 1 Tbsp. minced fresh gingerroot
- 2 garlic cloves, minced
- ¼ tsp. crushed red pepper flakes
- 1½ cups dried lentils, rinsed
- 1 tsp. ground turmeric
- ½ tsp. salt
- 5½ cups vegetable stock
- 2 large tomatoes, chopped
- ½ cup flaked coconut
- 2 Tbsp. minced fresh mint
- 3 cups hot cooked rice
- ⅓ cup plain Greek yogurt

1. In a large saucepan, heat the oil over medium heat; saute green onions, ginger, garlic and pepper flakes until onions are tender, 2-4 minutes. Stir in the lentils, turmeric, salt and stock; bring to a boil. Reduce heat; simmer, covered, until lentils are tender, 25-30 minutes, stirring occasionally.
2. Stir in tomatoes, coconut and mint. Serve with rice; top with yogurt.
1 SERVING: 374 cal., 7g fat (4g sat. fat), 3mg chol., 757mg sod., 63g carb. (7g sugars, 7g fiber), 16g pro.

FENNEL WILD RICE SALAD

This is a salad I invented years ago when my sister's family had to go gluten-free. It has since become a family favorite, and Thanksgiving just isn't the same without our wild rice salad!
—*Aimee Day, Ferndale, WA*

Prep: 15 min. • **Cook:** 55 min.
Makes: 2 servings

- ⅓ cup uncooked wild rice
- 1 cup water
- 1½ tsp. lemon juice
- 1½ tsp. olive oil
- ¼ cup thinly sliced fennel bulb
- 2 Tbsp. salted pumpkin seeds or pepitas
- 2 Tbsp. dried cherries
- 1 green onion, sliced
- 1 Tbsp. minced fresh parsley
- ⅛ tsp. salt
  Dash pepper

1. Rinse wild rice thoroughly; drain. In a small saucepan, combine water and rice; bring to a boil. Reduce heat; simmer, covered, 50-55 minutes or until rice is fluffy and tender. Drain if necessary.
2. Transfer rice to a small bowl. Drizzle with lemon juice and oil; toss to coat. Stir in remaining ingredients.
¾ CUP: 208 cal., 7g fat (1g sat. fat), 0 chol., 178mg sod., 31g carb. (8g sugars, 3g fiber), 7g pro. **DIABETIC EXCHANGES:** 2 starch, 1½ fat.

FESTIVE THREE-GRAIN SALAD

Wholesome ingredients and a festive appearance make this colorful side one of my holiday staples. Plus, I can assemble it the night before and store it in the refrigerator.
—Teri Kreyche, Tustin, CA

Prep: 15 min. • **Cook:** 1 hour + cooling
Makes: 8 servings

- ¾ cup uncooked wheat berries
- 5 cups water
- ½ cup uncooked medium pearl barley
- ⅓ cup uncooked long grain brown rice
- 1 medium apple, chopped
- ½ cup pomegranate seeds, dried cherries or dried cranberries
- 4 green onions, chopped
- ¼ cup finely chopped carrot
- ¼ cup finely chopped celery
- ¼ cup minced fresh parsley

DRESSING

- ⅓ cup cider vinegar
- 3 Tbsp. finely chopped red onion
- 3 Tbsp. canola oil
- 2 to 3 Tbsp. sugar
- 1 Tbsp. vegan Worcestershire sauce
- 2 garlic cloves, minced
- ½ tsp. salt
- ¼ tsp. pepper

1. In a large saucepan, combine wheat berries and water; bring to a boil. Reduce heat; simmer, covered, 10 minutes. Stir in barley; simmer, covered, 5 minutes. Stir in rice; simmer, covered, 40-45 minutes or until the grains are tender. Drain; transfer mixture to a large bowl. Cool to room temperature.

2. Add apple, pomegranate seeds, green onions, carrot, celery and parsley to the wheat berry mixture; toss to combine. In a small bowl, whisk dressing ingredients until blended. Pour over salad; toss to coat. Serve immediately or refrigerate and serve cold.

¾ CUP: 219 cal., 6g fat (0 sat. fat), 0 chol., 180mg sod., 38g carb. (8g sugars, 6g fiber), 5g pro.

YELLOW RICE & BLACK BEAN SALAD

Chipotle peppers turn up the heat on a colorful rice dish brimming with black beans. It can be served hot or cold.
—*Rose Rodwell, Bergen, NY*

Prep: 30 min. • **Cook:** 20 min.
Makes: 12 servings (½ cup each)

- 4   tsp. ground cumin, divided
- ¼   cup lime juice
- 2   Tbsp. plus 1½ tsp. canola oil
- ½   tsp. ground turmeric
- 1½ cups water
- 1   cup uncooked basmati rice
- 1   tsp. salt
- 4   green onions, sliced
- 1   can (15 oz.) black beans, rinsed and drained
- 1   small green pepper, chopped
- ½   cup chopped roasted sweet red peppers
- ⅓   cup minced fresh cilantro
- 1½ tsp. chopped chipotle pepper in adobo sauce

1. Place 3 tsp. cumin in a small skillet; cook over medium heat for 1 minute or until aromas are released. Stir in lime juice and oil; set aside.

2. In a large saucepan, combine turmeric and remaining 1 tsp. cumin. Cook over medium heat until aromatic, about 1 minute. Add the water, rice and salt; bring to a boil. Reduce heat to low; cover and simmer 15 minutes or until water is absorbed. Cool. Stir in onions and half of the lime juice mixture.

3. In a large bowl, combine remaining ingredients. Add the rice mixture and remaining lime juice mixture; toss salad to coat.

½ CUP: 126 cal., 3g fat (0 sat. fat), 0 chol., 307mg sod., 20g carb. (1g sugars, 2g fiber), 3g pro. **DIABETIC EXCHANGES:** 1 starch, 1 fat.

ASPARAGUS SOUP WITH
LEMON CREME FRAICHE P. 131

Heartwarming Soups

Endlessly adaptable, soups might just be
the perfect food. Clear broth soups, rich cream
soups, hearty chilis, light bisques and comforting
chowders—there's a soup for every occasion,
and at any time of the year!

VEGETARIAN SPLIT PEA SOUP

Even the pickiest pea soup lover will request this version time and again. Thick and well seasoned, it packs a nutritional punch, plus plenty of fiber and protein. It's wonderful with a slice of crusty French bread.

—*Michele Doucette, Stephenville, NL*

Prep: 15 min. • **Cook:** 1½ hours
Makes: 7 servings

- 6 cups vegetable broth
- 2 cups dried green split peas, rinsed
- 1 medium onion, chopped
- 1 cup chopped carrots
- 2 celery ribs with leaves, chopped
- 2 garlic cloves, minced
- ½ tsp. dried marjoram
- ½ tsp. dried basil
- ¼ tsp. ground cumin
- ½ tsp. salt
- ¼ tsp. pepper
  Optional: Shredded carrots and sliced green onions

1. In a large saucepan, combine the first 9 ingredients; bring to a boil. Reduce heat; cover and simmer until peas are tender, about 1 hour, stirring occasionally.

2. Add the salt and pepper; simmer 10 minutes longer. Remove soup from heat; cool slightly. Process in batches in a blender or food processor until smooth; return to the pan and heat through. If desired, garnish servings with carrots and green onions.

1 CUP: 227 cal., 1g fat (0 sat. fat), 0 chol., 771mg sod., 42g carb. (7g sugars, 15g fiber), 14g pro.

SLOW-COOKED BLACK BEAN SOUP

Life can get really crazy with young kids, but I never want to compromise when it comes to cooking. This recipe is healthy and so easy, thanks to the slow cooker!
—*Angela Lemoine, Howell, NJ*

Prep: 15 min. • **Cook:** 6 hours
Makes: 8 servings

- 2 cans (15 oz. each) black beans, rinsed and drained
- 1 medium onion, finely chopped
- 1 medium sweet red pepper, finely xchopped
- 4 garlic cloves, minced
- 2 tsp. ground cumin
- 2 cans (14½ oz. each) vegetable broth
- 1 tsp. olive oil
- 1 cup fresh or frozen corn
  Dash pepper
  Minced fresh cilantro

1. In a 3-qt. slow cooker, combine the first 6 ingredients. Cook, covered, on low until the vegetables are softened, 6-8 hours.

2. Puree soup using an immersion blender. Or, cool the soup slightly and puree in batches in a blender. Return to slow cooker and heat through.

3. In a small skillet, heat oil over medium heat. Add corn; cook and stir until golden brown, 4-6 minutes. Sprinkle soup with pepper. Garnish with corn and cilantro.

¾ CUP: 117 cal., 1g fat (0 sat. fat), 0 chol., 616mg sod., 21g carb. (3g sugars, 5g fiber), 6g pro. **DIABETIC EXCHANGES:** 1½ starch.

MEAT
LOVER
OPTION
PAGE 320

PASTA FAGIOLI SOUP MIX

This is what I call Italian chili. The dry ingredients, when artfully packaged, make a heartwarming gift for friends and family during the holidays.
—*Tamra Duncan, Lincoln, AR*

- -

Prep: 20 min. + soaking • **Cook:** 1¾ hours
Makes: 14 servings (3½ qt.)

- 1 cup small pasta shells
- ¾ cup dried great northern beans
- ¾ cup dried pinto beans
- ¾ cup dried kidney beans
- ¼ cup dried minced onion
- 3 Tbsp. dried parsley flakes
- 1 tsp. dried basil
- 1 tsp. dried oregano
- ½ tsp. dried rosemary, crushed
- ¼ tsp. dried minced garlic
- 1 bay leaf
  Dash crushed red pepper flakes

ADDITIONAL INGREDIENTS

- 14 cups water, divided
- 1 can (28 oz.) diced tomatoes, undrained
- 3 medium carrots, chopped
- 1 celery rib, chopped
- 1 tsp. salt
  Grated Parmesan cheese, optional

1. Place pasta in a small resealable plastic bag; place in a 1-qt. glass jar. Layer with the beans. Place seasonings in another plastic bag; place in jar. Cover and store in a cool, dry place for up to 3 months. Yield: 1 batch.

2. To prepare soup: Remove seasoning packet from jar. Remove beans; sort and rinse. Set pasta aside.
3. Place beans in a Dutch oven; add 6 cups water. Bring to a boil; boil for 2 minutes. Remove from heat; cover and let stand until beans are softened, 1-4 hours. Drain; discard liquid.
4. Return beans to the pot. Add contents of seasoning packet and the remaining water. Bring to a boil. Reduce heat; cover and simmer until beans are tender, about 1 hour. Add tomatoes, carrots, celery and salt; cover and simmer for 30 minutes longer, stirring occasionally.
5. Stir in pasta. Cover and simmer until the pasta and carrots are tender, 5-10 minutes, stirring occasionally. Remove the bay leaf before serving. Garnish with cheese if desired.
1 CUP: 148 cal., 0 fat (0 sat. fat), 0 chol., 256mg sod., 29g carb. (4g sugars, 7g fiber), 8g pro. **DIABETIC EXCHANGES:** 1½ starch, 1 vegetable, 1 lean meat.

TEST KITCHEN TIP

This recipe fits in a 1-qt. jar, perfect for gifting. But if you're making it to serve tonight, it's easy to cut the recipe in half.

🍲 PESTO BEAN SOUP

This is one of my favorite vegetarian recipes, especially on cold winter evenings. I make large batches and freeze it. Homemade pesto is tasty, but you can use store-bought to make the recipe really simple. Serve the soup with garlic toast and a green salad.
—*Liz Bellville, Tonasket, WA*

Prep: 10 min. • **Cook:** 4 hours
Makes: 8 servings (2½ qt.)

1 carton (32 oz.) reduced-sodium vegetable broth
1 large white onion, chopped
4 garlic cloves, minced
2½ cups sliced baby portobello mushrooms
3 cans (15 to 15½ oz. each) cannellini beans, rinsed and drained
¾ cup prepared pesto, divided
¼ cup grated Parmigiano-Reggiano cheese
Optional: Additional pesto and grated cheese

1. In a 4-qt. slow cooker, combine the first 5 ingredients. Stir in ½ cup pesto. Cook, covered, on low until vegetables are tender, 4-6 hours.
2. Before serving, stir in the remaining ¼ cup pesto and the cheese. If desired, serve with additional pesto and cheese.
1¼ CUPS: 244 cal., 9g fat (2g sat. fat), 2mg chol., 586mg sod., 30g carb. (3g sugars, 8g fiber), 9g pro. **DIABETIC EXCHANGES:** 2 starch, 1½ fat, 1 lean meat.

ASPARAGUS SOUP WITH LEMON CREME FRAICHE

Here is a definite winner—a silky-smooth fresh asparagus soup. Serve it warm or chilled depending on the weather.
—*Fern Vitense, Tipton, IA*

Prep: 25 min. • **Cook:** 25 min.
Makes: 6 servings

- 1 Tbsp. butter
- 1 Tbsp. olive oil
- 1 small onion, chopped
- 4 cups cut fresh asparagus (1-in. pieces)
- 3 medium red potatoes, peeled and cubed
- 2 cans (14½ oz. each) vegetable broth
- 2 tsp. grated lemon zest
- ½ tsp. salt
- ½ tsp. pepper
- ½ tsp. ground coriander
- ¼ tsp. ground ginger

GARNISH

- ¼ cup minced chives
- ¼ cup creme fraiche or sour cream
- 1 Tbsp. lemon juice
- ½ tsp. grated lemon zest

1. In a large saucepan, heat butter and oil over medium-high heat. Add onion; cook and stir until tender. Add asparagus and potatoes; cook 3 minutes longer. Stir in broth, lemon zest and seasonings. Bring to a boil. Reduce heat; simmer, covered, until potatoes are tender, 15-20 minutes.
2. Cool slightly. Process soup in batches in a blender until smooth. Return all to pan and heat through.
3. Combine garnish ingredients; serve with soup.
1 CUP: 155 cal., 8g fat (4g sat. fat), 13mg chol., 873mg sod., 17g carb. (4g sugars, 3g fiber), 4g pro.

⏱ ❄ CARIBBEAN POTATO SOUP

An interesting blend of veggies—including okra, kale and black-eyed peas—goes into this bright, hearty soup. Have no kale on hand? Use spinach instead.
—Crystal Jo Bruns, Iliff, CO

- -

Takes: 30 min.
Makes: 6 servings (2¼ qt.)

- 2 medium onions, chopped
- 2 tsp. canola oil
- 3 garlic cloves, minced
- 2 tsp. minced fresh gingerroot
- 2 tsp. ground coriander
- 1 tsp. ground turmeric
- ½ tsp. dried thyme
- ¼ tsp. ground allspice
- 5 cups vegetable broth
- 2 cups cubed peeled sweet potato
- 3 cups chopped fresh kale
- 1 cup frozen sliced okra
- 1 cup coconut milk
- 1 cup canned diced tomatoes, drained
- 1 cup canned black-eyed peas, rinsed and drained
- 2 Tbsp. lime juice

1. In a Dutch oven, saute onions in oil until tender. Add the garlic, ginger and spices; cook 1 minute longer.
2. Stir in broth and potato. Bring to a boil. Reduce heat; simmer, covered, for 5 minutes.
3. Stir in kale and okra. Return to a boil; simmer, covered, until potato is tender, about 10 minutes longer.
4. Add the milk, tomatoes, peas and lime juice; heat through.
FREEZE OPTION: Freeze cooled soup in freezer containers. To use, partially thaw in refrigerator overnight. Heat through in a saucepan, stirring occasionally; add broth or water if necessary.
1½ CUPS: 213 cal., 10g fat (7g sat. fat), 0 chol., 954mg sod., 28g carb. (9g sugars, 6g fiber), 5g pro.

CHEDDAR CAULIFLOWER SOUP

Cauliflower is often last on the list of vegetables my family will eat, but they adore this creamy, savory soup with tender leeks and shredded cheddar cheese.
—Kristin Rimkus, Snohomish, WA

- -

Prep: 20 min. • **Cook:** 45 min.
Makes: 8 servings (2 qt.)

- 1 Tbsp. olive oil
- 1½ cups thinly sliced leeks (white portion only)
- 1 medium head cauliflower, broken into florets
- 1 Tbsp. minced fresh thyme or 1 tsp. dried thyme
- 2 garlic cloves, minced
- 1 tsp. vegan Worcestershire sauce
- 1 carton (32 oz.) vegetable broth
- 1 can (12 oz.) reduced-fat evaporated milk
- 1 cup shredded sharp cheddar cheese
  Optional: Additional shredded sharp cheddar cheese and minced fresh thyme

1. In a large saucepan, heat oil over medium heat. Add leeks; cook and stir until tender, 3-5 minutes. Stir in the cauliflower, thyme, garlic and Worcestershire sauce. Add broth; bring to a boil. Reduce heat; simmer, covered, until vegetables are very tender, 30-35 minutes.
2. Puree soup using an immersion blender. Or, cool soup slightly and puree in batches in a blender; return to pan. Add the evaporated milk and cheese; cook and stir until the cheese is melted, 3-5 minutes. If desired, sprinkle individual servings with additional cheese and thyme.
1 CUP: 146 cal., 7g fat (3g sat. fat), 22mg chol., 643mg sod., 13g carb. (8g sugars, 2g fiber), 8g pro. **DIABETIC EXCHANGES:** 1½ fat, 1 vegetable, ½ reduced-fat milk.

SUCCULENT STRAWBERRY SOUP

This cool, creamy fruit soup makes a perfect summertime treat for family and friends. The strawberry base with a hint of orange appeals to all palates!
—*Paula Pelis, Lenhartsville, PA*

Prep: 30 min. + chilling
Makes: 4 servings

2 qt. hulled fresh strawberries, divided
½ cup water
5 Tbsp. sugar
1 Tbsp. all-purpose flour
1 tsp. grated orange zest
1 cup heavy whipping cream
Optional: Fresh mint and additional hulled strawberries, sliced

1. Mash half the strawberries with a potato masher or fork.
2. In a blender, combine the remaining strawberries, water, sugar, flour and orange zest; process until smooth. Pour into a 2-qt. saucepan. Bring to a boil over medium heat; boil for 2 minutes, stirring constantly. Add mashed strawberries. Reduce heat; simmer, uncovered, for 10 minutes, stirring constantly. Chill for at least 1 hour.
3. Stir in cream. Chill, covered, overnight. If desired, serve with mint and additional sliced strawberries.
1 CUP: 360 cal., 23g fat (14g sat. fat), 82mg chol., 26mg sod., 39g carb. (30g sugars, 7g fiber), 3g pro.

BROCCOLI CHOWDER

I like to serve this comforting soup on chilly stay-at-home evenings. Nutmeg seasons a light, creamy broth filled with tender broccoli florets and diced potatoes.
—*Sue Call, Beech Grove, IN*

Takes: 30 min. • **Makes:** 6 servings

3 cups fresh broccoli florets
2 cups diced peeled potatoes
2 cups water
⅓ cup sliced green onions
1 tsp. salt
½ tsp. pepper
3 Tbsp. butter
3 Tbsp. all-purpose flour
⅛ tsp. ground nutmeg
2 cups whole milk
½ cup shredded cheddar cheese

1. In a large saucepan, combine the first 6 ingredients. Bring to a boil. Reduce the heat; cover and simmer until vegetables are tender, 12-14 minutes.
2. Meanwhile, in another saucepan, melt the butter. Stir in flour and nutmeg until smooth. Gradually add milk. Bring to a boil; cook and stir for 2 minutes or until thickened. Stir into vegetable mixture; heat through. Sprinkle with cheese.
1 CUP: 200 cal., 11g fat (7g sat. fat), 36mg chol., 561mg sod., 19g carb. (5g sugars, 2g fiber), 7g pro.

🍲 ❄ TOMATO BASIL TORTELLINI SOUP

When my family first tried this soup, they all had to have seconds. My husband is happy any time I put the dish on the table. Sometimes I include crumbled bacon and serve it with mozzarella cheese.
—*Christy Addison, Clarksville, OH*

Prep: 25 min. • **Cook:** 6¼ hours
Makes: 18 servings (4½ qt.)

- 2 Tbsp. olive oil
- 1 medium onion, chopped
- 3 medium carrots, chopped
- 5 garlic cloves, minced
- 3 cans (28 oz. each) crushed tomatoes, undrained
- 1 carton (32 oz.) vegetable broth
- 1 Tbsp. sugar
- 1 tsp. dried basil
- 1 bay leaf
- 3 pkg. (9 oz. each) refrigerated cheese tortellini
- ¾ cup half-and-half cream
   Shredded Parmesan cheese
   minced fresh basil

1. In a large skillet, heat oil over medium-high heat. Add onion and carrots; cook and stir until crisp-tender, 5-6 minutes. Add garlic; cook 1 minute longer.
2. Transfer to a 6- or 7-qt. slow cooker. Add the tomatoes, broth, sugar, basil and bay leaf. Cook, covered, on low until vegetables are tender, 6-7 hours.
3. Stir in tortellini. Cook, covered, on high for 15 minutes. Reduce heat to low; stir in cream until heated through. Discard bay leaf. Top with Parmesan cheese and basil before serving.
FREEZE OPTION: Before stirring in the half-and-half, cool soup and freeze in freezer containers. To use, partially thaw in refrigerator overnight. Heat through in a saucepan, stirring occasionally; add half-and-half as directed.
1 CUP: 214 cal., 7g fat (3g sat. fat), 23mg chol., 569mg sod., 32g carb. (9g sugars, 4g fiber), 9g pro. **DIABETIC EXCHANGES:** 2 starch, 1 fat.

MEAT LOVER OPTION PAGE 320

🍲 VEGETARIAN PEA SOUP

I combined several recipes to make my own version of this soup. It was a real favorite when I was a vegetarian for health reasons. Even my meat-loving husband asked for seconds!
—*Corrie Gamache, Palmyra, VA*

Prep: 15 min. • **Cook:** 7 hours
Makes: 8 servings (2 qt.)

- 1 pkg. (16 oz.) dried green split peas, rinsed
- 1 medium leek (white portion only), chopped
- 3 celery ribs, chopped
- 1 medium potato, peeled and chopped
- 2 medium carrots, chopped
- 1 garlic clove, minced
- ¼ cup minced fresh parsley
- 2 cartons (32 oz. each) reduced-sodium vegetable broth
- 1½ tsp. ground mustard
- ½ tsp. pepper
- ½ tsp. dried oregano
- 1 bay leaf

In a 5-qt. slow cooker, combine all the ingredients. Cover and cook on low until peas are tender, 7-8 hours. Discard bay leaf. Stir before serving.
1 CUP: 248 cal., 1g fat (0 sat. fat), 0 chol., 702mg sod., 46g carb. (7g sugars, 16g fiber), 15g pro.

🗑 ❄ **PRESSURE-COOKER VEGETABLE WILD RICE SOUP**

PRESSURE-COOKER VEGETABLE WILD RICE SOUP

This thick and hearty soup is packed with colorful vegetables. It's wonderful for lunch alongside a healthy salad or a light sandwich.
—*Thomas Faglon, Somerset, NJ*

Prep: 25 min. • **Cook:** 20 min. + releasing
Makes: 12 servings (3 qt.)

- 6 cups reduced-sodium vegetable broth
- 2 cans (14½ oz. each) fire-roasted diced tomatoes, undrained
- 2 celery ribs, sliced
- 2 medium carrots, chopped
- 1¾ cups baby portobello mushrooms, sliced
- 1 medium onion, chopped
- 1 medium parsnip, peeled and chopped
- 1 medium sweet potato, peeled and cubed
- 1 medium green pepper, chopped
- 1 cup uncooked wild rice
- 2 garlic cloves, minced
- ¾ tsp. salt
- ¼ tsp. pepper
- 2 bay leaves
- 2 fresh thyme sprigs

Combine all the ingredients in a 6-qt. electric pressure cooker. Lock the lid; close pressure-release valve. Adjust to pressure-cook on high 20 minutes. Let the pressure release naturally for 10 minutes; quick-release any remaining pressure. Discard bay leaves and thyme sprigs before serving. If desired, serve with additional thyme.

FREEZE OPTION: Freeze cooled soup in freezer containers. To use, partially thaw in refrigerator overnight. Heat through in a saucepan, stirring occasionally; add broth if necessary.

1 CUP: 117 cal., 0 fat (0 sat. fat), 0 chol., 419mg sod., 25g carb. (7g sugars, 4g fiber), 4g pro. **DIABETIC EXCHANGES:** 2 vegetable, 1 starch.

🕐 5️ GRANDMA'S TOMATO SOUP

This recipe is one of my grandmother's favorites. She even made the tomato juice in it from scratch! Gram had this delicious soup cooking on the stove every time I visited her. She enjoyed making this and other wonderful dishes for family and friends, and she made everything with love.
—*Gerri Sysun, Narrragansett, RI*

Takes: 15 min. • **Makes:** 2 servings

- 2 Tbsp. butter
- 1 Tbsp. all-purpose flour
- 2 cups tomato juice
- ½ cup water
- 2 Tbsp. sugar
- ⅛ tsp. salt
- ¾ cup cooked wide egg noodles
  Chopped fresh parsley, optional

In a saucepan over medium heat, melt butter. Add flour; stir to form a smooth paste. Gradually add tomato juice and water, stirring constantly; bring to a boil. Cook and stir until thickened, about 2 minutes. Add sugar and salt. Stir in egg noodles and heat through. If desired, sprinkle with parsley.

1 CUP: 259 cal., 12g fat (7g sat. fat), 44mg chol., 1144mg sod., 36g carb. (20g sugars, 1g fiber), 4g pro.

READER RAVE

"I made this for Sunday dinner with grilled cheese sandwiches on homemade French bread. It's the most delicious tomato soup my husband and I have ever had!"

—JELLYBUG, TASTEOFHOME.COM

MOROCCAN CAULIFLOWER & ALMOND SOUP

This vegetable soup tastes rich and decadent but is really very healthy! There are bonuses—it's vegan, and it makes your house smell amazing!
—*Barbara Marynowski, Hutto, TX*

Prep: 20 min. • **Cook:** 6 hours
Makes: 8 servings

- 1 large head cauliflower (about 3½ lbs.), broken into florets
- 6 cups vegetable stock
- ¾ cup sliced almonds, toasted and divided
- ½ cup plus 2 Tbsp. minced fresh cilantro, divided
- 2 Tbsp. olive oil
- 1 to 3 tsp. harissa chili paste or hot pepper sauce
- ½ tsp. ground cinnamon
- ½ tsp. ground cumin
- ½ tsp. ground coriander
- 1¼ tsp. salt
- ½ tsp. pepper
- Additional harissa chili paste, optional

1. In a 5- or 6-qt. slow cooker, combine the cauliflower, vegetable stock, ½ cup almonds, ½ cup cilantro and the next 7 ingredients. Cook, covered, on low until cauliflower is tender, 6-8 hours.

2. Puree soup using an immersion blender. Or, cool slightly and puree soup in batches in a blender; return to the slow cooker and heat through. Serve with remaining ¼ cup almonds and 2 Tbsp. cilantro and, if desired, additional harissa.

NOTE: To toast nuts, bake in a shallow pan in a 350° oven for 5-10 minutes or cook in a skillet over low heat until lightly browned, stirring occasionally.

1¼ CUPS: 116 cal., 8g fat (1g sat. fat), 0 chol., 835mg sod., 9g carb. (2g sugars, 3g fiber), 4g pro.

VEGETARIAN RED BEAN CHILI

This vegetarian chili recipe is healthy and tastes wonderful. Even meat lovers would like it! I like to top my bowl with shredded cheddar cheese.
—*Connie Barnett, Athens, GA*

Prep: 10 min. • **Cook:** 5 hours
Makes: 6 servings (2 qt.)

- 1 can (16 oz.) red beans, rinsed and drained
- 2 cans (8 oz. each) no-salt-added tomato sauce
- 2 cups water
- 1 can (14½ oz.) diced tomatoes, undrained
- 1 pkg. (12 oz.) frozen vegetarian meat crumbles
- 1 large onion, chopped
- 1 to 2 Tbsp. chili powder
- 1 Tbsp. ground cumin
- 2 garlic cloves, minced
- 1 tsp. pepper
- ½ tsp. salt
- ½ tsp. cayenne pepper
  Optional: Sour cream and shredded cheddar cheese

In a 4-qt. slow cooker, combine the first 12 ingredients. Cover and cook on low until heated through, 5-6 hours. If desired, serve with sour cream and cheddar cheese.

FREEZE OPTION: Freeze the cooled chili in freezer containers. To use, partially thaw in refrigerator overnight. Heat through in a saucepan, stirring occasionally; add broth if necessary.

1⅓ CUPS: 201 cal., 3g fat (0 sat. fat), 0 chol., 1035mg sod., 27g carb. (5g sugars, 9g fiber), 17g pro.

TEST KITCHEN TIP

Vegetarian meat crumbles are a nutritious protein source made from soy. Look for them in the natural foods freezer section.

BULGUR CHILI

This vegetarian chili is zesty, but it also offers a slight hint of sweetness. It's an ideal recipe for when you have visitors because it doesn't have to simmer for hours like other chilis.

—*Jeraldine Hall, Ravenden Springs, AR*

- -

Prep: 10 min. + standing • **Cook:** 25 min.
Makes: 9 servings

- ¾ cup bulgur
- 2 cups boiling water
- 1½ cups finely chopped green peppers
- 1 large onion, chopped
- 2 tsp. canola oil
- 2 cups reduced-sodium tomato juice
- 1 can (16 oz.) kidney beans, rinsed and drained
- 1 can (15 oz.) Ranch Style beans (pinto beans in seasoned tomato sauce)
- 1 can (14½ oz.) diced tomatoes, undrained
- 1 can (8 oz.) tomato sauce
- 1 cup water
- 2 to 3 Tbsp. chili powder
- 2 garlic cloves, minced
- ½ tsp. ground cumin
- ⅛ to ¼ tsp. cayenne pepper
- ¾ cup shredded reduced-fat cheddar cheese

1. Place bulgur in a large bowl; stir in boiling water. Cover and let stand until most of the liquid is absorbed, about 30 minutes. Drain and squeeze dry.
2. In a large saucepan, saute green peppers and onion in oil until tender. Stir in the bulgur, tomato juice, beans, tomatoes, tomato sauce, water, chili powder, garlic, cumin and cayenne. Bring to a boil. Reduce heat; simmer, covered, for 20-25 minutes or until heated through. Sprinkle with cheese.
1 CUP: 195 cal., 3g fat (1g sat. fat), 5mg chol., 657mg sod., 33g carb. (0 sugars, 7g fiber), 11g pro. **DIABETIC EXCHANGES:** 2 vegetable, 1½ starch, 1 lean meat.

READER RAVE

"[This is] the best chili I've ever made—great for following a vegan/plant based lifestyle! It's very easy to make as well as simple to either add or leave out items depending upon personal preference. Simply delicious!"
—JULES77, TASTEOFHOME.COM

CARROT BROCCOLI SOUP

At our house this soup is a staple. It's fast, easy and filled to the brim with carrots and broccoli. Even picky eaters will like it.
—*Sandy Smith, London, ON*

Prep: 15 min. • **Cook:** 20 min.
Makes: 4 servings

- 1 medium onion, chopped
- 2 medium carrots, chopped
- 2 celery ribs, chopped
- 1 Tbsp. butter
- 3 cups fresh broccoli florets
- 3 cups fat-free milk, divided
- ¾ tsp. salt
- ½ tsp. dried thyme
- ⅛ tsp. pepper
- 3 Tbsp. all-purpose flour

1. In a large saucepan coated with cooking spray, cook the onion, carrots and celery in butter for 3 minutes. Add broccoli; cook 3 minutes longer. Stir in 2¾ cups milk, salt, thyme and pepper.
2. Bring to a boil. Reduce heat; cover and simmer until the vegetables are tender, 5-10 minutes.
3. Combine the flour and remaining milk until smooth; gradually stir into soup. Bring to a boil; cook until thickened, about 2 minutes longer.
1¼ CUPS: 168 cal., 4g fat (3g sat. fat), 14mg chol., 633mg sod., 24g carb. (15g sugars, 4g fiber), 10g pro. **DIABETIC EXCHANGES:** 2 vegetable, 1 fat-free milk, ½ fat.

TEST KITCHEN TIP

For a creamier soup, use 2% milk instead of the skim. If you like, replace the straight thyme with a blend that contains thyme, such as an Italian spice blend.

ROASTED PEPPER POTATO SOUP

I really enjoy potato soup, and this rich, creamy version is different from most I've tried. I like its lemon and cilantro flavors, but you can adjust the ingredients to best suit your family's taste buds.
—*Hollie Powell, St. Louis, MO*

Prep: 30 min. • **Cook:** 15 min.
Makes: 6 servings

- 2 medium onions, chopped
- 2 Tbsp. canola oil
- 1 jar (7 oz.) roasted sweet red peppers, undrained and chopped
- 1 can (4 oz.) chopped green chiles, drained
- 2 tsp. ground cumin
- 1 tsp. salt
- 1 tsp. ground coriander
- 3 cups diced peeled potatoes
- 3 cups vegetable broth
- 2 Tbsp. minced fresh cilantro
- 1 Tbsp. lemon juice
- ½ cup reduced-fat cream cheese, cubed

1. In a large saucepan, saute onions in oil until tender. Stir in the roasted peppers, chiles, cumin, salt and coriander. Cook and stir for 2 minutes. Stir in potatoes and broth; bring to a boil.
2. Reduce heat; cover and simmer until potatoes are tender, 10-15 minutes. Stir in cilantro and lemon juice. Cool slightly.
3. In a blender, process the cream cheese and half the soup until smooth. Return all to pan and heat through.
1 CUP: 204 cal., 9g fat (3g sat. fat), 11mg chol., 1154mg sod., 26g carb. (0 sugars, 4g fiber), 6g pro.

🍲 SLOW-COOKER THAI BUTTERNUT SQUASH PEANUT SOUP

This seemingly exotic dish is simple, vegan, healthy and hearty. The peanut butter blends beautifully with the sweetness of the squash and Thai seasonings. You can also serve this soup without pureeing it first.
—Kayla Capper, Ojai, CA

Prep: 25 min. • **Cook:** 5 hours
Makes: 8 servings

- 3 cups cubed peeled butternut squash
- 1 can (13.66 oz.) light coconut milk
- 1 medium sweet red pepper, finely chopped
- 1 medium onion, finely chopped
- 1 cup vegetable stock
- ½ cup chunky peanut butter
- 3 Tbsp. lime juice
- 2 Tbsp. red curry paste
- 4 garlic cloves, minced
- 1 Tbsp. reduced-sodium soy sauce
- 1 tsp. minced fresh gingerroot
- ½ tsp. salt
- ¼ tsp. pepper
  Optional: Chopped fresh cilantro and chopped salted peanuts

1. In a 4- or 5-qt. slow cooker, combine the first 13 ingredients. Cook, covered, on low until squash is tender, 5-6 hours.
2. Puree the soup using an immersion blender. Or, cool slightly and puree soup in batches in a blender. Return to slow cooker and heat through. If desired, garnish with cilantro and peanuts.
¾ CUP: 181 cal., 12g fat (4g sat. fat), 0 chol., 470mg sod., 16g carb. (5g sugars, 3g fiber), 5g pro. **DIABETIC EXCHANGES:** 1 starch, 1 high-fat meat, 1 fat.
HEALTH TIP: This brightly colored soup provides you with your total daily dose of vitamin A, thanks to the butternut squash and red pepper.

🍲 FIRE-ROASTED TOMATO MINESTRONE

This soup was created to accommodate special Christmas dinner guests who are vegetarians. It was so good we all enjoyed it. This can also be cooked on the stove for two hours on low simmer.
—DonnaMarie Ryan, Topsfield, MA

Prep: 20 min. • **Cook:** 4½ hours
Makes: 8 servings (about 3 qt.)

- 1 medium sweet onion, chopped
- 1 cup cut fresh green beans
- 1 small zucchini, cubed
- 1 medium carrot, chopped
- 1 celery rib, chopped
- 2 garlic cloves, minced
- 2 Tbsp. olive oil
- ¼ tsp. salt
- ¼ tsp. pepper
- 2 cans (14½ oz. each) fire-roasted diced tomatoes
- 1 can (15 oz.) cannellini beans, rinsed and drained
- 1 carton (32 oz.) vegetable broth
- 1 cup uncooked small pasta shells
- 1 cup chopped fresh spinach
  Shredded Parmesan cheese, optional

1. In a 5-qt. slow cooker, combine the first 9 ingredients. Add tomatoes and beans; pour in broth. Cook, covered, on low until vegetables are tender, 4-6 hours.
2. Stir in pasta; cook, covered, on low until pasta is tender, 30-40 minutes. Stir in spinach before serving. If desired, top with shredded Parmesan cheese.
1⅓ CUPS: 175 cal., 4g fat (1g sat. fat), 0 chol., 767mg sod., 29g carb. (7g sugars, 5g fiber), 6g pro.

MEAT
LOVER
OPTION
PAGE 320

❄ GINGER BUTTERNUT SQUASH BISQUE

This soup is filling enough for my husband, and it's vegetarian—which I love. The couple who introduced us made it for us on a freezing night, and we have been hooked ever since.
—*Cara McDonald, Winter Park, CO*

Prep: 25 min. • **Bake:** 40 min. + cooling
Makes: 6 servings

- 1   medium butternut squash (about 3 lbs.)
- 1   Tbsp. olive oil
- 2   medium carrots, finely chopped
- 1   medium onion, chopped
- 2   garlic cloves, minced
- 2   tsp. minced fresh gingerroot
- 2   tsp. curry powder
- 1   can (14½ oz.) vegetable broth
- 1   can (13.66 oz.) coconut milk
- 1   tsp. salt
- ½   tsp. pepper
- 2   cups hot cooked brown rice
- ¼   cup sweetened shredded coconut, toasted
- ¼   cup salted peanuts, coarsely chopped
- ¼   cup minced fresh cilantro

1. Preheat oven to 400°. Cut the squash lengthwise in half; remove and discard seeds. Place the squash in a greased shallow roasting pan, cut side down. Roast 40-45 minutes or until squash is tender. Cool slightly.
2. In a large saucepan, heat oil over medium heat. Add carrots and onion; cook and stir until tender. Add garlic, ginger and curry powder; cook and stir 1 minute longer. Add broth; bring to a boil. Reduce heat; simmer, uncovered, 10-12 minutes or until carrots are tender.
3. Scoop flesh from squash; discard skins. Add squash, coconut milk, salt and pepper to carrot mixture; bring just to a boil, stirring occasionally. Remove from heat; cool slightly. Process in batches in a blender until smooth.
4. Return to pan; heat through. Top individual servings with rice, coconut, peanuts and cilantro.

NOTE: To toast coconut, spread in a dry skillet; cook and stir over low heat until lightly browned.

1 CUP: 386 cal., 21g fat (14g sat. fat), 0 chol., 749mg sod., 48g carb. (10g sugars, 10g fiber), 7g pro.

This recipe makes a rich, thick bisque. If you prefer a thinner soup, just add a second 14½-oz. can of vegetable broth.

SPICY PEANUT SOUP

After enjoying a similar dish at a little cafe, I knew I had to try to duplicate it at home. I think my version comes pretty close. It's the best way I know to chase away winter's chill.
—*Lisa Meredith, St. Paul, MN*

Prep: 35 min. • **Cook:** 20 min.
Makes: 7 servings

- 2   medium carrots, chopped
- 1   small onion, chopped
- 2   Tbsp. olive oil
- 2   garlic cloves, minced
- 1   large sweet potato, peeled and cubed
- ½   cup chunky peanut butter
- 2   Tbsp. red curry paste
- 2   cans (14½ oz. each) vegetable broth
- 1   can (14½ oz.) fire-roasted diced tomatoes, undrained
- 1   bay leaf
- 1   fresh thyme sprig
- ½   tsp. pepper
- ½   cup unsalted peanuts

1. In a large saucepan, cook carrots and onion in oil over medium heat for 2 minutes. Add garlic; cook 1 minute longer. Stir in the sweet potato; cook 2 minutes longer. Stir in peanut butter and curry paste until blended. Add broth, tomatoes, bay leaf, thyme and pepper.
2. Bring to a boil. Reduce heat; cover and simmer until sweet potatoes and carrots are tender, 15-20 minutes. (Soup will appear curdled.)
3. Discard bay leaf and thyme sprig. Stir soup until blended. Sprinkle individual servings with peanuts.
1 CUP: 276 cal., 18g fat (3g sat. fat), 0 chol., 932mg sod., 22g carb. (9g sugars, 4g fiber), 8g pro.

BLACK BEAN-PUMPKIN SOUP

This recipe is packed with protein from the beans and with vitamins from the pumpkin. The dollop of light sour cream adds a satisfying touch.
—*Jennifer Fisher, Austin, TX*

Prep: 30 min. • **Cook:** 30 min.
Makes: 8 servings (2 qt.)

- 2 cans (15 oz. each) black beans, rinsed and drained
- 1 can (14½ oz.) diced tomatoes, drained
- 2 medium onions, finely chopped
- 1 tsp. olive oil
- 3 garlic cloves, minced
- 1 tsp. ground cumin
- 3 cups vegetable broth
- 1 can (15 oz.) pumpkin
- 2 Tbsp. cider vinegar
- ½ tsp. pepper
- 2 Tbsp. bourbon, optional
- ½ cup reduced-fat sour cream
- ½ cup thinly sliced green onions
- ½ cup roasted salted pumpkin seeds

1. Place beans and tomatoes in a food processor; cover and process until blended. Set aside.

2. In a Dutch oven, saute onions in oil until tender. Add the garlic and cumin; saute 1 minute longer. Stir in the broth, pumpkin, vinegar, pepper and bean mixture. Bring to a boil. Reduce heat; cover and simmer for 20 minutes.

3. Stir in bourbon if desired. Garnish each serving with sour cream, green onions and pumpkin seeds.

1 CUP: 238 cal., 8g fat (2g sat. fat), 5mg chol., 716mg sod., 30g carb. (9g sugars, 9g fiber), 13g pro.

READER RAVE

"This is so perfect for autumn! It's nutrient rich, healthy and, most importantly, affordable."
—MARYANNROWE-SMITH, TASTEOFHOME.COM

TURNIP GREENS SALAD
P. 174

Sides & Salads

These garden-fresh salads and sides complete any meal. Find favorites studded with corn, pasta, beans, broccoli and much more.

TOFU SALAD

To make the tofu extra crispy in this recipe, we recommend draining some of the liquid and cooking it in a generous amount of oil at high heat. It takes a little extra time, but it's worth it!
—Taste of Home *Test Kitchen*

- -

Prep: 15 min. + marinating • **Cook:** 10 min.
Makes: 4 servings

- 1 pkg. (16 oz.) extra-firm tofu, cut into 1-in. cubes
- ¼ cup rice vinegar
- ¼ cup reduced-sodium soy sauce
- 2 Tbsp. sesame oil
- 2 Tbsp. Sriracha chili sauce or 2 tsp. hot pepper sauce
- 2 Tbsp. creamy peanut butter
- ¼ tsp. ground ginger
- 2 Tbsp. canola oil
- 6 cups torn romaine
- 2 medium carrots, shredded
- 1 medium ripe avocado, peeled and sliced
- 1 cup cherry tomatoes, halved
- ½ small red onion, thinly sliced
- 2 Tbsp. sesame seeds, toasted

1. Blot tofu dry. Wrap in a clean kitchen towel; place on a plate and refrigerate for at least 1 hour. In a large shallow dish, whisk the vinegar, soy sauce, sesame oil, Sriracha, peanut butter and ginger until smooth. Add the tofu; turn to coat. Cover and refrigerate for 3-5 hours, turning occasionally. Drain the tofu, reserving marinade; pat dry.
2. In a large skillet, heat oil over medium-high heat. Add the tofu; cook until crisp and golden brown, 5-7 minutes, stirring occasionally. Remove from pan; drain on paper towels.
3. In a large bowl, combine the romaine, carrots, avocado, tomatoes, onion and tofu. Pour reserved marinade over salad; toss to coat. Sprinkle with the sesame seeds. Serve immediately.
2 CUPS: 414 cal., 31g fat (4g sat. fat), 0 chol., 1129mg sod., 24g carb. (12g sugars, 7g fiber), 15g pro.

AVOCADO & ARTICHOKE PASTA SALAD

A squeeze of lime, a sprinkle of fresh cilantro and a little avocado make this creamy, zingy pasta salad one to file with the keepers. Refrigerate until serving—if you can keep it that long!
—*Carrie Farias, Oak Ridge, NJ*

- -

Takes: 30 min. • **Makes:** 10 servings

2 cups uncooked gemelli or spiral pasta
1 can (14 oz.) water-packed artichoke hearts, drained and coarsely chopped
2 plum tomatoes, seeded and chopped
1 medium ripe avocado, peeled and cubed
¼ cup grated Romano cheese

DRESSING
¼ cup canola oil
2 Tbsp. lime juice
1 Tbsp. minced fresh cilantro
1½ tsp. grated lime zest
½ tsp. kosher salt
½ tsp. freshly ground pepper

1. Cook pasta according to the package directions. Drain; rinse with cold water.
2. In a large bowl, combine the pasta, artichoke hearts, tomatoes, avocado and cheese. In a small bowl, whisk dressing ingredients. Pour over the pasta mixture; toss gently to combine. Refrigerate, covered, until serving.
¾ CUP: 188 cal., 10g fat (1g sat. fat), 3mg chol., 248mg sod., 21g carb. (1g sugars, 2g fiber), 6g pro.

ZUCCHINI PATTIES

My sister gave me this recipe and I, in turn, have given it to many of my friends. These patties have a nice flavor and are compatible with just about any entree.
—*Annabelle Cripe, Goshen, IN*

Prep: 15 min. • **Cook:** 20 min.
Makes: 4 servings

- 2 cups shredded zucchini
- ½ cup biscuit/baking mix
- ½ cup shredded cheddar cheese
- 2 Tbsp. grated onion
- ½ tsp. salt
- ½ tsp. dried basil
- ¼ tsp. pepper
- 2 large eggs, lightly beaten
- 2 Tbsp. butter

In a bowl, combine the first 7 ingredients. Stir in the eggs; mix well. In a skillet over medium-high heat, melt butter. Working in batches, drop batter by ¼ cupfuls into the pan. Cook until the patties are lightly browned, 4-5 minutes on each side.
2 PATTIES: 214 cal., 14g fat (8g sat. fat), 122mg chol., 618mg sod., 14g carb. (3g sugars, 1g fiber), 8g pro.

AIR-FRYER ITALIAN BREAD SALAD WITH OLIVES

This salad recipe is quick and flavorful, and always gets rave reviews from my friends and family. It's a timesaver during the holidays since it can be made ahead.
—*Angela Spengler, Niceville, FL*

Takes: 25 min. • **Makes:** 4 servings

- 5 cups cubed ciabatta bread (½-in. cubes)
- ⅓ cup olive oil
- 1 garlic clove, minced
- ⅛ tsp. pepper
- 2 Tbsp. balsamic vinegar
- ⅛ tsp. salt
- 1 large tomato, chopped
- 2 Tbsp. sliced ripe olives
- 2 Tbsp. coarsely chopped fresh basil
- 1 Tbsp. chopped fresh Italian parsley
- 2 Tbsp. shredded Parmesan cheese

1. Preheat air fryer to 350°. Place bread cubes in a large bowl. In another bowl, mix oil, garlic and pepper; drizzle 2 Tbsp. over bread and toss to coat. Reserve remaining oil mixture.
2. Place the bread cubes on a greased tray in the air-fryer basket. Cook until crisp and light brown, 7-9 minutes, stirring occasionally.
3. Meanwhile, whisk vinegar and salt into reserved oil mixture. Add tomato, olives and herbs; toss to coat. Cool bread cubes slightly. Add to tomato mixture; toss to combine. Sprinkle with the cheese; serve immediately.
1 CUP: 308 cal., 21g fat (3g sat. fat), 2mg chol., 365mg sod., 26g carb. (6g sugars, 2g fiber), 5g pro.

BLACK BEAN VEGGIE BURGER SALAD

This lower-fat version of a traditional taco salad doesn't lose any of the flavor of the original. The creamy, flavorful dressing complements the unique use of a veggie burger as well.
—*Mary Bilyeu, Ann Arbor, MI*

Takes: 15 min. • **Makes:** 2 servings

2 frozen spicy black bean veggie burgers
3 cups spring mix salad greens
¾ cup grape tomatoes, halved
⅓ cup frozen corn, thawed
¼ cup finely chopped red onion
½ cup coarsely crushed nacho tortilla chips
½ cup shredded Mexican cheese blend
⅓ cup ranch salad dressing
⅓ cup salsa
1 tsp. taco seasoning

1. Cook veggie burgers according to package directions. Divide the salad greens, tomatoes, corn and onion between 2 serving plates. Crumble burgers; sprinkle each salad with burgers, chips and cheese.
2. In a small bowl, combine the salad dressing, salsa and taco seasoning; serve with salad.

1 SERVING: 395 cal., 13g fat (4g sat. fat), 20mg chol., 1454mg sod., 49g carb. (10g sugars, 9g fiber), 24g pro.

SIMPLE VEGETARIAN SLOW-COOKED BEANS

These tasty beans loaded with spinach, tomatoes and carrots are a go-to dish when I have a hungry family to feed. It's frequently on our menu.
—*Jennifer Reid, Farmington, ME*

Prep: 15 min. • **Cook:** 4 hours
Makes: 8 servings

- 4 cans (15½ oz. each) great northern beans, rinsed and drained
- 4 medium carrots, finely chopped (about 2 cups)
- 1 cup vegetable stock
- 6 garlic cloves, minced
- 2 tsp. ground cumin
- ¾ tsp. salt
- ⅛ tsp. chili powder
- 4 cups fresh baby spinach, coarsely chopped
- 1 cup oil-packed sun-dried tomatoes, patted dry and chopped
- ⅓ cup minced fresh cilantro
- ⅓ cup minced fresh parsley

In a 3-qt. slow cooker, combine the first 7 ingredients. Cook, covered, on low for 4-5 hours or until the carrots are tender, adding spinach and tomatoes during the last 10 minutes of cooking. Stir in cilantro and parsley.

¾ CUP. 229 cal., 3g fat (0 sat. fat), 0 chol., 672mg sod., 40g carb. (2g sugars, 13g fiber), 12g pro.

READER RAVE

"My three kids really liked this recipe! I served it with a side of couscous (and a dish of berries) for a wonderful warm meal to come home to. The sun-dried tomatoes add amazing flavor. I think I will add onion and maybe zucchini next time. So good!"
APRIL, TASTEOFHOME.COM

SHAVED FENNEL SALAD

This salad tastes even more impressive than it looks. It has an incredible crunch thanks to the cucumbers, radishes and apples, and the fennel fronds add just the faintest hint of licorice flavor.
—*William Milton III, Clemson, SC*

- -

Takes: 15 min. • **Makes:** 8 servings

- 1 large fennel bulb, fronds reserved
- 1 English cucumber
- 1 medium Honeycrisp apple
- 2 Tbsp. extra virgin olive oil
- ½ tsp. kosher salt
- ¼ tsp. coarsely ground pepper
- 2 radishes, thinly sliced

With a mandoline or vegetable peeler, cut the fennel, cucumber and apple into very thin slices. Transfer to a large bowl; toss with olive oil, salt and pepper. Top with radishes and reserved fennel fronds to serve.

¾ CUP: 55 cal., 4g fat (1g sat. fat), 0 chol., 138mg sod., 6g carb. (4g sugars, 2g fiber), 1g pro. **DIABETIC EXCHANGES:** 1 vegetable, 1 fat.

SMOKY CAULIFLOWER

The smoked Spanish paprika gives a simple side of cauliflower more depth of flavor. We're fans of roasted veggies, and this one is a definite winner.
—*Juliette Mulholland, Corvallis, OR*

- -

Takes: 30 min. • **Makes:** 8 servings

- 1 large head cauliflower, broken into 1-in. florets (about 9 cups)
- 2 Tbsp. olive oil
- 1 tsp. smoked paprika
- ¾ tsp. salt
- 2 garlic cloves, minced
- 2 Tbsp. minced fresh parsley

1. Place cauliflower in a large bowl. Combine oil, paprika and salt. Drizzle over cauliflower; toss to coat. Transfer to a 15x10x1-in. baking pan. Bake, uncovered, at 450° for 10 minutes.
2. Stir in the garlic. Bake 10-15 minutes longer or until cauliflower is tender and lightly browned, stirring occasionally. Sprinkle with parsley.

¾ CUP: 58 cal., 4g fat (0 sat. fat), 0 chol., 254mg sod., 6g carb. (3g sugars, 3g fiber), 2g pro. **DIABETIC EXCHANGES:** 1 vegetable, ½ fat.

CORN & BLACK BEAN SALAD

This colorful, crunchy salad is chock-full of easy-to-swallow nutrition that all ages will love. Try it with a variety of summer entrees, or as a wholesome salsa!
—Krista Frank, Rhododendron, OR

Prep: 15 min. + chilling
Makes: 8 servings

- 1 can (15½ oz.) black-eyed peas, rinsed and drained
- 1 can (15 oz.) black beans, rinsed and drained
- 2 large tomatoes, finely chopped
- 1½ cups fresh or frozen corn
- ½ cup finely chopped red onion
- ¼ cup minced fresh cilantro
- 2 garlic cloves, minced

DRESSING

- 2 Tbsp. sugar
- 2 Tbsp. white vinegar
- 2 Tbsp. canola oil
- 1½ tsp. lime juice
- ¼ tsp. salt
- ¼ tsp. ground cumin
- ¼ tsp. pepper

In a large bowl, combine the first 7 ingredients. In a small bowl, whisk dressing ingredients; pour over corn mixture and toss to coat. Cover and refrigerate at least 1 hour. Stir before serving. Serve with a slotted spoon.
¾ CUP: 167 cal., 4g fat (0 sat. fat), 0 chol., 244mg sod., 27g carb. (8g sugars, 5g fiber), 7g pro. **DIABETIC EXCHANGES:** 2 starch, 1 fat.

BRUSSELS SPROUTS SALAD

My husband and I like Brussels sprouts, so I'm always looking for new ways to use them. I most often serve this colorful salad with roast pork or duck.
—Nancy Korondan, Yorkville, IL

Takes: 20 min. • **Makes:** 8 servings

- 1½ lbs. fresh Brussels sprouts, trimmed and halved
- 2 green onions, chopped
- ½ cup olive oil
- 2 Tbsp. lemon juice
- 1 to 1½ tsp. Dijon mustard
- ½ tsp. salt
- ½ tsp. dried thyme
- ¼ tsp. pepper
- 1 bunch red leaf lettuce or radicchio, torn
- 2 Tbsp. slivered almonds, toasted

1. Place the Brussels sprouts in a large saucepan; add 1 in. water. Bring to a boil. Reduce the heat; simmer, covered, until tender, 8-10 minutes. Drain; rinse with cold water and pat dry. Combine with green onions.
2. Meanwhile, whisk together the next 6 ingredients. Toss 2 Tbsp. dressing with lettuce; transfer to a serving bowl. Pour remaining dressing over the Brussels sprouts and onions; toss to coat. Mound on lettuce. Sprinkle with almonds.
NOTE: To toast nuts, bake in a shallow pan in a 350° oven for 5-10 minutes or cook in a skillet over low heat until lightly browned, stirring occasionally.
1 CUP: 171 cal., 15g fat (2g sat. fat), 0 chol., 192mg sod., 9g carb. (2g sugars, 4g fiber), 4g pro. **DIABETIC EXCHANGES:** 3 fat, 2 vegetable.

51 FRESH FRUIT BOWL

The glorious colors of the fruit make this a festive salad. Slightly sweet and chilled, it makes a nice accompaniment to almost any entree.

—*Marion Kirst, Troy, MI*

Prep: 15 min. + chilling
Makes: 16 servings

- 8   cups fresh melon cubes
- 1   to 2 Tbsp. corn syrup
- 1   pint fresh strawberries, halved
- 2   cups fresh pineapple chunks
- 2   oranges, sectioned
      Fresh mint leaves, optional

In a large bowl, combine melon cubes and corn syrup. Cover and refrigerate overnight. Just before serving, stir in remaining fruit. Garnish with fresh mint leaves if desired.

¾ CUP: 56 cal., 0 fat (0 sat. fat), 0 chol., 14mg sod., 14g carb. (11g sugars, 2g fiber), 1g pro. **DIABETIC EXCHANGES:** 1 fruit.

EGGPLANT PARMESAN

We really like eggplant and would rather have it baked than fried. This can be served as a side dish or a main dish.
—*Donna Wardlow-Keating, Omaha, NE*

- -

Prep: 10 min. • **Bake:** 45 min. + cooling
Makes: 2 servings

- 2 Tbsp. olive oil
- 1 garlic clove, minced
- 1 small eggplant, peeled and cut into ¼-in. slices
- 1 Tbsp. minced fresh basil or 1 tsp. dried basil
- 1 Tbsp. grated Parmesan cheese
- 1 medium tomato, thinly sliced
- ½ cup shredded mozzarella cheese Additional basil, optional

1. Combine oil and garlic; brush over both sides of eggplant slices. Place on a greased baking sheet. Bake at 425° for 15 minutes; turn. Bake until golden brown, about 5 minutes longer. Cool on a wire rack.
2. Place half the eggplant in a greased 1-qt. baking dish. Sprinkle with half the basil and Parmesan cheese. Arrange tomato slices over top; sprinkle with remaining basil and Parmesan. Layer with half the mozzarella cheese and the remaining eggplant; top with remaining mozzarella. Cover and bake at 350° for 20 minutes. Uncover; bake until cheese is melted, 5-7 minutes longer. Garnish with additional basil if desired.
1 SERVING: 275 cal., 21g fat (6g sat. fat), 24mg chol., 164mg sod., 16g carb. (9g sugars, 5g fiber), 9g pro.

CURRIED COLESLAW

I came up with this recipe by combining my classic coleslaw with my mom's favorite curried chicken salad. It's a special spin on plain slaw and a terrific side salad to take to potlucks. Use golden raisins if you don't have cranberries.
—*Robin Haas, Hyde Park, MA*

- -

Prep: 25 min. + standing
Makes: 16 servings

- 1 medium head cabbage, thinly sliced
- 1 Tbsp. plus ½ tsp. kosher salt, divided
- 2 celery ribs, chopped
- 1 large carrot, shredded
- ½ cup dried cranberries
- ¼ cup chopped onion
- ½ cup mayonnaise
- 2 Tbsp. white vinegar
- 1 Tbsp. sugar
- 1 tsp. celery seed
- 1 tsp. curry powder
- ½ tsp. Dijon mustard

1. Place cabbage in a colander over a plate. Sprinkle with 1 Tbsp. kosher salt; toss to coat. Let stand 1 hour.
2. Rinse cabbage and drain well; pat dry. Place in a large bowl. Add celery, carrot, cranberries and onion. In a small bowl, whisk the remaining ingredients and remaining ½ tsp. kosher salt. Drizzle over coleslaw; toss to coat. Refrigerate until serving.
1 CUP: 82 cal., 5g fat (1g sat. fat), 1mg chol., 477mg sod., 9g carb. (7g sugars, 2g fiber), 1g pro. **DIABETIC EXCHANGES:** 1 vegetable, 1 fat.

GRILLED ROMAINE SALAD

For a great-tasting salad, try this recipe on the grill! It's equally good with any dressing of your choice.
—*Susan Court, Pewaukee, WI*

Takes: 20 min. • **Makes:** 12 servings

- ⅓ cup plus 3 Tbsp. olive oil, divided
- 2 Tbsp. white wine vinegar
- 1 Tbsp. dill weed
- ½ tsp. garlic powder
- ⅛ tsp. crushed red pepper flakes
- ⅛ tsp. salt
- 6 green onions
- 4 plum tomatoes, halved
- 1 large cucumber, peeled and halved lengthwise
- 2 romaine hearts, halved lengthwise

1. In a small bowl, whisk ⅓ cup olive oil, vinegar and seasonings.

2. Brush onions, tomatoes, cucumber and romaine with remaining oil. Grill the onions, tomatoes and cucumber, uncovered, over medium heat for 4-5 minutes on each side or until the onions are crisp-tender. Grill romaine for 30 seconds on each side or until heated through.

3. Place romaine on a serving platter. Chop vegetables and sprinkle over romaine. Drizzle salad with dressing. Serve immediately.

¾ CUP: 98 cal., 10g fat (1g sat. fat), 0 chol., 30mg sod., 3g carb. (1g sugars, 1g fiber), 1g pro.

HUMMUS PASTA SALAD

Adding the dressing while the pasta is still warm allows the pasta to absorb some of the dressing. This is a hearty side but could be a nice meatless main dish as well.

—*Michelle Morrow, Newmarket, NH*

Prep: 25 min. • **Bake:** 20 min. + chilling
Makes: 18 servings

- 2 cans (16 oz. each) garbanzo beans or chickpeas, rinsed and drained
- 2 Tbsp. olive oil
- ¾ tsp. salt, divided
- ½ tsp. pepper, divided
- 1 pkg. (16 oz.) uncooked whole wheat spiral pasta
- 4 cups chopped fresh kale
- 2 medium lemons
- ½ cup water
- 6 Tbsp. tahini
- 4 garlic cloves, minced
- 2 Tbsp. Greek olive juice
- 1 pint cherry tomatoes, quartered
- 1 cup Greek olives, chopped

1. Preheat oven to 350°. Place garbanzo beans on a parchment-lined rimmed baking sheet. Drizzle with oil and sprinkle with ½ tsp. salt and ¼ tsp. pepper; toss to coat. Bake until golden brown, about 20 minutes.

2. Meanwhile, cook pasta according to package directions for al dente. Drain pasta; rinse with cold water and drain well. Place kale in a large mixing bowl; massage until tender, 3-5 minutes. Add the pasta.

3. Finely grate zest from 1 lemon. Cut lemons crosswise in half; squeeze juice from lemons. In a small bowl, whisk the water, tahini, garlic, olive juice, lemon juice and zest, and remaining ¼ tsp. salt and ¼ tsp. pepper. Pour over pasta mixture; toss to coat. Stir in garbanzo beans, tomatoes and olives. Refrigerate, covered, at least 3 hours.

¾ CUP: 219 cal., 8g fat (1g sat. fat), 0 chol., 316mg sod., 30g carb. (2g sugars, 6g fiber), 7g pro. **DIABETIC EXCHANGES:** 2 starch, 1½ fat.

MEAT LOVER OPTION
PAGE 320

MARINATED CAULIFLOWER SALAD

I serve this as an appetizer alongside a charcuterie tray. But it also makes a delicious side dish.
—*Stephanie Hase, Lyons, CO*

Prep: 20 min. + marinating
Makes: 12 servings

- ¼ cup red wine vinegar
- ¼ cup olive oil
- 2 Tbsp. water
- 5 cups fresh cauliflowerets
- 1 bay leaf
- 1 garlic clove, minced
- ¼ tsp. salt
- ¼ tsp. coarsely ground pepper
- 1 medium carrot, shredded
- 1 small red onion, chopped
- ¼ cup minced fresh parsley
- ¼ tsp. dried basil

1. In a small saucepan, bring vinegar, oil and water just to a boil.
2. Meanwhile, place next 5 ingredients in a large heatproof bowl. Add the hot oil mixture; toss to coat. Refrigerate, covered, at least 6 hours or overnight, stirring occasionally.
3. Add the carrot, onion, parsley and basil; toss to coat. Refrigerate, covered, 2 hours longer. Discard bay leaf. Serve with a slotted spoon.
⅔ CUP: 58 cal., 5g fat (1g sat. fat), 0 chol., 67mg sod., 4g carb. (1g sugars, 1g fiber), 1g pro. **DIABETIC EXCHANGES:** 1 vegetable, 1 fat.

SHREDDED KALE & BRUSSELS SPROUTS SALAD

This salad is a simple and delicious way to eat your superfoods! It gets even better in the fridge, so I make it ahead. I use my homemade honey mustard dressing, but any type works just fine.
—*Alexandra Weisser, New York, NY*

Takes: 15 min. • **Makes:** 6 servings

- 1 small bunch kale (about 8 oz.), stemmed and thinly sliced (about 6 cups)
- ½ lb. fresh Brussels sprouts, thinly sliced (about 3 cups)
- ½ cup pistachios, coarsely chopped
- ½ cup honey mustard salad dressing
- ¼ cup shredded Parmesan cheese

In a large bowl, combine the first 3 ingredients. Add the dressing and cheese; toss before serving.
1 CUP: 207 cal., 14g fat (2g sat. fat), 8mg chol., 235mg sod., 16g carb. (5g sugars, 4g fiber), 7g pro. **DIABETIC EXCHANGES:** 3 fat, 2 vegetable, ½ starch.

TEST KITCHEN TIP

It's easy to prepare the kale for this salad. Begin by washing and destemming the kale. Then chop it into small pieces, or stack and roll the leaves (think of a cigar) and slice into thin ribbons.

SUMMER SQUASH SALAD

Packing the perfect crunch, this salad is a healthier alternative to coleslaw. Like most gardeners, we usually have an abundance of squash and zucchini in summer, so this dish is an amazing way to use our fresh produce.
—*Diane Hixon, Niceville, FL*

Prep: 15 min. + chilling
Makes: 12 servings

4   cups julienned zucchini
4   cups julienned yellow squash
2   cups sliced radishes
1   cup canola oil
⅓   cup cider vinegar
2   Tbsp. Dijon mustard
2   Tbsp. snipped fresh parsley
1½ tsp. salt
1   tsp. dill weed
½   tsp. pepper

In a large bowl, toss zucchini, squash and radishes. In a small bowl, whisk remaining ingredients. Pour over the vegetables. Cover and refrigerate for at least 2 hours. If desired, top with additional snipped fresh parsley.

¾ CUP: 188 cal., 19g fat (1g sat. fat), 0 chol., 368mg sod., 4g carb. (3g sugars, 1g fiber), 1g pro.

HEIRLOOM TOMATO SALAD

This is a simple yet elegant dish that always pleases my guests. Not only is it tasty, but it is healthy too. The more varied the colors of the tomatoes you choose, the prettier the salad will be.
—*Jessie Apfel, Berkeley, CA*

Prep: 20 min. + chilling
Makes: 6 servings

- 2 cups cut-up heirloom tomatoes
- 1 cup multicolored cherry tomatoes, halved
- 2 cups fresh baby spinach
- ½ cup sliced red onion

DRESSING

- 3 Tbsp. olive oil
- 2 Tbsp. white balsamic vinegar
- 1 garlic clove, minced
- ½ tsp. salt
- ¼ tsp. dried basil
- ¼ tsp. dried oregano
- ¼ tsp. dried rosemary, crushed
- ¼ tsp. dried thyme
- ¼ tsp. pepper
- ⅛ tsp. rubbed sage

Place the tomatoes, spinach and onion in a large bowl. Whisk together dressing ingredients; toss with salad. Refrigerate, covered, 2 hours. Serve the salad with a slotted spoon.

⅔ CUP: 75 cal., 5g fat (1g sat. fat), 0 chol., 161mg sod., 7g carb. (4g sugars, 2g fiber), 1g pro. **DIABETIC EXCHANGES:** 1 vegetable, 1 fat.

KALE SLAW SPRING SALAD

My parents and in-laws are retired and like to spend winters in Florida. This tangy spring salad brings the snowbirds back for our Easter celebration!
—*Jennifer Gilbert, Brighton, MI*

Takes: 25 min. • **Makes:** 10 servings

- 5 cups chopped fresh kale
- 3 cups torn romaine
- 1 pkg. (14 oz.) coleslaw mix
- 1 medium fennel bulb, thinly sliced
- 1 cup chopped fresh broccoli
- ½ cup shredded red cabbage
- 1 cup crumbled feta cheese
- ¼ cup sesame seeds, toasted
- ⅓ cup extra virgin olive oil
- 3 Tbsp. sesame oil
- 2 Tbsp. honey
- 2 Tbsp. cider vinegar
- 2 Tbsp. lemon juice
- ⅓ cup pureed strawberries
  Sliced fresh strawberries

1. Combine kale and romaine. Add the coleslaw mix, fennel, broccoli and red cabbage; sprinkle with feta cheese and sesame seeds. Toss to combine.
2. Stir together olive oil and sesame oil. Whisk in honey, vinegar and lemon juice. Add pureed strawberries. Whisk until combined. Dress salad just before serving; top with sliced strawberries.
1⅓ CUPS: 192 cal., 15g fat (3g sat. fat), 6mg chol., 140mg sod., 12g carb. (7g sugars, 3g fiber), 4g pro. **DIABETIC EXCHANGES:** 3 fat, 1 starch.

COOL BEANS SALAD

This protein-filled dish could be served as a colorful side dish or a meatless main entree. Double the recipe because it will be gone in a flash! The basmati rice adds a unique flavor and the dressing gives it a bit of a tang.
—*Janelle Lee, Appleton, WI*

Takes: 20 min. • **Makes:** 6 servings

- ½ cup olive oil
- ¼ cup red wine vinegar
- 1 Tbsp. sugar
- 1 garlic clove, minced
- 1 tsp. salt
- 1 tsp. ground cumin
- 1 tsp. chili powder
- ¼ tsp. pepper
- 3 cups cooked basmati rice
- 1 can (16 oz.) kidney beans, rinsed and drained
- 1 can (15 oz.) black beans, rinsed and drained
- 1½ cups frozen corn, thawed
- 4 green onions, sliced
- 1 small sweet red pepper, chopped
- ¼ cup minced fresh cilantro

In a large bowl, whisk the first 8 ingredients. Add the remaining ingredients; toss to coat. Chill salad until serving.
1⅓ CUPS: 440 cal., 19g fat (3g sat. fat), 0 chol., 659mg sod., 58g carb. (5g sugars, 8g fiber), 12g pro.

ONION ORANGE SALAD

People always enjoy the bold flavors in this delightful salad. It's both delicious and beautiful.

—Zita Wilensky, North Miami Beach, FL

Takes: 15 min. • **Makes:** 8 servings

- ⅓ cup olive oil
- ¼ cup orange juice
- 3 Tbsp. vinegar
- 1 garlic clove, minced
- 1 tsp. minced fresh parsley
- ¼ tsp. salt
  Dash pepper
- 8 cups torn spinach or mixed greens
- 3 medium oranges, peeled and sliced
- 1 cup sliced red onion
- ½ cup crumbled blue cheese
- ¼ cup slivered almonds, toasted

In a small bowl, whisk the first 7 ingredients. On a serving platter or individual plates, arrange greens, oranges and onion. Drizzle with the dressing. Sprinkle with the cheese and almonds.

1 SERVING: 162 cal., 13g fat (3g sat. fat), 6mg chol., 216mg sod., 8g carb. (6g sugars, 2g fiber), 4g pro. **DIABETIC EXCHANGES:** 2½ fat, 1 vegetable, ½ starch.

TURNIP GREENS SALAD

I created this recipe using items from my garden. Although most people cook turnip greens, I wanted to present those same greens in a way that would retain the nutrients. The salad can also have different kinds of meat added. I have used cooked shrimp, chicken or beef.
—*James McCarroll, Murfreesboro, TN*

Takes: 30 min. • **Makes:** 8 servings

- 1 bunch fresh turnip greens (about 10 oz.)
- 5 oz. fresh baby spinach (about 8 cups)
- 1 medium cucumber, halved and thinly sliced
- 1 cup cherry tomatoes, halved
- ¾ cup dried cranberries
- ½ medium red onion, thinly sliced
- ⅓ cup crumbled feta cheese
- 1 garlic clove
- ½ tsp. kosher salt
- ⅓ cup extra virgin olive oil
- 2 Tbsp. sherry vinegar
- 1 tsp. Dijon mustard
- ¼ tsp. pepper
- ⅛ tsp. cayenne pepper

1. Trim and discard root end of turnip greens. Coarsely chop leaves and cut stalks into 1-in. pieces. Place in a large bowl. Add spinach, cucumber, tomatoes, cranberries, red onion and feta.

2. Place the garlic on a cutting board; sprinkle with salt. Using the flat side of a knife, mash garlic. Continue to mash until it reaches a paste consistency. Transfer to a small bowl. Whisk in oil, vinegar, mustard, pepper and cayenne until blended. Drizzle over salad; toss to coat. Serve immediately.

1¼ CUPS: 161 cal., 10g fat (2g sat. fat), 3mg chol., 203mg sod., 17g carb. (12g sugars, 3g fiber), 3g pro. **DIABETIC EXCHANGES:** 2 vegetable, 2 fat, ½ starch.

HERBY PEA SALAD

We love spring vegetables. One Mother's Day I came up with this flavorful green salad that everyone enjoyed. You could increase the dressing and mix in some cooked small cooked pasta, like acini de pepe, for a pasta salad.
—*Ann Sheehy, Lawrence, MA*

Takes: 30 min. • **Makes:** 8 servings

- 1 Tbsp. olive oil
- 2 medium leeks (white portion only), thinly sliced
- 3 small zucchini, halved and sliced
- ½ lb. fresh asparagus, trimmed and cut into 2-in. pieces
- 3 cups frozen petite peas (about 16 oz.), thawed
- 2 Tbsp. each minced fresh chives and parsley
- 1 to 2 Tbsp. minced fresh tarragon

DRESSING
- 3 Tbsp. olive oil
- 2 Tbsp. rice or white wine vinegar
- ¾ tsp. salt
- ½ tsp. Dijon mustard
- ¼ tsp. pepper

1. In a large skillet, heat the oil over medium heat. Add leeks; cook and stir 4-6 minutes or until tender. In a Dutch oven, place steamer basket over 1 in. water. In batches, place zucchini and asparagus in basket. Bring water to a boil. Reduce heat to maintain a low boil; steam, covered, 4-5 minutes or until crisp-tender. Remove and immediately drop into ice water. Drain and pat dry.
2. In a large bowl, combine peas, leeks, zucchini mixture and herbs. In a small bowl, whisk dressing ingredients. Pour over the salad; toss to coat. Serve the salad immediately.

¾ CUP: 129 cal., 7g fat (1g sat. fat), 0 chol., 353mg sod., 13g carb. (6g sugars, 3g fiber), 4g pro. **DIABETIC EXCHANGES:** 1½ fat, 1 vegetable, ½ starch.

GRILLED POTATOES & PEPPERS

My husband, Matt, grills this recipe for both breakfast and dinner gatherings. Besides our company, his potatoes are one of the best parts of the event!
—*Susan Nordin, Warren, PA*

- -

Prep: 20 min. • **Grill:** 40 min.
Makes: 10 servings

- 8 medium red potatoes, cut into wedges
- 2 medium green peppers, sliced
- 1 medium onion, cut into thin wedges
- 2 Tbsp. olive oil
- 5 garlic cloves, thinly sliced
- 1 tsp. paprika
- 1 tsp. steak seasoning
- 1 tsp. Italian seasoning
- ¼ tsp. salt
- ¼ tsp. pepper

1. In a large bowl, combine all the ingredients. Divide between 2 pieces of heavy-duty foil (about 18 in. square). Fold foil around potato mixture and crimp the edges to seal.
2. Grill, covered, over medium heat until potatoes are tender, 40-45 minutes. Open the foil carefully to allow steam to escape.
¾ CUP: 103 cal., 3g fat (0 sat. fat), 0 chol., 134mg sod., 18g carb. (2g sugars, 2g fiber), 2g pro. **DIABETIC EXCHANGES:** 1 starch, ½ fat.

SUMMER AVOCADO SALAD

Garden-fresh veggies, creamy avocado and a sprinkling of feta cheese make this salad a healthy summer standout!
—*Deborah Williams, Peoria, AZ*

- -

Takes: 30 min. • **Makes:** 2 servings

- ½ cup chopped seeded peeled cucumber
- ⅓ cup chopped sweet yellow pepper
- 6 cherry tomatoes, seeded and quartered
- 2 Tbsp. finely chopped sweet onion
- 1 Tbsp. minced fresh basil or 1 tsp. dried basil
- 1½ tsp. lemon juice
- 1½ tsp. olive oil
- Dash garlic powder
- 1 medium ripe avocado, peeled and chopped
- 2 Tbsp. crumbled feta cheese

In a small bowl, combine the first 8 ingredients; cover and refrigerate 15-20 minutes. Add avocado; toss gently. Sprinkle with feta. Serve immediately.
1 CUP: 186 cal., 15g fat (3g sat. fat), 4mg chol., 77mg sod., 12g carb. (4g sugars, 6g fiber), 4g pro. **DIABETIC EXCHANGES:** 3 fat, 1 vegetable.

ITALIC TOMATO CUCUMBER SALAD

This medley of vegetables is a cool and refreshing complement to zesty dishes.
—*Florine Bruns, Fredericksburg, TX*

Takes: 10 min. • **Makes:** 4 servings

- 2 medium cucumbers, sliced
- 1 large tomato, cut into wedges
- 1 small red onion, cut into thin strips
- ¼ cup Italian salad dressing or salad dressing of your choice

In a large bowl, combine the vegetables. Add dressing; toss to coat.

½ CUP: 93 cal., 6g fat (1g sat. fat), 0 chol., 257mg sod., 9g carb. (6g sugars, 2g fiber), 2g pro. **DIABETIC EXCHANGES:** 1 vegetable, 1 fat.

TEX-MEX POTATO SALAD

I created this recipe for my cooking class, and it was a hit. It's perfect for a backyard cookout or potluck. The secret ingredient is pickled jalapenos—they add so much interest and flavor. Add a can of black beans for more protein.

—*Dianna Ackerley, Cibolo, TX*

Prep: 20 min. • **Cook:** 20 min. + chilling
Makes: 12 servings

- 2 medium ears sweet corn
- 1 large sweet red pepper
- 2 lbs. small red potatoes
- 1 medium ripe avocado, peeled and cubed
- 1 cup grape tomatoes, halved
- 2 green onions, cut into ½-in. slices
- ¼ cup reduced-fat sour cream or fat-free plain Greek yogurt
- ¼ cup reduced-fat mayonnaise
- ¼ cup salsa
- 2 Tbsp. lime juice
- 1 Tbsp. red wine vinegar
- 2 tsp. chopped pickled jalapeno slices
- ½ tsp. salt
- ¼ tsp. garlic powder
- ¼ tsp. onion powder
- ¼ tsp. ground cumin
- ¼ tsp. pepper
  Dash cayenne pepper
  Fresh cilantro leaves

1. Preheat oven to 400°. Place corn and red pepper on a greased baking sheet. Roast for 20-25 minutes until lightly charred, turning once. Let cool. Peel off and discard skin from pepper. Remove stem and seeds. Cut pepper into ½-in. pieces. Cut corn from cobs; set aside.

2. Place potatoes in a large saucepan; add water to cover. Bring to a boil. Reduce heat; cook, uncovered, until tender, 10-12 minutes. Drain and cool. Cut potatoes in half; place in a large bowl. Add sliced red pepper, corn, avocado, tomatoes and green onions.

3. Place the sour cream, mayonnaise, salsa, lime juice, vinegar, jalapenos, salt and seasonings in a blender. Cover and process until blended. Pour over the potato mixture; toss to coat. Refrigerate, covered, until chilled. Serve with cilantro.
¾ CUP: 120 cal., 4g fat (1g sat. fat), 2mg chol., 168mg sod., 19g carb. (4g sugars, 3g fiber), 3g pro. **DIABETIC EXCHANGES:** 1 starch, 1 fat.

TASTY MARINATED TOMATOES

My niece introduced me to this colorful recipe some time ago. I now make it when I have buffets or large gatherings because it can be prepared hours ahead. This is a great way to use a bumper crop of tomatoes.

—*Myrtle Matthews, Marietta, GA*

Prep: 10 min. + marinating
Makes: 8 servings

- 3 large or 5 medium fresh tomatoes, thickly sliced
- ⅓ cup olive oil
- ¼ cup red wine vinegar
- 1 tsp. salt, optional
- ¼ tsp. pepper
- ½ garlic clove, minced
- 2 Tbsp. chopped onion
- 1 Tbsp. minced fresh parsley
- 1 Tbsp. minced fresh basil or 1 tsp. dried basil

Arrange tomatoes in a large shallow dish. Combine remaining ingredients in a jar; cover tightly and shake well. Pour over tomato slices. Cover and refrigerate for several hours.
2 PIECES: 91 cal., 9g fat (0 sat. fat), 0 chol., 6mg sod., 3g carb. (0 sugars, 0 fiber), 1g pro.

SUNFLOWER STRAWBERRY SALAD

We have an annual strawberry festival in our town, so recipes with strawberries are quite popular here. I've served this salad at luncheons, and I've always received compliments.
—*Betty Malone, Humboldt, TN*

Prep: 10 min. + chilling
Makes: 6 servings

- 2 cups sliced fresh strawberries
- 1 medium apple, diced
- 1 cup seedless green grapes, halved
- ½ cup thinly sliced celery
- ¼ cup raisins
- ½ cup strawberry yogurt
- 2 Tbsp. sunflower kernels

In a large bowl, combine strawberries, apple, grapes, celery and raisins. Stir in the yogurt. Cover and refrigerate for at least 1 hour. Add the sunflower kernels and toss.

¾ CUP: 107 cal., 2g fat (0 sat. fat), 1mg chol., 43mg sod., 22g carb. (17g sugars, 3g fiber), 2g pro. **DIABETIC EXCHANGES:** 1½ fruit, ½ fat.

TEST KITCHEN TIP

Sunflower seed shells aren't toxic, so it's OK if you accidentally eat a few. But don't make a habit of it because the shells are a choking hazard and could cause a blockage or obstruction in your esophagus. To quickly shell the sunflower seeds, add half a cup or so of sunflower seeds to a bag and seal the bag shut. Use a rolling pin to gently roll over the seeds, cracking each shell open. Then, pour the contents of the bag into a bowl of water—the shells will rise while the kernels will sink. Skim the shells from the surface to discard, and drain the kernels for use.

GARDEN SALAD WITH CHICKPEAS

Toss crisp veggies in a light vinaigrette for a chickpea salad that tastes as if it's straight from your garden.
—*Taste of Home Test Kitchen*

Takes: 25 min. • **Makes:** 6 servings

- ⅓ cup olive oil
- ¼ cup lemon juice
- 2 Tbsp. red wine vinegar
- ½ tsp. salt
- ¼ tsp. pepper
- ¼ tsp. garlic powder

SALAD
- 1 can (15 oz.) chickpeas or garbanzo beans, rinsed and drained
- 2 medium carrots, julienned
- 1 medium zucchini, julienned
- ½ cup chopped tomato
- 4 green onions, thinly sliced
- 4 radishes, thinly sliced
- ½ cup chopped pecans, toasted
- ½ cup coarsely chopped fresh parsley
- ½ cup crumbled goat cheese
- 6 cups spring mix salad greens

1. In a small bowl, whisk oil, lemon juice, vinegar, salt, pepper and garlic powder.
2. In a large bowl, combine chickpeas, carrots, zucchini, tomato, green onions, radishes, pecans, parsley and cheese. Stir in ½ cup dressing. Arrange greens in a serving bowl; top with the chickpea mixture. Drizzle the salad with the remaining dressing.

1 SERVING: 294 cal., 23g fat (4g sat. fat), 12mg chol., 394mg sod., 21g carb. (5g sugars, 7g fiber), 7g pro.

MEAT LOVER OPTION PAGE 320

EDAMAME CORN CARROT SALAD

I created my salad recipe by trying to think of a protein-filled, nutritious and light dish. It was super easy and visually appealing.

—*Maiah Miller, Montclair, VA*

Prep: 25 min. + chilling
Makes: 8 servings

2½ cups frozen shelled edamame
3 cups julienned carrots
1½ cups frozen corn, thawed
4 green onions, chopped
2 Tbsp. minced fresh cilantro
VINAIGRETTE
3 Tbsp. rice vinegar
3 Tbsp. lemon juice
4 tsp. canola oil
2 garlic cloves, minced
½ tsp. salt
½ tsp. pepper

1. Place edamame in a small saucepan; add water to cover. Bring to a boil; cook 4-5 minutes or until tender. Drain and place in a large bowl; cool slightly.
2. Add carrots, corn, green onions and cilantro. Whisk together the vinaigrette ingredients; toss with salad. Refrigerate, covered, at least 2 hours before serving.
⅔ CUP: 111 cal., 5g fat (0 sat. fat), 0 chol., 135mg sod., 14g carb. (4g sugars, 3g fiber), 5g pro. **DIABETIC EXCHANGES:** 1 starch, ½ fat.

MARINATED BROCCOLI

This festive side dish couldn't be easier to throw together. But because it's so pretty, it's perfect for special occasions.

—Edna Hoffman, Hebron, IN

- -

Prep: 15 min. + chilling
Makes: 2 servings

4 tsp. olive oil
1 Tbsp. water
1 Tbsp. white wine vinegar
1½ tsp. lemon juice
1 tsp. honey
1 garlic clove, minced
¼ tsp. salt
Dash cayenne pepper
2 cups fresh broccoli florets
2 Tbsp. chopped sweet red pepper

In a jar with a tight-fitting lid, combine the first 8 ingredients; shake well. In a small bowl, combine broccoli and red pepper; add dressing and toss to coat. Cover and refrigerate for at least 1 hour. Serve with a slotted spoon.

1 CUP: 119 cal., 9g fat (1g sat. fat), 0 chol., 315mg sod., 9g carb. (5g sugars, 2g fiber), 2g pro. **DIABETIC EXCHANGES:** 1½ fat, 1 vegetable.

SWEET POTATOES WITH CILANTRO BLACK BEANS

I'm a vegan, and I'm always looking for impressive, satisfying dishes that all my friends can enjoy. Sweet potatoes with black beans and a touch of peanut butter is one of my standout recipes.
—Kayla Capper, Ojai, CA

- -

Takes: 20 min. • **Makes:** 4 servings

- 4 medium sweet potatoes (about 8 oz. each)
- 1 Tbsp. olive oil
- 1 small sweet red pepper, chopped
- 2 green onions, chopped
- 1 can (15 oz.) black beans, rinsed and drained
- ½ cup salsa
- ¼ cup frozen corn
- 2 Tbsp. lime juice
- 1 Tbsp. creamy peanut butter
- 1 tsp. ground cumin
- ¼ tsp. garlic salt
- ¼ cup minced fresh cilantro
  Additional minced fresh cilantro, optional

1. Scrub sweet potatoes; pierce several times with a fork. Place on a microwave-safe plate. Microwave, uncovered, on high for 6-8 minutes or until tender, turning once.

2. Meanwhile, in a large skillet, heat oil over medium-high heat. Add pepper and green onions; cook and stir 3-4 minutes or until tender. Stir in beans, salsa, corn, lime juice, peanut butter, cumin and garlic salt; heat through. Stir in cilantro.

3. With a sharp knife, cut an "X" in each sweet potato. Fluff the pulp with a fork. Spoon bean mixture over potatoes. If desired, sprinkle with additional cilantro.

1 POTATO WITH ½ CUP BLACK BEAN MIXTURE: 400 cal., 6g fat (1g sat. fat), 0 chol., 426mg sod., 77g carb. (26g sugars, 12g fiber), 11g pro.

MEAT LOVER OPTION
PAGE 320

GREEN BEANS & RADISH SALAD WITH TARRAGON PESTO

Whichever way my garden grows, I build my salad with green beans, radishes and a pesto made with tarragon. That adds a hint of licorice.
—*Lily Julow, Lawrenceville, GA*

Takes: 25 min. • **Makes:** 10 servings

1½ lbs. fresh green beans, trimmed
2 cups thinly sliced radishes
½ cup pecan or walnut pieces, toasted
¼ cup tarragon leaves
3 Tbsp. grated Parmesan cheese
½ garlic clove
¼ tsp. coarse sea salt or kosher salt
⅛ tsp. crushed red pepper flakes
1½ tsp. white wine vinegar
¼ cup olive oil

1. In a 6-qt. stockpot, bring 8 cups water to a boil. Add beans in batches; cook, uncovered, 2-3 minutes or just until crisp-tender. Remove the beans and immediately drop into ice water. Drain and pat dry. Toss together the beans and radishes.

2. Place the pecans, tarragon, cheese, garlic, salt and pepper flakes in a small food processor; pulse until chopped. Add vinegar; process until blended. Continue processing while gradually adding oil in a steady stream. Toss with bean mixture.

1 CUP: 115 cal., 10g fat (1g sat. fat), 1mg chol., 89mg sod., 7g carb. (2g sugars, 3g fiber), 2g pro. **DIABETIC EXCHANGES:** 2 fat, 1 vegetable.

OPEN-FACED FRICO
EGG SANDWICH
P. 218

Brunch Time

Whether you're craving sweet oats or a savory egg bake stuffed with veggies and cheese, these vegetarian breakfast recipes are the perfect way to start the day.

SWEET POTATO PANCAKES WITH CINNAMON CREAM

Topped with a rich cinnamon cream, these sweet potato pancakes are an ideal dish for celebrating the tastes and aromas of fall.
—*Tammy Rex, New Tripoli, PA*

Prep: 25 min. • **Cook:** 5 min./batch
Makes: 12 servings

- 1 pkg. (8 oz.) cream cheese, softened
- ¼ cup packed brown sugar
- ½ tsp. ground cinnamon
- ½ cup sour cream

PANCAKES

- 6 large eggs
- ¾ cup all-purpose flour
- ½ tsp. ground nutmeg
- ½ tsp. salt
- ¼ tsp. pepper
- 6 cups shredded peeled sweet potatoes (about 3 large)
- 3 cups shredded peeled apples (about 3 large)
- ⅓ cup grated onion
- ½ cup canola oil

1. In a bowl, beat the cream cheese, brown sugar and cinnamon until blended; beat in sour cream. Set aside.
2. In a large bowl, whisk the eggs, flour, nutmeg, salt and pepper. Add the sweet potatoes, apples and onion; toss to coat.
3. In a large nonstick skillet, heat 2 Tbsp. oil over medium heat. Working in batches, drop sweet potato mixture by ⅓ cupfuls into oil; press slightly to flatten. Using the remaining oil as needed, fry until golden brown, 2-3 minutes on each side. Drain on paper towels. Serve pancakes with cinnamon topping.

2 PANCAKES WITH 2 TBSP. TOPPING: 325 cal., 21g fat (7g sat. fat), 114mg chol., 203mg sod., 30g carb. (15g sugars, 3g fiber), 6g pro.

MEAT LOVER OPTION
PAGE 320

CHEESY VEGETABLE EGG DISH

I'm a cook at a Bible camp, and this is one of my most popular recipes with the youngsters. What touched me the most was when a 10-year-old boy asked me for the recipe so he could have his mother make it at home.
—Elsie Campbell, Dulzura, CA

- -

Prep: 20 min. • **Bake:** 35 min.
Makes: 10 servings

1   medium zucchini, diced
1   medium onion, chopped
1   can (4 oz.) mushroom stems and pieces, drained
¼   cup chopped green pepper
½   cup butter, cubed
½   cup all-purpose flour
1   tsp. baking powder
½   tsp. salt
10   large eggs, lightly beaten
2   cups 4% cottage cheese
4   cups shredded Monterey Jack cheese

1. In a large skillet, saute the zucchini, onion, mushrooms and green pepper in butter until tender. Stir in the flour, baking powder and salt until blended.
2. In a large bowl, combine eggs and cottage cheese. Stir in vegetables and Monterey Jack cheese.
3. Transfer to a greased 2½-qt. baking dish. Bake, uncovered, at 350° for 35-45 minutes or until a thermometer reads 160°.
1 PIECE: 407 cal., 30g fat (17g sat. fat), 287mg chol., 759mg sod., 10g carb. (4g sugars, 1g fiber), 24g pro.

THREE-CHEESE QUICHE

Savor eggs and cheese at their best. Guests often describe this crustless entree as tall, light and fluffy. Everyone loves it!

—Judy Reagan, Hannibal, MO

- -

Prep: 15 min. • **Bake:** 45 min. + standing
Makes: 6 servings

- 7 large eggs
- 5 large egg yolks
- 1 cup heavy whipping cream
- 1 cup half-and-half cream
- 1 cup shredded part-skim mozzarella cheese
- ¾ cup shredded sharp cheddar cheese, divided
- ½ cup shredded Swiss cheese
- 2 Tbsp. finely chopped oil-packed sun-dried tomatoes
- 1½ tsp. salt-free seasoning blend
- ¼ tsp. dried basil

1. Preheat oven to 350°. In a large bowl, combine the eggs, egg yolks, whipping cream, half-and-half, mozzarella cheese, ½ cup cheddar cheese, Swiss cheese, tomatoes, seasoning blend and basil; pour into a greased 9-in. deep-dish pie plate. Sprinkle with remaining ¼ cup cheddar cheese.
2. Bake 45-50 minutes or until a knife inserted in the center comes out clean. Let stand 10 minutes before cutting.
1 PIECE: 449 cal., 37g fat (21g sat. fat), 524mg chol., 316mg sod., 5g carb. (3g sugars, 0 fiber), 22g pro.

COLORFUL BRUNCH FRITTATA

A friend asked me for a special recipe that could be served at his daughter's wedding brunch. I created this frittata for the occasion. Loaded with colorful veggies, it looks beautiful on a buffet.

—Kristin Arnett, Elkhorn, WI

- -

Prep: 15 min. • **Bake:** 50 min. + standing
Makes: 12 servings

- 1 lb. fresh asparagus, trimmed and cut into 1-in. pieces
- ½ lb. sliced fresh mushrooms
- 1 medium sweet red pepper, diced
- 1 medium sweet yellow pepper, diced
- 1 small onion, chopped
- 3 green onions, chopped
- 3 Tbsp. olive oil
- 2 garlic cloves, minced
- 3 plum tomatoes, seeded and chopped
- 14 large eggs, lightly beaten
- 2 cups half-and-half cream
- 2 cups shredded Colby-Monterey Jack cheese
- 3 Tbsp. minced fresh parsley
- 3 Tbsp. minced fresh basil
- ½ tsp. salt
- ¼ tsp. pepper
- ½ cup shredded Parmesan cheese

1. Preheat oven to 350°. In a large skillet, saute asparagus, mushrooms, peppers and onions in oil until tender. Add garlic; cook 1 minute longer. Add the tomatoes; set aside.
2. In a large bowl, whisk eggs, cream, Colby-Monterey Jack cheese, parsley, basil, salt and pepper; stir into the vegetable mixture.
3. Pour into a greased 13x9-in. baking dish. Bake, uncovered, 45 minutes.
4. Sprinkle with Parmesan cheese. Bake 5 minutes longer or until a knife inserted in the center comes out clean. Let stand 10 minutes before cutting.
1 PIECE: 270 cal., 19g fat (10g sat. fat), 256mg chol., 377mg sod., 7g carb. (4g sugars, 1g fiber), 16g pro.

ARUGULA & MUSHROOM BREAKFAST PIZZA

It's a challenge to be creative with breakfast every morning, and I like to come up with fun foods the kids will love. This is a great recipe for them to join in and help make for breakfast. It's also convenient to make ahead and freeze for a weekday.
—*Melissa Pelkey Hass, Waleska, GA*

Prep: 20 min. • **Bake:** 15 min.
Makes: 6 servings

- 1   prebaked 12-in. thin whole wheat pizza crust
- ¾   cup reduced-fat ricotta cheese
- 1   tsp. garlic powder
- 1   tsp. paprika, divided
- 1   cup sliced baby portobello mushrooms
- ½   cup julienned soft sun-dried tomatoes (not packed in oil)
- 3   cups fresh arugula or baby spinach
- 2   Tbsp. balsamic vinegar
- 2   Tbsp. olive oil
- ¼   tsp. salt, divided
- ¼   tsp. pepper, divided
- 6   large eggs

1. Preheat the oven to 450°. Place crust on a pizza pan. Spread with the ricotta cheese; sprinkle with garlic powder and ½ tsp. paprika. Top with the mushrooms and tomatoes.
2. With clean hands, massage arugula with vinegar, oil and ⅛ tsp. each salt and pepper until softened; arrange over the pizza.
3. Using a spoon, make 6 indentations in arugula; carefully break an egg into each. Sprinkle with the remaining paprika, salt and pepper. Bake until egg whites are completely set and yolks begin to thicken but are not hard, 12-15 minutes.
1 PIECE: 299 cal., 13g fat (4g sat. fat), 194mg chol., 464mg sod., 31g carb. (8g sugars, 5g fiber), 15g pro. **DIABETIC EXCHANGES:** 2 medium-fat meat, 1½ starch, 1 vegetable, 1 fat.

MIGAS BREAKFAST TACOS

Unless you grew up in the Southwest or visit there often, you might be hearing of *migas* for the first time. Think of them as the best scrambled eggs ever. The secret ingredient: corn tortillas!
—*Stephen Exel, Des Moines, IA*

Takes: 30 min. • **Makes:** 3 servings

- ¼   cup finely chopped onion
- 1   jalapeno pepper, seeded and chopped
- 1   Tbsp. canola oil
- 2   corn tortillas (6 in.), cut into thin strips
- 4   large eggs
- ¼   tsp. salt
- ⅛   tsp. pepper
- ½   cup crumbled queso fresco or shredded Monterey Jack cheese
- ¼   cup chopped seeded tomato
- 6   flour tortillas (6 in.), warmed
  Optional toppings: Refried beans, sliced avocado, sour cream and minced fresh cilantro

1. In a large skillet, saute onion and jalapeno in oil until tender. Add tortilla strips; cook 3 minutes longer. In a small bowl, whisk the eggs, salt and pepper. Add to skillet; cook and stir until almost set. Stir in cheese and tomato.
2. Serve in flour tortillas with toppings as desired.
NOTE: Wear disposable gloves when cutting hot peppers; the oils can burn skin. Avoid touching your face.
2 TACOS: 424 cal., 21g fat (5g sat. fat), 295mg chol., 821mg sod., 39g carb. (2g sugars, 1g fiber), 21g pro.

READER RAVE

"I made this for myself, freezing them for a few breakfasts pleasantly full of southwestern flavor! I will definitely try this again, served with a side medley of fruit and sweet muffins for my family when they come for a Saturday morning breakfast!"
—ARTGIRL26, TASTEOFHOME.COM

ITALIAN GARDEN FRITTATA

I serve this pretty frittata with melon wedges for a delicious breakfast or brunch. Feel free to add additional fresh veggies or a pinch of oregano.
—*Sally Maloney, Dallas, GA*

Takes: 30 min. • **Makes:** 4 servings

4 large eggs
6 large egg whites
½ cup grated Romano cheese, divided
1 Tbsp. minced fresh sage
½ tsp. salt
¼ tsp. pepper
1 tsp. olive oil
1 small zucchini, sliced
2 green onions, chopped
2 plum tomatoes, thinly sliced

1. Preheat broiler. In a large bowl, whisk eggs, egg whites, ¼ cup cheese, sage, salt and pepper until blended.
2. In a 10-in. broiler-safe skillet coated with cooking spray, heat the oil over medium-high heat. Add zucchini and green onions; cook and stir 2 minutes. Reduce heat to medium-low. Pour in egg mixture. Cook, covered, 4-7 minutes or until eggs are nearly set.
3. Uncover; top with the tomatoes and remaining cheese. Broil 3-4 in. from heat 2-3 minutes or until eggs are completely set. Let stand 5 minutes. Cut the frittata into wedges.

1 PIECE: 183 cal., 11g fat (5g sat. fat), 228mg chol., 655mg sod., 4g carb. (3g sugars, 1g fiber), 18g pro. **DIABETIC EXCHANGES:** 2 medium-fat meat, 1 vegetable.
HEALTH TIP: Using 6 egg whites, which is equivalent to 3 whole eggs, saves almost 30 calories and 4 grams fat per serving.

BROCCOLI-MUSHROOM BUBBLE BAKE

I got bored with the same old breakfast casseroles served at our monthly moms' meeting, so I decided to create something new. Judging by the reactions of the other moms, this one's a keeper.
—*Shannon Koene, Blacksburg, VA*

Prep: 20 min. • **Bake:** 25 min.
Makes: 12 servings

- 1 tsp. canola oil
- ½ lb. fresh mushrooms, finely chopped
- 1 medium onion, finely chopped
- 1 tube (16.3 oz.) large refrigerated flaky biscuits
- 1 pkg. (10 oz.) frozen broccoli with cheese sauce
- 3 large eggs
- 1 can (5 oz.) evaporated milk
- 1 tsp. Italian seasoning
- ½ tsp. garlic powder
- ½ tsp. salt
- ¼ tsp. pepper
- 1½ cups shredded Colby-Monterey Jack cheese

1. Preheat oven to 350°. In a large skillet, heat oil over medium-high heat. Add mushrooms and onion; cook and stir until tender, 4-6 minutes.
2. Cut each biscuit into 8 pieces; place in a greased 13x9-in. baking dish. Top with mushroom mixture.
3. Cook the broccoli with cheese sauce according to package directions. Spoon over mushroom mixture.
4. In a large bowl, whisk eggs, milk and seasonings; pour over top. Sprinkle with cheese. Bake casserole until golden brown, 25-30 minutes.
1 SERVING: 233 cal., 13g fat (6g sat. fat), 64mg chol., 648mg sod., 21g carb. (6g sugars, 1g fiber), 9g pro.

GREEK TOFU SCRAMBLE

I created this recipe over a decade ago when I was in college, and it was the first time I ever had tofu. I wanted to eat tofu and be earthy like all my cool vegetarian friends. Well, the vegetarian diet may not have stuck with me, but this recipe is still popular with my family!
—*Jennifer Garcia, Franklin, MA*

Takes: 25 min. • **Makes:** 2 servings

- 1 pkg. (9 oz.) fresh spinach (about 10 cups)
- 1 Tbsp. butter
- ⅔ lb. firm tofu, drained and crumbled
- ¼ cup coarsely chopped kalamata olives
- 2 Tbsp. fresh lemon juice
- 2 tsp. minced fresh oregano or 1 tsp. dried oregano
- ¼ tsp. pepper
- ¼ cup crumbled feta cheese
  Optional: Grated lemon zest and diced tomatoes

1. Place spinach and 1 Tbsp. water in a large skillet. Cook over medium-high heat until spinach is wilted, 2-3 minutes. Transfer to a colander; drain, pressing out as much liquid as possible. Coarsely chop spinach.
2. In same skillet, melt butter over medium-high heat. Add tofu, olives, lemon juice, oregano, pepper and spinach. Cook, stirring frequently, until heated through, 3-4 minutes. Add the feta; cook until slightly melted. Serve immediately; sprinkle with lemon zest and tomatoes if desired.
NOTE: Tofu is made from soybeans and does not contain animal products, yet it is high in protein. This makes it popular in vegetarian recipes, but it's nutritious and tasty in conventional recipes, too.
1½ CUPS: 240 cal., 17g fat (6g sat. fat), 23mg chol., 481mg sod., 9g carb. (2g sugars, 3g fiber), 17g pro.

FETA ASPARAGUS FRITTATA

Asparagus and feta cheese come together to make this frittata extra special. Perfect for a lazy Sunday or to serve with a salad for a light lunch!
—*Mildred Sherrer, Fort Worth, TX*

Takes: 30 min. • **Makes:** 2 servings

- 12 fresh asparagus spears, trimmed
- 6 large eggs
- 2 Tbsp. heavy whipping cream
  Dash salt
  Dash pepper
- 1 Tbsp. olive oil
- 2 green onions, chopped
- 1 garlic clove, minced
- ½ cup crumbled feta cheese

1. Preheat the oven to 350°. In a large skillet, place asparagus in ½ in. water; bring to a boil. Cook, covered, until the asparagus is crisp-tender, 3-5 minutes; drain. Cool slightly.
2. In a bowl, whisk together eggs, cream, salt and pepper. Chop 2 asparagus spears. In an 8-in. cast-iron or other ovenproof skillet, heat oil over medium heat until hot. Saute green onions, garlic and chopped asparagus 1 minute. Stir in the egg mixture; cook, covered, over medium heat until the eggs are nearly set, 3-5 minutes. Top with whole asparagus spears and cheese.
3. Bake until eggs are completely set, 7-9 minutes.
½ FRITTATA: 425 cal., 31g fat (12g sat. fat), 590mg chol., 1231mg sod., 8g carb. (3g sugars, 3g fiber), 27g pro.

ASPARAGUS & RED PEPPER FRITTATA

Here's a tasty way to start the morning. This frittata is enhanced with asparagus, potatoes, peppers, herbs and a rich blend of cheeses. Serve with a side of fruit.
—*Toni Donahue, Westerville, OH*

- -

Prep: 20 min. • **Cook:** 25 min.
Makes: 6 servings

12 fresh asparagus spears, trimmed
½ tsp. plus 3 Tbsp. olive oil, divided
10 large eggs
3 large egg whites
¾ cup 2% milk
½ cup shredded Parmesan cheese
¾ tsp. salt
½ tsp. pepper
1 pkg. (20 oz.) refrigerated shredded hash brown potatoes
½ large sweet red pepper, julienned
3 fresh basil leaves, thinly sliced
½ cup shredded pepper jack cheese

1. Place asparagus on an ungreased baking sheet; drizzle with ½ tsp. oil. Bake at 400° for 10-12 minutes or until tender, stirring once.
2. In a large bowl, whisk the eggs, egg whites, milk, Parmesan cheese, salt and pepper; set aside. Heat 2 Tbsp. oil in a 12-in. ovenproof skillet over medium heat. Add the potatoes and press down lightly. Cook, uncovered, until bottom is golden brown, 6-7 minutes. Drizzle with remaining oil; turn over.
3. Pour egg mixture over potatoes. Cover and cook for 9-11 minutes or until nearly set. Arrange asparagus and red pepper over top. Sprinkle with basil and pepper jack cheese.
4. Broil 3-4 in. from the heat until eggs are completely set, 2-3 minutes. Let stand for 5 minutes. Cut into wedges.
1 WEDGE: 371 cal., 21g fat (7g sat. fat), 370mg chol., 692mg sod., 24g carb. (3g sugars, 2g fiber), 22g pro.

APPLE-HONEY DUTCH BABY

I love to make this treat on Sunday morning. It's so impressive when it's served warm right out of the oven, and the honey and apple filling is yummy.
—*Kathy Fleming, Lisle, IL*

- -

Takes: 30 min. • **Makes:** 4 servings

3 large eggs, room temperature
¾ cup 2% milk
¾ cup all-purpose flour
1 Tbsp. sugar
2 Tbsp. butter
TOPPING
1 Tbsp. butter
2 large apples, sliced
½ cup honey
2 to 3 tsp. lemon juice
½ tsp. ground cardamom
1 tsp. cornstarch
2 tsp. cold water

1. Preheat oven to 400°. In a large bowl, whisk together the first 4 ingredients until smooth. Place the butter in a 10-in. ovenproof skillet; heat in oven until melted, 2-3 minutes.
2. Tilt pan to coat the bottom and side. Pour batter into hot skillet. Bake until puffed and edge is lightly browned, 16-20 minutes.
3. Meanwhile, for the topping, in a large saucepan, heat butter over medium heat; saute apples until lightly browned. Stir in honey, lemon juice and cardamom. Mix cornstarch and water until smooth; stir into apple mixture. Bring to a boil; cook and stir until thickened, 1-2 minutes. Spoon into pancake; serve immediately.
1 SERVING: 429 cal., 14g fat (7g sat. fat), 166mg chol., 146mg sod., 72g carb. (50g sugars, 3g fiber), 9g pro.

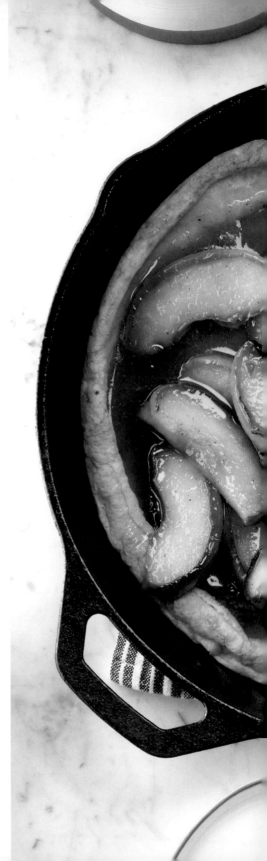

🍲 PRESSURE-COOKER RAISIN NUT OATMEAL

There's no better feeling than starting off the day with a terrific breakfast. I love that the oats, fruit and spices in this homey meal cook together on their own.
—*Valerie Sauber, Adelanto, CA*

Prep: 10 min. + standing
Cook: 5 min. + releasing
Makes: 6 servings

3	cups vanilla almond milk
¾	cup steel-cut oats
¾	cup raisins
3	Tbsp. brown sugar
4½	tsp. butter
¾	tsp. ground cinnamon
½	tsp. salt
1	large apple, peeled and chopped
¼	cup chopped pecans

1. In a 6-qt. electric pressure cooker, combine the first 7 ingredients. Lock lid; close pressure-release valve. Adjust to pressure-cook on high for 5 minutes. Let pressure release naturally. Press cancel.
2. Stir in apple. Let stand 10 minutes before serving (oatmeal will thicken upon standing). Spoon oatmeal into bowls; sprinkle with pecans.
¾ CUP: 272 cal., 9g fat (2g sat. fat), 8mg chol., 298mg sod., 47g carb. (29g sugars, 4g fiber), 4g pro.

SWEET POTATO & EGG SKILLET

I try to incorporate nutritious sweet potatoes in meals as often as possible, especially with breakfast! I came up with this recipe to feed my family a healthy, hearty breakfast—and it worked!
—*Jeanne Larson,*
Rancho Santa Margarita, CA

Takes: 25 min. • **Makes:** 4 servings

- 2 Tbsp. butter
- 2 medium sweet potatoes, peeled and shredded (about 4 cups)
- 1 garlic clove, minced
- ½ tsp. salt, divided
- ⅛ tsp. dried thyme
- 2 cups fresh baby spinach
- 4 large eggs
- ⅛ tsp. coarsely ground pepper

1. In a large cast-iron or other heavy skillet, heat butter over low heat. Add sweet potatoes, garlic, ¼ tsp. salt and thyme; cook, covered, until potatoes are almost tender, 4-5 minutes, stirring occasionally. Stir in spinach just until wilted, 2-3 minutes.
2. With the back of a spoon, make 4 wells in potato mixture. Break an egg into each well. Sprinkle eggs with pepper and remaining ¼ tsp. salt. Cook, covered, over medium-low heat until egg whites are completely set and yolks begin to thicken but are not hard, 5-7 minutes.
1 SERVING: 224 cal., 11g fat (5g sat. fat), 201mg chol., 433mg sod., 24g carb. (10g sugars, 3g fiber), 8g pro.
DIABETIC EXCHANGES: 1½ starch, 1½ fat, 1 medium-fat meat.
HEALTH TIP: With the sweet potatoes and spinach, this dish meets the daily requirement for vitamin A.

MUSHROOM-GOUDA QUICHE

For a laid-back Sunday brunch, we make a quiche in no time using refrigerated pie crust. Load it up with mushrooms, aromatic arugula and creamy Gouda.
—*Thomas Faglon, Somerset, NJ*

Prep: 15 min. • **Bake:** 30 min. + standing
Makes: 6 servings

- 1 sheet refrigerated pie crust
- 4 large eggs
- 1 cup heavy whipping cream
- ¼ tsp. salt
- ¼ tsp. pepper
- 2 cups sliced fresh shiitake mushrooms (about 4 oz.)
- 1 cup shredded Gouda or Monterey Jack cheese
- 1 cup chopped arugula or fresh baby spinach

1. Preheat oven to 350°. Unroll crust into a 9-in. pie plate; flute edge. Refrigerate while preparing filling.
2. In a large bowl, whisk the eggs, cream, salt and pepper until blended. Stir in the remaining ingredients. Pour into crust.
3. Bake on a lower oven rack until crust is golden brown and a knife inserted in center comes out clean, 30-35 minutes. Let the quiche stand for 10 minutes before cutting.
FREEZE OPTION: Cover and freeze the unbaked quiche. To use, remove from freezer 30 minutes before baking (do not thaw). Preheat oven to 350°. Place quiche on a baking sheet; cover quiche crust loosely with foil. Bake as directed, increasing time as necessary for a knife inserted in the center to come out clean.
1 PIECE: 422 cal., 33g fat (18g sat. fat), 207mg chol., 452mg sod., 21g carb. (4g sugars, 1g fiber), 12g pro.

BLUEBERRY CORNMEAL PANCAKES

These blueberry cornmeal pancakes are one of my family's favorite breakfasts. No time to make them from scratch? No problem! My grandmother's standby of store-bought corn muffin mix makes quick work of the job.
—*Carolyn Eskew, Dayton, OH*

Takes: 30 min. • **Makes:** 10 pancakes

- 1 pkg. (8½ oz.) cornbread/muffin mix
- 1 cup fresh or frozen blueberries
- ⅓ cup canned white or shoepeg corn
  Maple syrup

In a large bowl, prepare muffin mix according to package directions. Gently stir in blueberries and corn. Lightly grease a griddle; warm over medium heat. Pour batter by ¼ cupfuls onto griddle; flatten slightly. Cook until bottoms are golden brown. Turn; cook until second sides are golden brown. Serve with syrup.

2 PANCAKES: 251 cal., 7g fat (2g sat. fat), 39mg chol., 454mg sod., 41g carb. (14g sugars, 4g fiber), 6g pro.

STRAWBERRY BLISS OMELET

Instead of the usual ham and cheese, try dressing up eggs with strawberries and cream cheese. I first tasted this dish while vacationing at the beach.
—*Selina Smith, Frostburg, MD*

Takes: 15 min. • **Makes:** 3 servings

- 6 large eggs
- 2 Tbsp. water
- ½ tsp. salt
  Dash pepper
- 2 Tbsp. butter
- 2 oz. cream cheese, cut into ½-in. cubes
- 3 Tbsp. brown sugar
- 1½ cups sliced fresh strawberries, divided
  Confectioners' sugar

1. In a large bowl, whisk the eggs, water, salt and pepper. Heat butter in a 10-in. nonstick skillet over medium heat; add egg mixture. As the eggs set, lift the edge, letting uncooked portion flow underneath.

2. When the eggs are almost set, sprinkle cream cheese, brown sugar and 1 cup strawberries over 1 side. Fold omelet in half. Cover and cook for 1-2 minutes or until brown sugar begins to melt. Slide the omelet onto a plate; top with the remaining strawberries and dust with confectioners' sugar.

⅓ OMELET: 378 cal., 24g fat (12g sat. fat), 466mg chol., 659mg sod., 26g carb. (23g sugars, 2g fiber), 15g pro.

VEGGIE FRITTATA

I was impressed with myself that I could omit dairy and still create something so good! Use any vegetables in this recipe, then add a salad, fruit cup or yogurt on the side.
—*Kizmet Byrd, Fort Wayne, IN*

Takes: 30 min. • **Makes:** 6 servings

- 9 large eggs, room temperature
- ½ tsp. salt, divided
- ¼ tsp. pepper, divided
- 1 Tbsp. olive oil
- ½ cup chopped carrot
- ½ cup chopped sweet red pepper
- ⅓ cup chopped red onion
- ½ cup sliced zucchini
- 2 Tbsp. chopped fresh basil, divided
- 2 garlic cloves, minced
- ½ cup grape tomatoes, halved

1. Preheat the broiler. In a large bowl, whisk the eggs, ¼ tsp. salt and ⅛ tsp. pepper until blended.
2. In a 10-in. broiler-safe skillet, heat oil over medium-high heat. Add carrot; cook and stir until crisp-tender, 4-5 minutes. Add the red pepper and red onion; cook and stir until crisp-tender, 1-2 minutes. Add zucchini, 1 Tbsp. basil, garlic, and the remaining ¼ tsp. salt and ⅛ tsp. pepper; cook and stir until vegetables are tender.
3. Reduce heat to medium low; pour in egg mixture. Cook, covered, until nearly set, 4-6 minutes. Add tomatoes; cook, uncovered, until edge begins to pull away from the pan, about 3 minutes.
4. Broil 3-4 in. from heat until eggs are completely set, 1-2 minutes. Let stand 5 minutes. Sprinkle with the remaining 1 Tbsp. basil; cut into wedges.
1 WEDGE: 145 cal., 10g fat (3g sat. fat), 279mg chol., 313mg sod., 4g carb. (2g sugars, 1g fiber), 10g pro. **DIABETIC EXCHANGES:** 1 vegetable, 1 medium-fat meat, 1 fat.

SPICED BLUEBERRY QUINOA

I took up eating quinoa when I found out how much protein it has. This is an easy dish to experiment with; I made the first version of the recipe with shredded apples instead of blueberries. It's delicious either way!
—*Shannon Copley, Upper Arlington, OH*

Prep: 10 min. • **Cook:** 30 min.
Makes: 2 servings

- ½ cup quinoa, rinsed and well drained
- 2 cups unsweetened almond milk
- 2 Tbsp. honey
- ½ tsp. ground cinnamon
- ¼ tsp. salt
- 1 cup fresh or frozen blueberries, thawed
- ¼ tsp. vanilla extract
- 2 Tbsp. chopped almonds, toasted

1. In a small saucepan, cook and stir quinoa over medium heat until lightly toasted, 5-7 minutes. Stir in almond milk, honey, cinnamon and salt; bring to a boil. Reduce heat; simmer, uncovered, until quinoa is tender and liquid is almost absorbed, 20-25 minutes, stirring occasionally.
2. Remove from heat; stir in blueberries and vanilla. Sprinkle with almonds.
1 CUP: 352 cal., 10g fat (1g sat. fat), 0 chol., 479mg sod., 59g carb. (25g sugars, 7g fiber), 9g pro.
HEALTH TIP: Quinoa is a good source of trace minerals—specifically manganese and copper—that are important in turning carbohydrates into energy.

GREEN CHILE QUICHE SQUARES

Chiles add spark to this cheesy quiche. You can vary the flavor based on the kind of croutons you buy. I like to serve fresh fruit on the side.

—*Connie Wilson, Huntington Beach, CA*

Prep: 15 min. + chilling
Bake: 40 min. + standing
Makes: 12 servings

- 3 cups salad croutons
- 4 cups shredded cheddar cheese
- 1 can (4 oz.) chopped green chiles
- 6 large eggs
- 3 cups 2% milk
- 2 tsp. ground mustard
- 1 tsp. salt
- ¼ tsp. garlic powder

1. Arrange croutons in a greased 13x9-in. baking dish. Sprinkle with cheese and chiles. In a bowl, beat the remaining ingredients. Pour egg mixture over the cheese. Refrigerate, covered, 8 hours or overnight.

2. Remove dish from the refrigerator 30 minutes before baking. Preheat oven to 350°. Bake, uncovered, until a knife inserted in center comes out clean, 40-45 minutes. Let stand 10 minutes before cutting.

1 PIECE: 270 cal., 18g fat (9g sat. fat), 136mg chol., 653mg sod., 11g carb. (4g sugars, 1g fiber), 15g pro.

WATERMELON FRUIT PIZZA

Fruit pizza is an easy and refreshing way to end a summer meal. Top it with any fruit you may have on hand and add other toppings like fresh mint, toasted shredded coconut or chopped nuts.
—Taste of Home *Test Kitchen*

Takes: 10 min. • **Makes:** 8 servings

    4 oz. cream cheese, softened
    4 oz. frozen whipped topping, thawed
    ½ tsp. vanilla extract
    3 Tbsp. confectioners' sugar
    1 round slice of whole seedless
       watermelon, about 1 in. thick
       Assorted fresh fruit
       Fresh mint leaves, optional

1. In a small bowl, beat cream cheese until smooth. Gently fold in the whipped topping, then vanilla and confectioners' sugar until combined.
2. To serve, spread watermelon slice with cream cheese mixture. Cut into 8 wedges and top with your fruit of choice. If desired, garnish pizza with fresh mint.
1 PIECE: 140 cal., 7g fat (5g sat. fat), 14mg chol., 45mg sod., 17g carb. (16g sugars, 0 fiber), 1g pro. **DIABETIC EXCHANGES:** 1½ fat, 1 fruit.

BLUEBERRY CRUNCH BREAKFAST BAKE

Fresh blueberries make this a special breakfast, but I find that frozen berries work just as well. My grandma used to make this with strawberries, and I always loved to eat it at her house.
—Marsha Ketaner, Henderson, NV

Prep: 15 min. • **Bake:** 30 min.
Makes: 12 servings

    1 loaf (16 oz.) day-old French bread,
       cut into 1-in. slices
    8 large eggs, room temperature
    1 cup half-and-half cream
    ½ tsp. vanilla extract
    1 cup old-fashioned oats
    1 cup packed brown sugar
    ¼ cup all-purpose flour
    ½ cup cold butter
    2 cups fresh or frozen blueberries
    1 cup chopped walnuts

1. Arrange half the bread slices in a greased 13x9-in. baking dish.
2. In a large bowl, whisk the eggs, cream and vanilla. Slowly pour half the cream mixture over bread. Top with remaining bread and egg mixture. Let stand until liquid is absorbed, about 5 minutes.
3. Meanwhile, in a small bowl, combine the oats, brown sugar and flour; cut in butter until crumbly. Sprinkle over top. Top with blueberries and walnuts.
4. Bake, uncovered, at 375° until a knife inserted in the center comes out clean, 30-35 minutes. Let stand for 5 minutes before serving.
1 SERVING: 427 cal., 21g fat (8g sat. fat), 154mg chol., 351mg sod., 50g carb. (23g sugars, 3g fiber), 12g pro.

MEAT
LOVER
OPTION
PAGE 320

MINI ITALIAN FRITTATAS

I created this recipe for a picnic breakfast with friends. I wanted an egg meal that was portable and easy to make. These crowd-pleasing frittatas were the result!
—*Jess Apfe, Berkeley, CA*

- -

Prep: 20 min. • **Bake:** 20 min.
Makes: 1 dozen

- ¼ cup sun-dried tomatoes (not packed in oil)
- ¾ cup shredded part-skim mozzarella cheese, divided
- ½ cup chopped fresh spinach
- ⅓ cup water-packed artichoke hearts, rinsed, drained and chopped
- ⅓ cup chopped roasted sweet red peppers
- ¼ cup grated Parmesan cheese
- ¼ cup ricotta cheese
- 2 Tbsp. minced fresh basil
- 1 Tbsp. prepared pesto
- 2 tsp. Italian seasoning
- ¼ tsp. garlic powder
- 8 large eggs
- ½ tsp. pepper
- ¼ tsp. salt

1. Preheat the oven to 350°. Pour ½ cup boiling water over tomatoes in a small bowl; let stand for 5 minutes. Drain and chop the tomatoes.
2. In a small bowl, combine ½ cup mozzarella cheese, spinach, artichokes hearts, red peppers, Parmesan cheese, ricotta cheese, basil, pesto, Italian seasoning, garlic powder and tomatoes. In a large bowl, whisk eggs, pepper and salt until blended; stir in cheese mixture.
3. Fill 12 greased or foil-lined muffin cups three-fourths full. Sprinkle with the remaining mozzarella cheese. Bake until set, 18-22 minutes. Cool 5 minutes before removing from pan. Serve warm, with additional pesto if desired.
1 MINI FRITTATA: 95 cal., 6g fat (3g sat. fat), 149mg chol., 233mg sod., 2g carb. (1g sugars, 0 fiber), 8g pro. **DIABETIC EXCHANGES:** 1 lean meat, 1 fat.

ONION-GARLIC HASH BROWNS

Quick to assemble, these slow-cooked hash browns are one of my go-to sides. Stir in hot sauce if you like a bit of heat. I top my finished dish with a sprinkling of shredded cheddar cheese.
—*Cindi Boger, Ardmore, AL*

- -

Prep: 20 min. • **Cook:** 3 hours
Makes: 12 servings

- ¼ cup butter, cubed
- 1 Tbsp. olive oil
- 1 large red onion, chopped
- 1 small sweet red pepper, chopped
- 1 small green pepper, chopped
- 4 garlic cloves, minced
- 1 pkg. (30 oz.) frozen shredded hash brown potatoes
- ½ tsp. salt
- ½ tsp. pepper
- 3 drops hot pepper sauce, optional
- 2 tsp. minced fresh parsley

1. In a large skillet, heat butter and oil over medium heat. Add the onion and peppers. Cook and stir until crisp-tender. Add garlic; cook 1 minute longer. Stir in hash browns, salt, pepper and, if desired, pepper sauce.
2. Transfer to a 5-qt. slow cooker coated with cooking spray. Cook, covered, 3-4 hours or until heated through. Sprinkle with parsley just before serving.
½ CUP: 110 cal., 5g fat (3g sat. fat), 10mg chol., 136mg sod., 15g carb. (1g sugars, 1g fiber), 2g pro. **DIABETIC EXCHANGES:** 1 starch, 1 fat.

GREAT GRANOLA

Nuts and dried fruit make a crunchy homemade topping for yogurt or for eating by the handful. It also makes a delicious gift.
—*Johnna Johnson, Scottsdale, AZ*

Prep: 25 min. • **Bake:** 25 min. + cooling
Makes: 7 cups

- 2 cups old-fashioned oats
- ½ cup chopped almonds
- ½ cup salted pumpkin seeds or pepitas
- ½ cup chopped walnuts
- ¼ cup chopped pecans
- ¼ cup sesame seeds
- ¼ cup sunflower kernels
- ⅓ cup honey
- ¼ cup packed brown sugar
- ¼ cup maple syrup
- 2 Tbsp. toasted wheat germ
- 2 Tbsp. canola oil
- 1 tsp. ground cinnamon
- 1 tsp. vanilla extract
- 7 oz. mixed dried fruit (about 1⅓ cups)

1. In a large bowl, combine the first 7 ingredients; set aside.
2. In a small saucepan, combine the honey, brown sugar, syrup, wheat germ, oil and cinnamon. Cook and stir over medium heat until smooth, 4-5 minutes. Remove from the heat; stir in vanilla. Pour over oat mixture and toss to coat.
3. Transfer to a greased 15x10x1-in. baking pan. Bake at 350° until golden brown, stirring occasionally, 22-27 minutes. Cool completely on a wire rack. Stir in dried fruit. Store granola in an airtight container.

½ CUP: 290 cal., 14g fat (2g sat. fat), 0 chol., 49mg sod., 38g carb. (25g sugars, 4g fiber), 6g pro.

VEGGIE-PACKED STRATA

People are always eager to try this deliciously different casserole featuring eggs and cheese. Baked in a springform pan, the colorful strata catches folks' attention no matter where it's served.
—*Jennifer Unsell, Vance, AL*

Prep: 25 min.
Bake: 1 hour 20 minutes + standing
Makes: 8 servings

- 2 medium sweet red peppers, julienned
- 1 medium sweet yellow pepper, julienned
- 1 large red onion, sliced
- 3 Tbsp. olive oil, divided
- 3 garlic cloves, minced
- 2 medium yellow summer squash, thinly sliced
- 2 medium zucchini, thinly sliced
- ½ lb. fresh mushrooms, sliced
- 1 pkg. (8 oz.) cream cheese, softened
- ¼ cup heavy whipping cream
- 2 tsp. salt
- 1 tsp. pepper
- 6 large eggs, room temperature
- 8 slices bread, cut into ½-in. cubes (about 6 cups), divided
- 2 cups shredded Swiss cheese

1. In a large skillet, saute the peppers and onion in 1 Tbsp. oil until tender. Add the garlic; cook 1 minute longer. Drain; pat dry and set aside. In the same skillet, saute the yellow squash, zucchini and mushrooms in the remaining 2 Tbsp. oil until tender. Drain; pat dry and set aside.

2. Preheat oven to 325°. In a large bowl, beat cream cheese, cream, salt and pepper until smooth. Beat in eggs. Stir in vegetables, half of the bread cubes and Swiss cheese. Arrange remaining bread cubes in a greased 10-in. springform pan. Place on a baking sheet. Pour egg mixture into pan.

3. Bake, uncovered, until set and a thermometer reads 160°, 80-95 minutes. Let stand 10-15 minutes before serving. Run a knife around side of pan to loosen; remove side. Cut into wedges.

1 PIECE: 453 cal., 31g fat (15g sat. fat), 202mg chol., 938mg sod., 26g carb. (8g sugars, 3g fiber), 19g pro.

FREEZE OPTION: Cover and freeze the unbaked casserole and the remaining chopped sweet red pepper separately. To use, partially thaw both in refrigerator overnight. Remove from refrigerator 30 minutes before baking. Bake casserole as directed, increasing time as necessary to heat through and for a thermometer inserted in center to read 165°. Finely chop the remaining sweet red pepper; combine with vinaigrette as directed and serve with casserole.

1 PIECE WITH 1½ TSP. VINAIGRETTE MIXTURE: 281 cal., 17g fat (8g sat. fat), 175mg chol., 656mg sod., 16g carb. (6g sugars, 2g fiber), 14g pro.

PECAN WHEAT WAFFLES

Your hungry bunch will say a big yes to breakfast when these wonderful waffles are on the menu.

—*Susan Bell, Spruce Pine, NC*

- -

Takes: 30 min. • **Makes:** 6 servings

     1¼   cups all-purpose flour
      ¼   cup wheat bran
      1   Tbsp. sugar
     2½   tsp. baking powder
      ½   tsp. salt
      1   large egg, room temperature
      1   large egg white, room temperature
     1½   cups fat-free milk
      2   Tbsp. canola oil
      ⅓   cup chopped pecans

1. In a bowl, whisk together the first 5 ingredients. In another bowl, whisk together egg, egg white, milk and oil; add to flour mixture, stirring just until moistened. Fold in pecans.
2. Bake in a preheated waffle maker according to manufacturer's directions until golden.

1 ROUND WAFFLE: 227 cal., 10g fat (1g sat. fat), 32mg chol., 444mg sod., 28g carb. (6g sugars, 2g fiber), 7g pro. **DIABETIC EXCHANGES:** 2 starch, 2 fat.

❄ MEDITERRANEAN VEGGIE BRUNCH PUFF

I love making breakfast casseroles with whatever I have, and that's often spinach, sweet red pepper and cheddar. I also like to add a burst of flavor with vinaigrette.
—*Angela Robinson, Findlay, OH*

- -

Prep: 25 min. + chilling • **Bake:** 25 min.
Makes: 8 servings

      6   large eggs
      2   large egg whites
      1   cup 2% milk
      1   garlic clove, minced
      ½   tsp. salt
      ¼   tsp. pepper
      5   cups cubed croissants (about 6 oz.)
      ¾   cup chopped roasted sweet red peppers, divided
      ½   cup finely chopped sweet onion
      1   pkg. (10 oz.) frozen chopped spinach, thawed and squeezed dry
      1   cup shredded cheddar cheese
      ½   cup crumbled feta cheese
      3   Tbsp. Greek vinaigrette

1. Whisk the first 6 ingredients until blended. Place croissant pieces in a single layer in a greased 11x7-in. baking dish; top with ½ cup red pepper, onion and spinach. Pour egg mixture over top. Sprinkle with the cheeses. Refrigerate, covered, overnight.
2. Finely chop the remaining ¼ cup red pepper; place in a jar with a tight-fitting lid. Add the vinaigrette and shake to combine. Refrigerate until serving.
3. Preheat the oven to 350°. Remove casserole from the refrigerator while the oven heats. Bake, uncovered, for 25-30 minutes or until a knife inserted in the center comes out clean. Let stand for 5-10 minutes before cutting. Serve with the vinaigrette mixture.

EGG-FREE SPICED PANCAKES

Golden brown and fluffy, these pancakes are ideal served with syrup or berries. You'll never guess the eggs are missing!
—Taste of Home *Test Kitchen*

Prep: 10 min. • **Cook:** 10 min./batch
Makes: 8 pancakes

- 1 cup all-purpose flour
- 2 Tbsp. brown sugar
- 2½ tsp. baking powder
- ½ tsp. pumpkin pie spice
- ¼ tsp. salt
- 1 cup fat-free milk
- 2 Tbsp. canola oil
  Maple syrup, optional

1. In a large bowl, combine flour, brown sugar, baking powder, pie spice and salt. In another bowl, combine the milk and oil; stir into the dry ingredients just until moistened.

2. Preheat griddle over medium heat. Lightly grease griddle. Pour the batter by ¼ cupfuls onto griddle; cook until bubbles begin to pop and bottoms are golden brown. Turn; cook until second side is golden brown. If desired, serve with syrup.

FREEZE OPTION: Allow pancakes to cool. Arrange cooled pancakes in a single layer on sheet pans. Freeze overnight or until frozen. Transfer to an airtight container. Freeze for up to 2 months. To use, place pancake on a microwave-safe plate; microwave on high until heated through, 40-50 seconds.

2 PANCAKES: 223 cal., 7g fat (1g sat. fat), 1mg chol., 476mg sod., 34g carb. (10g sugars, 1g fiber), 5g pro. **DIABETIC EXCHANGES:** 2 starch, 1½ fat.

PEAR-STUFFED FRENCH TOAST WITH BRIE, CRANBERRIES & PECANS

This French toast is stuffed with fresh pears, dried cranberries, pecans, Brie and cream cheese. It's an easy overnight recipe that's so elegant and rich, it also makes an indulgent dessert!
—*Lindsay Sprunk, Rochelle, IL*

Prep: 35 min. + chilling
Bake: 35 min. + standing
Makes: 10 servings

- 2 Tbsp. butter
- 4 medium pears, peeled and thinly sliced
- 3 Tbsp. brown sugar, divided
- 1 pkg. (8 oz.) cream cheese, softened
- ½ cup dried cranberries
- ⅓ cup chopped pecans, toasted
- 20 slices French bread (½ in. thick)
- 1 round (8 oz.) Brie cheese, rind removed and thinly sliced
- 3 large eggs
- 2 cups 2% milk
- 3 tsp. vanilla extract
- ½ tsp. ground cinnamon
- ¼ tsp. salt
  Maple syrup, optional

1. In a large skillet, heat butter over medium heat. Add pears and 2 Tbsp. brown sugar; cook and stir until pears are tender, 4-6 minutes. In a bowl, mix cream cheese, cranberries and pecans.

2. Place half the French bread slices in a greased 13x9-in. baking dish. Layer with cream cheese mixture, pear mixture and Brie. Top with remaining bread slices. Whisk together next 5 ingredients and remaining brown sugar. Pour over bread. Refrigerate, covered, overnight.

3. Preheat oven to 375°. Remove the French toast from refrigerator while oven heats. Bake, uncovered, until top is golden brown, 35-40 minutes. Let stand 10 minutes before serving. If desired, serve French toast with syrup.

1 SERVING: 393 cal., 22g fat (11g sat. fat), 111mg chol., 476mg sod., 38g carb. (20g sugars, 4g fiber), 12g pro.

⏱ ❄ WHOLE GRAIN BANANA PANCAKES

My kids love homemade banana bread, so why not make it in pancake form? These freeze well, so stash some away for a future breakfast.
—*Ally Billhorn, Wilton, IA*

- -

Takes: 30 min. • **Makes:** 8 servings

1   cup whole wheat flour
1   cup all-purpose flour
4   tsp. baking powder
1   tsp. ground cinnamon
½   tsp. salt
2   large eggs, room temperature
2   cups fat-free milk
⅔   cup mashed ripe banana
      (about 1 medium)
1   Tbsp. olive oil
1   Tbsp. maple syrup
½   tsp. vanilla extract
      Optional: Sliced bananas and
      additional syrup

1. Whisk together the first 5 ingredients. In another bowl, whisk together eggs, milk, mashed banana, oil, 1 Tbsp. syrup and vanilla. Add to flour mixture; stir just until moistened.
2. Preheat a griddle coated with cooking spray over medium heat. Pour batter by ¼ cupfuls onto griddle; cook until bubbles on top begin to pop and bottoms are golden brown. Turn; cook until the second side is golden brown. If desired, serve pancakes with sliced bananas and additional syrup.
FREEZE OPTION: Freeze cooled pancakes between layers of waxed paper in a freezer container. To use, place pancakes on an ungreased baking sheet, cover with foil and reheat in a preheated 375° oven until heated through, 10-15 minutes. Or, place 2 pancakes on a microwave-safe plate and microwave on high until heated through, 45-60 seconds.
2 PANCAKES: 186 cal., 4g fat (1g sat. fat), 48mg chol., 392mg sod., 32g carb. (7g sugars, 3g fiber), 7g pro. **DIABETIC EXCHANGES:** 2 starch, ½ fat.

🟡 SMOKY TEMPEH BACON

Even meat eaters will love this! The meatless bacon made with tempeh gets its smoky flavor from liquid smoke and smoked paprika, and then it is crisped in a hot skillet. Eat it alone or use it on a sandwich or salad.
—*Rashanda Cobbins, Milwaukee, WI*

- -

Prep: 5 min. + chilling • **Cook:** 15 min.
Makes: 6 servings

3   Tbsp. liquid smoke
1   Tbsp. maple syrup
2   tsp. smoked paprika
½   tsp. ground cumin
1   pkg. (8 oz.) tempeh, thinly sliced
2   Tbsp. canola oil

1. Whisk together liquid smoke, maple syrup, paprika and cumin in an 8-in. square baking dish; add sliced tempeh. Gently toss to coat. Cover and refrigerate at least 1 hour.
2. Heat the oil in large saucepan over medium heat. In batches, cook tempeh until golden brown, 2-3 minutes per side. Serve immediately.
1 SERVING: 125 cal., 9g fat (1g sat. fat), 0 chol., 5mg sod., 6g carb. (2g sugars, 0 fiber), 8g pro.

TEST KITCHEN TIP

Liquid smoke is concentrated and often potent. We recommend starting with a small amount. You can always add more to adjust to your taste preferences.

OPEN-FACED FRICO EGG SANDWICH

The layer of melted and crisped cheese—the frico—is what makes this creamy sandwich unique. If you like spicy aoli, add two large cloves of garlic.
—*Julie Solis, Congers, NY*

Takes: 30 min. • **Makes:** 4 servings

- ¼ cup mayonnaise
- 1 Tbsp. olive oil
- 1 garlic clove, minced
- ⅛ tsp. salt
  Dash pepper
- ½ cup shredded Parmesan cheese
- 4 large eggs
- 4 slices Italian bread (1 in. thick), lightly toasted
- ½ cup sandwich giardiniera, drained and finely chopped
- 4 thin slices tomato
  Minced fresh parsley

1. For aioli, in a small bowl, combine the mayonnaise, olive oil, garlic, salt and pepper.

2. Sprinkle the Parmesan into a large nonstick skillet; heat over medium heat. Cook just until melted, about 2 minutes.

Break eggs, 1 at a time, into a custard cup or saucer, then gently slide into pan over Parmesan. Immediately reduce heat to low. To prepare eggs sunny-side up, cover pan and cook until yolks thicken but are not hard, 4-5 minutes.

3. Spread aioli over the toasted bread. Top each with giardiniera, a tomato slice and an egg. Sprinkle with parsley.

1 SANDWICH: 408 cal., 23g fat (5g sat. fat), 194mg chol., 1188mg sod., 33g carb. (3g sugars, 2g fiber), 16g pro.

MEAT LOVER OPTION
PAGE 320

OATMEAL BREAKFAST BARS

These soft and chewy treats have a hint of orange marmalade, so they're a fun change of pace from typical granola bars. They're so easy to put together and so delicious, you'll find yourself making them all the time.
—*Barbara Nowakowski,*
North Tonawanda, NY

Takes: 25 min. • **Makes:** 2½ dozen

- 4 cups quick-cooking oats
- 1 cup packed brown sugar
- 1 tsp. salt
- 1½ cups chopped walnuts
- 1 cup sweetened shredded coconut
- ¾ cup butter, melted
- ¾ cup orange marmalade

In a large bowl, combine the oats, brown sugar and salt. Stir in the remaining ingredients. Press into a greased 15x10x1-in. baking pan. Bake at 425° for 15-17 minutes or until golden brown. Cool on a wire rack. Cut into 30 bars.

1 BAR: 182 cal., 10g fat (4g sat. fat), 12mg chol., 141mg sod., 22g carb. (13g sugars, 1g fiber), 3g pro.

TEST KITCHEN TIP

If you want to jazz up these breakfast bars, stir in raisins, dried cranberries, sunflower kernels, mini chocolate chips or chopped pecans.

TEX-MEX GRAIN BOWL

This recipe is special because it is not only healthy but also delicious. Oatmeal is a dish often eaten sweetened. People are always pleasantly surprised when they taste this savory version.
—*Athena Russell, Greenville, SC*

Takes: 20 min. • **Makes:** 4 servings

- 4 cups water
- 2 Tbsp. reduced-sodium taco seasoning
- 2 cups old-fashioned oats or multigrain hot cereal
- 1 cup black beans, rinsed, drained and warmed
- 1 cup salsa
- ½ cup finely shredded cheddar cheese
- 1 medium ripe avocado, peeled and cubed
  Optional: Pitted ripe olives, sour cream and chopped cilantro

In a large saucepan, bring the water and taco seasoning to a boil. Stir in oats; cook 5 minutes over medium heat, stirring occasionally. Remove from heat. Divide oatmeal among 4 bowls. Top with beans, salsa, cheese, avocado, and optional toppings as desired. Serve immediately.
1 SERVING: 345 cal., 13g fat (4g sat. fat), 14mg chol., 702mg sod., 46g carb. (5g sugars, 9g fiber), 12g pro.

ROASTED VEGETABLE & CHEVRE QUICHE

Roasting the veggies in this rich-yet-bright quiche intensifies their flavors. The addition of fresh goat cheese lends a wonderful creamy tang.
—*Laura Davis, Chincoteague, VA*

Prep: 45 min. + chilling
Bake: 25 min. + standing
Makes: 6 servings

- 1 sheet refrigerated pie crust
- 1 small eggplant, cut into 1-in. pieces
- 1 poblano pepper, cut into 1-in. pieces
- 1 medium tomato, cut into 1-in. pieces
- 2 garlic cloves, minced
- 1 Tbsp. olive oil
- 2 large eggs plus 2 large egg yolks
- ¾ cup half-and-half cream
- 1 tsp. kosher salt
- ½ tsp. pepper
- 1 log (4 oz.) fresh goat cheese, crumbled

1. Unroll pie crust into an ungreased 9-in. tart pan. Refrigerate 30 minutes. Preheat oven to 425°.

2. Line unpricked crust with a double thickness of foil. Fill with pie weights, dried beans or uncooked rice. Bake on a lower oven rack until edge is golden brown, 10-12 minutes. Remove foil and weights; bake until bottom is golden brown, 3-5 minutes longer. Cool on a wire rack.
3. In a large bowl, combine eggplant, pepper, tomato and garlic. Add oil; toss to coat. Transfer to a greased 15x10x1-in. baking pan. Roast the vegetables until tender, 15-20 minutes, stirring halfway.
4. Reduce oven setting to 375°. Spoon roasted vegetables into crust. In a large bowl, whisk eggs, egg yolks, cream, salt and pepper until blended; pour over top. Sprinkle with goat cheese.
5. Bake on a lower oven rack on a baking sheet until a knife inserted near the center comes out clean, 25-30 minutes. Cover the edge with foil if needed to prevent overbrowning. Let quiche stand for 10 minutes before cutting.
1 PIECE: 219 cal., 14g fat (7g sat. fat), 83mg chol., 471mg sod., 19g carb. (2g sugars, 0 fiber), 3g pro.

CRISP CARAWAY
TWISTS
P. 248

Small Bites & Snacks

From healthy veggie-filled appetizers to savory game-day dunkables, these easy, fresh and flavorful recipes will satisfy everyone at the party—even meat lovers!

FETA BRUSCHETTA

You won't believe the compliments you'll receive when you greet guests with these warm appetizers. Every crispy bite offers the savory tastes of feta, tomatoes, basil and garlic. They're wonderful for holiday parties or any gathering.
—*Stacey Rinehart, Eugene, OR*

Takes: 30 min. • **Makes:** 10 appetizers

- ¼ cup butter, melted
- ¼ cup olive oil
- 10 slices French bread (1 in. thick)
- 1 pkg. (4 oz.) crumbled feta cheese
- 2 to 3 garlic cloves, minced
- 1 Tbsp. minced fresh basil or 1 tsp. dried basil
- 1 large tomato, seeded and chopped

1. Preheat oven to 350°. In a small bowl, combine butter and oil; brush onto both sides of bread. Place on a baking sheet. Bake at 350° for 8-10 minutes or until lightly browned on top.

2. Combine the feta cheese, garlic and basil; sprinkle over toast. Top with the tomato. Bake 8-10 minutes longer or until heated through. Serve warm.

1 SERVING: 296 cal., 14g fat (5g sat. fat), 18mg chol., 547mg sod., 35g carb. (1g sugars, 3g fiber), 8g pro.

ONION BRIE APPETIZERS

Guests will think you spent hours making these appetizers, but they're super easy to assemble using purchased puff pastry. The combination of Brie, caramelized onions and caraway is terrific.
—Carole Resnick, Cleveland, OH

- -

Prep: 25 min. + chilling • **Bake:** 15 min.
Makes: 1½ dozen

- 2   medium onions, thinly sliced
- 3   Tbsp. butter
- 2   Tbsp. brown sugar
- ½   tsp. white wine vinegar
- 1   sheet frozen puff pastry, thawed
- 4   oz. Brie cheese, rind removed, softened
- 1   to 2 tsp. caraway seeds
- 1   large egg
- 2   tsp. water

1. In a large skillet, cook onions, butter, brown sugar and vinegar over medium-low heat until onions are golden brown, stirring frequently. Remove with a slotted spoon; cool to room temperature.
2. On a lightly floured surface, roll puff pastry into an 11x8-in. rectangle. Cut Brie into thin slices; distribute evenly over pastry. Cover with the onions; sprinkle with caraway seeds.
3. Roll up 1 long side to the middle of the dough; roll up the other side so the 2 rolls meet in the center. Using a serrated knife, cut into ½-in. slices.

Place on parchment-lined baking sheets; flatten to ¼-in. thickness. Refrigerate for 15 minutes. Preheat oven to 375°.
4. In a small bowl, whisk egg and water; brush over slices. Bake until puffed and golden brown, 12-14 minutes. Serve appetizers warm.
1 APPETIZER: 121 cal., 8g fat (3g sat. fat), 23mg chol., 109mg sod., 11g carb. (3g sugars, 1g fiber), 3g pro.

FRESH HERB VEGETABLE DIP

I often entertain and am always looking for an easy crowd-pleaser. If it's one where I use fresh ingredients from my garden, it's even better! I serve this dip in individual servings for large parties so each person has their own cup.
—*Isabel Minunni, Poughkeepsie, NY*

Takes: 15 min. • **Makes:** 3 cups

- ¼ cup olive oil
- 3 Tbsp. lemon juice
- 1½ cups sour cream
- 2 medium ripe avocados, peeled and cubed
- 2 Tbsp. chopped chives
- 2 Tbsp. chopped fresh parsley
- 2 Tbsp. chopped fresh basil
- 1 Tbsp. chopped fresh tarragon
- 1 Tbsp. chopped fresh thyme
- 1 garlic clove, halved
- ½ tsp. salt
- ¼ tsp. pepper
  Assorted fresh vegetables

Place the first 12 ingredients in a food processor; process until smooth. Refrigerate until serving. Serve with vegetables of your choice.
¼ CUP: 140 cal., 14g fat (5g sat. fat), 21mg chol., 111mg sod., 3g carb. (1g sugars, 2g fiber), 2g pro. **DIABETIC EXCHANGES:** 1½ fat.

RAVIOLI APPETIZER POPS

Ravioli on a stick is a tasty appetizer everyone talks about. They're simple and fun. You can use packaged dipping sauces or make your own.
—*Erika Monroe-Williams, Scottsdale, AZ*

Prep: 25 min. • **Cook:** 5 min./batch
Makes: 3½ dozen

- ½ cup dry bread crumbs
- 2 tsp. pepper
- 1½ tsp. dried oregano
- 1½ tsp. dried parsley flakes
- 1 tsp. salt
- 1 tsp. crushed red pepper flakes
- ⅓ cup all-purpose flour
- 2 large eggs, lightly beaten
- 1 pkg. (9 oz.) refrigerated cheese ravioli
  Oil for frying
  Grated Parmesan cheese, optional
- 42 lollipop sticks
  Warm marinara sauce and prepared pesto

1. In a shallow bowl, mix bread crumbs and seasonings. Place flour and eggs in separate shallow bowls. Dip the ravioli in flour to coat both sides; shake off excess. Dip in egg, then crumb mixture, patting to help coating adhere.
2. In a large electric or cast-iron skillet, heat ½ in. oil to 375°. Fry ravioli, a few at a time, until golden brown, 1-2 minutes on each side. Drain on paper towels. Immediately sprinkle with cheese if desired. Carefully insert a lollipop stick into the back of each ravioli. Serve warm with marinara sauce and pesto.
1 APPETIZER: 32 cal., 1g fat (0 sat. fat), 9mg chol., 97mg sod., 4g carb. (0 sugars, 0 fiber), 1g pro.

MEAT LOVER OPTION
PAGE 320

APPETIZER WREATH

I have lots of fun with this festive appetizer wreath. I place a bowl of stuffed olives in the center.
—*Shirley Privratsky, Dickinson, ND*

Prep: 20 min. • **Bake:** 15 min. + cooling
Makes: 16 servings

- 2 tubes (8 oz. each) refrigerated crescent rolls
- 1 pkg. (8 oz.) cream cheese, softened
- ½ cup sour cream
- 1 tsp. dill weed
- ⅛ tsp. garlic powder
- 1½ cups chopped fresh broccoli florets
- ½ cup finely chopped sweet red pepper
- 1 cup finely chopped celery
  Celery leaves

1. Remove the crescent dough from the packaging (do not unroll). Cut each tube into 8 slices. Arrange in an 11-in. circle on an ungreased 14-in. pizza pan.
2. Bake at 375° for 15-20 minutes or until golden brown. Cool for 5 minutes before carefully removing to a serving platter; cool completely.
3. In a small bowl, beat cream cheese, sour cream, dill and garlic powder until smooth. Spread on the wreath; top with broccoli, red pepper, chopped celery and celery leaves.
1 PIECE: 125 cal., 9g fat (5g sat. fat), 21mg chol., 166mg sod., 7g carb. (2g sugars, 0 fiber), 3g pro.

BAKED BRIE WITH MUSHROOMS

My sister craves this appetizer so much that I once made a batch and carried it on the plane when I flew to New Mexico to visit her. The combination of creamy Brie with earthy sauteed mushrooms is out of this world.
—*Melody Ansell, Portland, OR*

Prep: 30 min. • **Bake:** 15 min.
Makes: 8 servings

- 1 Tbsp. butter
- 1 Tbsp. olive oil
- 1 lb. sliced fresh assorted mushrooms
- 2 small red onions, chopped
- ¼ tsp. salt
- ¼ tsp. pepper
- 5 garlic cloves, minced
- ⅔ cup port wine
- 1 round (8 oz.) Brie cheese
  Toasted French bread baguette slices

1. Preheat oven to 400°. In a large skillet, heat butter and oil over medium-high heat. Add the mushrooms, onions, salt and pepper; cook until golden brown, stirring occasionally, 12-14 minutes. Add garlic; cook 1 minute longer. Stir in wine. Bring to a boil; cook until the liquid is almost evaporated.
2. Remove rind from top of the cheese. Transfer to a 1½-qt. round baking dish. Top with the mushroom mixture. Bake, uncovered, until the cheese is melted, 15-20 minutes. Serve the Brie with baguette slices.
1 SERVING: 157 cal., 11g fat (6g sat. fat), 32mg chol., 266mg sod., 6g carb. (2g sugars, 1g fiber), 8g pro.

MARINATED MOZZARELLA & TOMATO APPETIZERS

This is best served chilled, and should marinate for a few days—the longer the better. My daughter puts the mozzarella on her antipasto platter.
—*Mary Ann Lee, Clifton Park, NY*

Prep: 15 min. + marinating • **Bake:** 5 min.
Makes: 16 servings

- ½ cup Italian salad dressing
- 2 Tbsp. minced fresh basil
- 2 Tbsp. minced fresh chives
- ½ tsp. coarsely ground pepper
- 2 cartons (8 oz. each) miniature fresh mozzarella cheese balls, drained
- 2 cups cherry tomatoes
- 12 slices French bread baguette (½ in. thick), cut into quarters
- 2 tsp. olive oil
- ⅛ tsp. salt

1. Preheat oven to 450°. Combine salad dressing, basil, chives and pepper. Add the cheese and tomatoes; toss to coat. Refrigerate, covered, at least 3 hours to let flavors blend.

2. Meanwhile, toss baguette pieces with oil and salt; arrange on a baking sheet. Bake until toasted, 4-5 minutes. Cool completely. Just before serving, add the toasted bread to cheese mixture; toss to combine. If desired, thread tomatoes, cheese and bread pieces on skewers for serving.

¼ CUP: 119 cal., 8g fat (4g sat. fat), 22mg chol., 171mg sod., 5g carb. (2g sugars, 0 fiber), 6g pro.

LENTIL TACO CUPS

My trusty muffin tin never fails to help me make fun and easy hand-held snacks. These festive vegetarian cups are so flavorful, nobody misses the meat. They are always a hit with my kids. Serve two per serving as a main dish.
—*Shauna Havey, Roy, UT*

- -

Prep: 25 min. • **Bake:** 15 min.
Makes: 1 dozen

12	mini flour tortillas, warmed
1	can (15 oz.) lentils, drained
¾	cup pico de gallo
½	cup enchilada sauce
2	Tbsp. taco seasoning
2	cups shredded Mexican cheese blend, divided

CREMA

1	cup sour cream
½	cup minced fresh cilantro
1	Tbsp. lime juice
¼	tsp. sea salt
	Shredded lettuce, sliced ripe olives and chopped tomatoes

1. Preheat oven to 425°. Press warm tortillas into 12 greased muffin cups, pleating sides as needed. In a large bowl, combine the lentils, pico de gallo, enchilada sauce and taco seasoning. Stir in 1½ cups cheese. Divide lentil mixture among cups. Sprinkle cups with the remaining cheese.
2. Bake until heated through and cheese is melted, 12-15 minutes. Meanwhile, for the crema, combine sour cream, cilantro, lime juice and sea salt. Serve cups with crema, lettuce, olives and tomatoes.
1 TACO CUP: 215 cal., 12g fat (6g sat. fat), 31mg chol., 498mg sod., 16g carb. (2g sugars, 4g fiber), 9g pro.
HEALTH TIP: Skip the ½ cup cheese on top and switch to low-fat Greek yogurt to cut the saturated fat by more than 50%.

MOROCCAN STUFFED MUSHROOMS

Coriander and cumin are zesty updates to the familiar stuffed mushrooms. The addition of couscous makes them very filling and delicious.
—*Raymonde Bourgeois, Swastika, ON*

Prep: 45 min. • **Bake:** 10 min.
Makes: 2 dozen

24 medium fresh mushrooms
½ cup chopped onion
⅓ cup finely shredded carrot
1 tsp. canola oil
1 garlic clove, minced
½ tsp. salt
½ tsp. ground cumin
¼ tsp. ground coriander
¾ cup vegetable broth
2 Tbsp. dried currants
½ cup uncooked couscous
2 Tbsp. minced fresh parsley
2 Tbsp. minced fresh mint

1. Remove stems from mushrooms and finely chop stems; set the caps aside. In a large nonstick skillet, saute the onion, carrot and chopped stems in oil until crisp-tender.
2. Add garlic, salt, cumin and coriander. Cook and stir for 1 minute. Add broth and currants; bring to a boil. Stir in couscous. Remove from heat; cover and let stand for 5-10 minutes or until the broth is absorbed. Fluff with a fork. Stir in the parsley and mint. Stuff the couscous mixture into the mushroom caps.
3. Place on a baking sheet. Bake at 400° until the mushrooms are tender, 10-15 minutes.
1 STUFFED MUSHROOM: 25 cal., 0 fat (0 sat. fat), 0 chol., 81mg sod., 5g carb. (1g sugars, 1g fiber), 1g pro.

PULL-APART HERB BREAD

The ingredients for this recipe are so simple and yet the result is spectacular, I'm always willing to share the secret. It's a variation of a doughnut recipe I made years ago, using refrigerated biscuits. The best part? Tearing the bread apart and eating it warm.
—*Evelyn Kenney, Hamilton, NJ*

Takes: 30 min. • **Makes:** 10 servings

1 garlic clove, minced
¼ cup butter, melted
2 tubes (10.2 oz. each) refrigerated biscuits
1 cup shredded cheddar cheese
¼ tsp. dried basil
¼ tsp. fennel seed
¼ tsp. dried oregano

1. In a 10-in. cast-iron or other ovenproof skillet, saute the garlic in butter for 1 minute; remove from the pan and set aside. Separate the biscuits; cut in half horizontally. Place half in an even layer in the skillet, overlapping as necessary. Brush with butter mixture; sprinkle with half the cheese and herbs. Repeat layers.
2. Bake at 375° for 20-25 minutes or until bread is golden brown. Place the pan on a wire rack; serve warm.
1 PIECE: 257 cal., 14g fat (8g sat. fat), 23mg chol., 569mg sod., 25g carb. (4g sugars, 1g fiber), 6g pro.

⏱ 🄵 GARLIC-HERB MINI QUICHES

Looking for a wonderful little bite to dress up the brunch buffet? These delectable tartlets are irresistible!
—*Josephine Piro, Easton, PA*

- -

Takes: 25 min. • **Makes:** 45 mini quiches

- 1 pkg. (6½ oz.) reduced-fat garlic-herb spreadable cheese
- ¼ cup fat-free milk
- 2 large eggs
- 3 pkg. (1.9 oz. each) frozen miniature phyllo tart shells
- 2 Tbsp. minced fresh parsley
  Minced chives, optional

1. Preheat oven to 350°. In a small bowl, beat the spreadable cheese, milk and eggs. Place tart shells on an ungreased baking sheet; fill each with 2 tsp. mixture. Sprinkle with parsley.
2. Bake for 10-12 minutes or until filling is set and shells are lightly browned. Sprinkle with chives if desired. Serve quiches warm.
1 MINI QUICHE: 31 cal., 2g fat (0 sat. fat), 12mg chol., 32mg sod., 2g carb. (0 sugars, 0 fiber), 1g pro.

MINI MAC & CHEESE BITES

Young relatives were coming for a Christmas party, so I wanted something fun for them to eat. Instead, the adults devoured these tasty bites.
—*Kate Mainiero, Elizaville, NY*

- -

Prep: 35 min. • **Bake:** 10 min.
Makes: 3 dozen

- 2 cups uncooked elbow macaroni
- 1 cup seasoned bread crumbs, divided
- 2 Tbsp. butter
- 2 Tbsp. all-purpose flour
- ½ tsp. onion powder
- ½ tsp. garlic powder
- ½ tsp. seasoned salt
- 1¾ cups 2% milk
- 2 cups shredded sharp cheddar cheese, divided
- 1 cup shredded Swiss cheese
- ¾ cup biscuit/baking mix
- 2 large eggs, room temperature, lightly beaten

1. Preheat oven to 425°. Cook macaroni according to package directions; drain.
2. Meanwhile, sprinkle ¼ cup bread crumbs into 36 greased mini-muffin cups. In a large saucepan, melt butter over medium heat. Stir in flour and seasonings until smooth; gradually whisk in milk. Bring to a boil, stirring constantly; cook and stir until thickened, 1-2 minutes. Stir in 1 cup cheddar cheese and Swiss cheese until melted.
3. Remove from heat; stir in biscuit mix, eggs and ½ cup bread crumbs. Add the macaroni; toss to coat. Spoon about 2 Tbsp. macaroni mixture into prepared mini-muffin cups; sprinkle with the remaining cheddar cheese and the seasoned bread crumbs.
4. Bake until golden brown, 8-10 minutes. Cool in pans 5 minutes before serving.
1 APPETIZER: 91 cal., 5g fat (3g sat. fat), 22mg chol., 162mg sod., 8g carb. (1g sugars, 0 fiber), 4g pro.

TEST KITCHEN TIP

You can add mix-ins such as chopped jalapenos, sliced chives or minced garlic.

♥ MEAT LOVER OPTION
PAGE 320

51 CHEESE-STUFFED CHERRY TOMATOES

We grow plenty of cherry tomatoes, so my husband and I handpick enough for these easy appetizers. This is one of our favorite recipes, and it's impossible to eat just one.
—*Mary Lou Robison, Greensboro, NC*

Prep: 15 min. + chilling • **Makes:** 1 dozen

- 1 pint cherry tomatoes
- 1 pkg. (4 oz.) crumbled feta cheese
- ½ cup finely chopped red onion
- ½ cup olive oil
- ¼ cup red wine vinegar
- 1 Tbsp. dried oregano
  Salt and pepper to taste

1. Cut a thin slice off the top of each tomato. Scoop out and discard pulp. Invert tomatoes onto paper towels to drain. Combine cheese and onion; spoon into tomatoes.
2. In a small bowl, whisk the oil, vinegar, oregano, salt and pepper. Spoon over tomatoes. Cover and refrigerate for 30 minutes or until ready to serve.
1 TOMATO: 111 cal., 11g fat (2g sat. fat), 5mg chol., 93mg sod., 2g carb. (1g sugars, 1g fiber), 2g pro.

ROASTED BUFFALO CAULIFLOWER BITES

Try these savory bites for a kickin' appetizer that's healthy too!
—*Emily Tyra, Lake Ann, MI*

Takes: 25 min. • **Makes:** 8 servings

- 1   medium head cauliflower (about 2¼ lbs.), cut into florets
- 1   Tbsp. canola oil
- ½   cup Buffalo wing sauce
     Blue cheese salad dressing

1. Preheat oven to 400°. Toss cauliflower with oil; spread in a 15x10x1-in. pan. Roast until tender and lightly browned, stirring once, 20-25 minutes.

2. Transfer to a bowl; toss with the wing sauce. Serve with dressing.

⅓ CUP: 39 cal., 2g fat (0 sat. fat), 0 chol., 474mg sod., 5g carb. (2g sugars, 2g fiber), 2g pro.

MEAT
LOVER
OPTION
PAGE 320

51 ROASTED PUMPKIN NACHOS

Previously, I had made this dish with black beans and corn off the cob in the summer. Wanting to try it with fresh fall ingredients, I replaced the corn with roasted pumpkin—yum! It's also good with butternut squash.
—*Lesle Harwood, Douglassville, PA*

Prep: 40 min. • **Bake:** 10 min.
Makes: 12 servings

- 4 cups cubed fresh pumpkin or butternut squash (about 1 lb.)
- 2 Tbsp. olive oil
- ¼ tsp. salt
- ⅛ tsp. pepper
- 1 pkg. (13 oz.) tortilla chips
- 1 can (15 oz.) black beans, rinsed and drained
- 1 jar (16 oz.) salsa
- 3 cups shredded Mexican cheese blend
   Optional toppings: Minced fresh cilantro, sliced green onions and hot pepper sauce

1. Preheat oven to 400°. Place pumpkin in a greased 15x10x1-in. baking pan. Drizzle with oil; sprinkle with salt and pepper. Toss to coat. Roast until tender, 25-30 minutes, stirring occasionally.
2. Reduce oven setting to 350°. On a greased 15x10x1-in. baking pan, layer half each of the chips, beans, pumpkin, salsa and cheese. Repeat layers. Bake until cheese is melted, 8-10 minutes. Add toppings as desired; serve the nachos immediately.
1 SERVING: 347 cal., 18g fat (6g sat. fat), 25mg chol., 559mg sod., 36g carb. (3g sugars, 4g fiber), 10g pro.

MARINATED ALMOND-STUFFED OLIVES

Marinated stuffed olives go over so well with company that I try to keep a batch in the fridge at all times.
—*Larissa Delk, Columbia, TN*

Prep: 15 min. + marinating
Makes: 8 cups

- 1 cup blanched almonds, toasted
- 3 cans (6 oz. each) pitted ripe olives, drained
- 3 jars (7 oz. each) pimiento-stuffed olives, undrained
- ½ cup white balsamic vinegar
- ½ cup dry red wine
- ½ cup canola oil
- 1 medium garlic clove, minced
- ½ tsp. sugar
- 1 tsp. dried oregano
- 1 tsp. pepper
- ½ tsp. dill weed
- ½ tsp. dried basil
- ½ tsp. dried parsley flakes

Insert an almond into each ripe olive; place in a large bowl. Add pimiento-stuffed olives with olive juice. In a small bowl, whisk the vinegar, wine, oil, garlic, sugar and seasonings. Pour mixture over olives. Refrigerate, covered, 8 hours or overnight, stirring occasionally. Transfer to a serving bowl.
¼ CUP: 78 cal., 7g fat (0 sat. fat), 0 chol., 455mg sod., 3g carb. (0 sugars, 1g fiber), 1g pro.

51 GARLIC TOMATO BRUSCHETTA

I drew inspiration from my grandma's recipe for this garden-fresh bruschetta. The tomato goodness makes a great party appetizer, or you can serve it as a side with your favorite Italian entree.
—*Jean Franzoni, Rutland, VT*

Prep: 30 min. + chilling • **Makes:** 2 dozen

- ¼ cup olive oil
- 3 Tbsp. chopped fresh basil
- 3 to 4 garlic cloves, minced
- ½ tsp. salt
- ¼ tsp. pepper
- 4 medium tomatoes, diced
- 2 Tbsp. grated Parmesan cheese
- 1 loaf (1 lb.) unsliced French bread

1. In a large bowl, combine oil, basil, garlic, salt and pepper. Add tomatoes and toss gently. Sprinkle with cheese. Refrigerate at least 1 hour.

2. Bring to room temperature before serving. Slice bread into 24 pieces; toast under broiler until lightly browned. Top with tomato mixture. Serve immediately.

1 PIECE: 77 cal., 3g fat (0 sat. fat), 0 chol., 172mg sod., 11g carb. (1g sugars, 1g fiber), 2g pro. **DIABETIC EXCHANGES:** ½ starch, ½ fat.

TEST KITCHEN TIP

Make the tomato mixture a few hours ahead of time if you want the flavors to meld before serving. Prep it any further in advance than that, though, and the tomatoes will get too juicy. Either way, you'll want to scoop the mixture onto the toast with a slotted spoon to strain any liquid.

GARBANZO-STUFFED MINI PEPPERS

Mini peppers are the perfect size for a two-bite appetizer. They have the crunch of pita chips, without the extra calories.
—*Christine Hanover, Lewiston, CA*

Takes: 20 min. • **Makes:** 32 appetizers

1 tsp. cumin seeds
1 can (15 oz.) garbanzo beans or chickpeas, rinsed and drained
¼ cup fresh cilantro leaves
3 Tbsp. water
3 Tbsp. cider vinegar
¼ tsp. salt
16 miniature sweet peppers, halved lengthwise
Additional fresh cilantro leaves

1. In a dry small skillet, toast the cumin seeds over medium heat until aromatic, 1-2 minutes, stirring frequently. Transfer to a food processor. Add garbanzo beans, cilantro, water, vinegar and salt; pulse until blended.

2. Spoon into pepper halves. Top with additional cilantro. Refrigerate peppers until serving.

1 APPETIZER: 15 cal., 0 fat (0 sat. fat), 0 chol., 36mg sod., 3g carb. (1g sugars, 1g fiber), 1g pro.

SAVORY PARTY BREAD

It's impossible to stop nibbling on warm pieces of this cheesy, oniony loaf. The bread fans out for a fun presentation.
—*Kay Daly, Raleigh, NC*

Prep: 10 min. • **Bake:** 25 min.
Makes: 8 servings

- 1 unsliced round loaf sourdough bread (1 lb.)
- 1 lb. Monterey Jack cheese
- ½ cup butter, melted
- ½ cup chopped green onions
- 2 to 3 tsp. poppy seeds

1. Preheat oven to 350°. Cut bread widthwise into 1-in. slices to within ½ in. of bottom of loaf. Repeat cuts in opposite direction. Cut cheese into ¼-in. slices; cut the slices into small pieces. Place cheese in cuts in bread.
2. In a small bowl, mix butter, green onions and poppy seeds; drizzle over bread. Wrap in foil; place on a baking sheet. Bake for 15 minutes. Unwrap; bake until the cheese is melted, about 10 minutes longer.
1 SERVING: 481 cal., 31g fat (17g sat. fat), 91mg chol., 782mg sod., 32g carb. (1g sugars, 2g fiber), 17g pro.

VEGETARIAN BUFFALO DIP

A friend made Buffalo chicken dip and that got me thinking about creating a vegetarian dip with the same flavors. This addictive dip is so amazing, no one will miss the meat.
—*Amanda Silvers, Oldfort, TN*

Prep: 10 min. • **Cook:** 1½ hours
Makes: 6 cups

- 1 cup sour cream
- 8 oz. cream cheese, softened
- 1 envelope ranch salad dressing mix
- 2 cups shredded sharp cheddar cheese
- 1 can (15 oz.) black beans, rinsed and drained
- 8 oz. fresh mushrooms, chopped
- 1 cup Buffalo wing sauce
   Optional: Sliced green onions and tortilla chips

Combine sour cream, cream cheese and ranch dressing mix in a bowl until smooth. Stir in the next 4 ingredients. Transfer to a 3- or 4-qt. slow cooker. Cook, covered, on high for 1½ hours. If desired, sprinkle with green onions and serve with tortilla chips.
¼ CUP: 113 cal., 8g fat (5g sat. fat), 21mg chol., 526mg sod., 5g carb. (1g sugars, 1g fiber), 4g pro.

TEST KITCHEN TIP

To soften cream cheese, unwrap the block and slice it into several small cubes. Lightly cover the cubes with a paper towel and leave out at room temperature until soft, 35-45 minutes.

51 CAYENNE PRETZELS

These seasoned pretzels were a huge hit at my daughter's graduation party. The longer they sit, the spicier they get!
—*Gayle Zebo, Warren, PA*

Prep: 10 min. • **Bake:** 1¼ hours
Makes: 3½ qt.

- 1 cup canola oil
- 1 envelope ranch salad dressing mix
- 1 tsp. garlic salt
- 1 tsp. cayenne pepper
- 1 lb. (12 cups) pretzel sticks

1. In a small bowl, combine the oil, dressing mix, garlic salt and cayenne. Divide pretzels between 2 ungreased 15x10x1-in. baking pans. Pour oil mixture over pretzels; stir to coat.

2. Bake at 200° for 1¼-1½ hours or until golden brown, stirring occasionally. Cool completely. Store in an airtight container.

¾ CUP: 236 cal., 15g fat (2g sat. fat), 0 chol., 690mg sod., 24g carb. (1g sugars, 1g fiber), 3g pro.

DILLY VEGGIE PIZZA

Always popular at special events and a cinch to prep, this pizza is one of my favorite ways to use leftover veggies. You can change the mixture to match your kids' tastes, and it's just as yummy the next day.
—*Heather Ahrens, Columbus, OH*

Prep: 20 min. • **Bake:** 10 min. + cooling
Makes: 12 servings

- 1 tube (8 oz.) refrigerated crescent rolls
- 1½ cups vegetable dill dip
- 2 medium carrots, chopped
- 1 cup finely chopped fresh broccoli
- 1 cup chopped seeded tomatoes
- 4 green onions, sliced
- 1 can (2¼ oz.) sliced ripe olives, drained

1. Unroll crescent dough into 1 long rectangle. Press onto the bottom of a greased 13x9-in. baking pan; seal seams. Bake at 375° until golden brown, 10-12 minutes. Cool completely on a wire rack.
2. Spread dip over crust; sprinkle with the carrots, broccoli, tomatoes, onions and olives. Cut into squares. Refrigerate any leftovers.
1 PIECE: 185 cal., 14g fat (3g sat. fat), 15mg chol., 332mg sod., 13g carb. (4g sugars, 1g fiber), 3g pro.

READER RAVE

"Great and easy recipe! I used red bell peppers and celery instead of the tomatoes and black olives. Everybody raved about it. This recipe is a keeper!"
—KATHLEENBRAUN, TASTEOFHOME.COM

CIDER CHEESE FONDUE

Cheese lovers are sure to enjoy dipping into this creamy, quick-to-fix fondue that has just a hint of apple. You can also serve the appetizer with pear wedges.
—*Kenny Van Rheenen, Mendota, IL*

Takes: 15 min. • **Makes:** 2⅔ cups

- ¾ cup apple cider or apple juice
- 2 cups shredded cheddar cheese
- 1 cup shredded Swiss cheese
- 1 Tbsp. cornstarch
- ⅛ tsp. pepper
  Cubed French bread and sliced apples and green peppers

1. In a large saucepan, bring cider to a boil. Reduce heat to medium-low. Toss the cheeses with cornstarch and pepper; stir into cider. Cook and stir until cheese is melted, 3-4 minutes.
2. Transfer to a small fondue pot or 1½-qt. slow cooker; keep warm. Serve with bread cubes and sliced apples and green peppers.
¼ CUP: 111 cal., 8g fat (6g sat. fat), 28mg chol., 138mg sod., 3g carb. (2g sugars, 0 fiber), 7g pro.

BUTTERY RADISH BAGUETTE

My dad and brother are crazy for radishes, and this peppery baguette appetizer is a big-time favorite. Add a sprinkle of fresh dill or parsley on top.
—*Kathy Hewitt, Cranston, RI*

- -

Takes: 15 min. • **Makes:** about 1½ dozen

 1 sourdough or French bread baguette (about 10 oz.), cut diagonally into ¾-in. slices
 6 Tbsp. unsalted butter, softened
2¼ cups thinly sliced radishes (about 18 medium)
    Sea salt
    Snipped fresh dill, optional

Spread baguette slices with butter. Top with radishes. Sprinkle lightly with salt and, if desired, top with dill.

1 APPETIZER: 76 cal., 4g fat (2g sat. fat), 10mg chol., 107mg sod., 9g carb. (1g sugars, 0 fiber), 1g pro.

CHIPOTLE FOCACCIA WITH GARLIC-ONION TOPPING

Chipotle peppers make some people grab their water glasses; others can't get enough of the smoky heat. I came up with this recipe to fit right in the middle. Add more chipotle if you crave spiciness.
—*Frances Kay Bouma, Trail, BC*

- -

Prep: 1¼ hours + rising • **Bake:** 20 min.
Makes: 1 loaf (16 pieces)

 1 cup water (70° to 80°)
 2 Tbsp. olive oil
2½ cups all-purpose flour
 1 tsp. salt
 1 Tbsp. chopped chipotle pepper in adobo sauce
1½ tsp. active dry yeast
TOPPING
 6 garlic cloves, peeled
 ¼ tsp. plus 7 Tbsp. olive oil, divided
 2 large onions, cut into ¼-in. slices
 2 Tbsp. chopped chipotle peppers in adobo sauce
 ¼ tsp. salt
    Chopped chives, optional

1. In bread machine pan, place the first 6 ingredients in order suggested by the manufacturer. Select the dough setting (check dough after 5 minutes of mixing; add 1-2 Tbsp. water or flour if needed).

2. When cycle is completed, turn dough onto a lightly floured surface. Punch down the dough; cover and let rest for 15 minutes.

3. Meanwhile, place garlic in a small microwave-safe bowl. Drizzle with ¼ tsp. oil. Microwave on high for 20-60 seconds or until softened. Mash the garlic.

4. Roll dough into a 12x10-in. rectangle. Transfer to a well-greased baking sheet. Cover and let rise in a warm place until slightly risen, about 20 minutes.

5. With fingertips, make several dimples over top of dough. Brush dough with 1 Tbsp. oil. Bake at 400° for 10 minutes or until lightly browned.

6. Meanwhile, in a large skillet, saute onions in remaining oil until tender. Add the chipotle peppers, salt and mashed garlic; saute 2-3 minutes longer. Sprinkle over dough.

7. Bake until golden brown, 10-15 minutes longer. If desired, top with the chopped chives. Cut into serving portions; serve focaccia warm.

FREEZE OPTION: Freeze cooled focaccia squares in freezer containers, separating layers with waxed paper. To use, reheat the squares on an ungreased baking sheet in a preheated 400° oven until heated through.

1 PIECE: 159 cal., 8g fat (1g sat. fat), 0 chol., 206mg sod., 19g carb. (2g sugars, 1g fiber), 3g pro.

RUSTIC TUSCAN PEPPER BRUSCHETTA

If you love sweet red, yellow and orange peppers, pair them with fresh mint for a cold kitchen appetizer. Marinate for up to one hour before assembling.
—*Noelle Myers, Grand Forks, ND*

Takes: 30 min. • **Makes:** 10 servings

- 2 Tbsp. olive oil
- 2 Tbsp. balsamic vinegar
- 1 Tbsp. honey
- 1 Tbsp. minced fresh mint
- 1 each medium sweet yellow, orange and red pepper, cut into thin 1-in. strips
- 6 oz. fresh goat cheese
- ⅔ cup whipped cream cheese
- 48 assorted crackers

1. In a large bowl, whisk oil, vinegar, honey and mint. Add peppers; toss to coat. Let stand 15 minutes.
2. Meanwhile, in a small bowl, beat the goat cheese and cream cheese. Spread 1 rounded tsp. on each cracker. Drain peppers well. Arrange peppers on cheese-topped crackers.
1 APPETIZER: 34 cal., 2g fat (1g sat. fat), 5mg chol., 60mg sod., 3g carb. (1g sugars, 0 fiber), 1g pro.

TEST KITCHEN TIP

A chipotle pepper is a smoked and dried jalapeno pepper from the region surrounding Mexico City. Often found canned in chile sauce in the U.S., chipotles are medium to hot in heat levels and are used in a variety of Mexican and American dishes that require a hot, spicy flavor.

MEAT LOVER OPTION
PAGE 320

CHEESY QUESADILLAS

You can slice these into thin wedges to use as party appetizers or dippers for chili, or serve them with extra salsa and sour cream for a main dish.
—*Terri Keeney, Greeley, CO*

Takes: 15 min. • **Makes:** 12 pieces

- 4 flour tortillas (8 in.), warmed
- 1½ cups shredded Mexican cheese blend
- ½ cup salsa

1. Place tortillas on a greased baking sheet. Combine the cheese and salsa; spread over half of each tortilla. Fold tortilla over.
2. Broil 4 in. from the heat for 3 minutes on each side or until golden brown. Cut into wedges.
1 PIECE: 111 cal., 6g fat (3g sat. fat), 13mg chol., 203mg sod., 10g carb. (0g sugars, 1g fiber), 4g pro.

CASHEW CHEESE

Spread this vegan cashew cheese on crackers, over a toasted bagel or serve with fresh vegetables. It also makes a terrific sandwich topper.
—Taste of Home *Test Kitchen*

Prep: 1 hour + chilling • **Makes:** ¾ cup

- 1 cup raw cashews
- ⅓ cup water
- 2 Tbsp. nutritional yeast
- 2 tsp. lemon juice
- ½ tsp. salt
- ⅛ tsp. garlic powder

Place cashews in a small bowl. Add enough warm water to cover completely. Soak cashews for 1-2 hours; drain and discard water. Add cashews and the remaining 5 ingredients to the food processor. Cover and process until smooth, 1-2 minutes, scraping down sides occasionally. Transfer to serving dish. Cover and refrigerate for at least 1 hour before serving.

1 TBSP: 56 cal., 4g fat (1g sat. fat), 0 chol., 101mg sod., 3g carb. (1g sugars, 0 fiber), 2g pro. **DIABETIC EXCHANGES:** 1 fat.

TEST KITCHEN TIP

Add your favorite herbs and spices to the cashew cheese to create different flavors.

CRISP CARAWAY TWISTS

These twists are always a hit when I serve them on holidays or special occasions. The flaky cheese-filled twists (made with convenient puff pastry) bake to a crispy golden brown. When our big family gets together, I make two batches.
—Dorothy Smith, El Dorado, AR

Takes: 30 min. • **Makes:** about 1½ dozen

- 1 large egg
- 1 Tbsp. water
- 1 tsp. country-style Dijon mustard
- ¾ cup shredded Swiss cheese
- ¼ cup finely chopped onion
- 2 tsp. minced fresh parsley
- 1½ tsp. caraway seeds
- ¼ tsp. garlic salt
- 1 sheet frozen puff pastry, thawed

1. In a small bowl, beat egg, water and mustard; set aside. In another bowl, combine the cheese, onion, parsley, caraway seeds and garlic salt.

2. Unfold pastry sheet; brush with egg mixture. Sprinkle cheese mixture lengthwise over half the pastry. Fold pastry over filling; press edges to seal. Brush top with remaining egg mixture. Cut widthwise into ½-in. strips; twist each strip several times.

3. Place 1 in. apart on greased baking sheets, pressing ends down. Bake at 375° for 15-20 minutes or until golden brown. Serve warm.

1 TWIST: 90 cal., 5g fat (2g sat. fat), 15mg chol., 91mg sod., 8g carb. (0 sugars, 1g fiber), 3g pro.

STRAWBERRY SALSA

My deliciously different salsa is versatile, fresh-tasting and colorful. People are surprised to see a salsa made with strawberries, but it's excellent as a dip with corn chips. We also enjoy it over grilled chicken and pork.

—*Jean Giroux, Belchertown, MA*

Prep: 15 min. + chilling • **Makes:** 4 cups

1 pint fresh strawberries, chopped
4 plum tomatoes, seeded and chopped
1 small red onion, finely chopped
1 to 2 medium jalapeno peppers, minced
2 Tbsp. lime juice
1 Tbsp. olive oil
2 garlic cloves, minced

In a large bowl, combine strawberries, tomatoes, onion and jalapenos. Stir in the lime juice, oil and garlic. Cover and refrigerate for 2 hours before serving.

NOTE: Wear disposable gloves when cutting hot peppers; the oils can burn skin. Avoid touching your face.

¼ CUP: 19 cal., 1g fat (0 sat. fat), 0 chol., 1mg sod., 3g carb. (2g sugars, 1g fiber), 0 pro. **DIABETIC EXCHANGES:** 1 free food.

AIR-FRYER CHICKPEA FRITTERS WITH SWEET-SPICY SAUCE

Chickpeas are a common ingredient in many dishes in Pakistan, where I grew up. I like to incorporate the tastes of my home country in my cooking. Here I combined the light spice of Pakistani foods with my love of deep-fried finger foods that many people, including my American-born daughters, enjoy.
—*Shahrin Hasan, York, PA*

Prep: 20 min. • **Cook:** 5 min./batch
Makes: 2 dozen (1 cup sauce)

- 1 cup plain yogurt
- 2 Tbsp. sugar
- 1 Tbsp. honey
- ½ tsp. salt
- ½ tsp. pepper
- ½ tsp. crushed red pepper flakes

FRITTERS
- 1 can (15 oz.) chickpeas or garbanzo beans, rinsed and drained
- 1 tsp. ground cumin
- ½ tsp. salt
- ½ tsp. garlic powder
- ½ tsp. ground ginger
- 1 large egg, room temperature
- ½ tsp. baking soda
- ½ cup chopped fresh cilantro
- 2 green onions, thinly sliced

1. Preheat air fryer to 400°. In a small bowl, combine the first 6 ingredients; refrigerate until serving.
2. Place chickpeas and seasonings in a food processor; process until finely ground. Add egg and baking soda; pulse until blended. Transfer to a bowl; stir in cilantro and green onions.
3. In batches, drop the chickpea mixture by rounded tablespoonfuls onto greased tray in air-fryer basket. Cook until lightly browned, 5-6 minutes. Serve with sauce.
1 FRITTER WITH 2 TSP. SAUCE: 34 cal., 1g fat (0 sat. fat), 9mg chol., 156mg sod., 5g carb. (3g sugars, 1g fiber), 1g pro.

SPICY ROASTED CARROT HUMMUS

This is a wonderful appetizer for Easter, Mother's Day or any spring gathering. The roasted carrots give this hummus such a bright, fresh flavor. People who say they don't like hummus end up loving this version.
—*Anne Ormond, Dover, NH*

Prep: 20 min. • **Bake:** 15 min. + cooling
Makes: 2 cups

    1   cup chopped carrots
    3   garlic cloves, peeled
    3   Tbsp. olive oil, divided
    1   can (15 oz.) garbanzo beans or
        chickpeas, rinsed and drained
    2   Tbsp. lemon juice
    2   Tbsp. tahini
    1   Tbsp. water
    1   tsp. hot pepper sauce,
        such as Tabasco
    ¼   tsp. sea salt
    ¼   tsp. ground turmeric
    ¼   tsp. ground cumin
    ⅛   tsp. cayenne pepper
    ¼   cup sunflower kernels
        Assorted fresh vegetables
        and pita wedges

1. Preheat the oven to 400°. Place the carrots and garlic in a rimmed baking sheet. Drizzle with 2 Tbsp. oil; toss to coat. Roast until the carrots are soft, 15-20 minutes. Cool on a wire rack.
2. Transfer the carrot mixture to a food processor. Add garbanzo beans, lemon juice, tahini, water, hot sauce, salt and spices. While processing, add remaining 1 Tbsp. oil. Process until the desired consistency is reached. Transfer to a serving dish. If desired, drizzle with additional oil and hot sauce. Top with sunflower kernels. Serve warm or chilled with vegetables and pita wedges.
¼ CUP: 155 cal., 11g fat (1g sat. fat), 0 chol., 175mg sod., 12g carb. (2g sugars, 3g fiber), 4g pro. **DIABETIC EXCHANGES:** 2 fat, 1 starch.

✻ SPANAKOPITA PINWHEELS

I just love spanakopita, and these spinach and feta pinwheels are a quick and easy way to enjoy it. I make them for teacher get-togethers and family events.
—*Ryan Palmer, Windham, ME*

Prep: 30 min. + cooling • **Bake:** 20 min.
Makes: 2 dozen

    1   medium onion, finely chopped
    2   Tbsp. olive oil
    1   tsp. dried oregano
    1   garlic clove, minced
    2   pkg. (10 oz. each) frozen chopped
        spinach, thawed and squeezed dry
    2   cups crumbled feta cheese
    2   large eggs, lightly beaten
    1   pkg. (17.3 oz.) frozen puff pastry,
        thawed

1. In a small skillet, saute onion in oil until tender. Add oregano and garlic; cook 1 minute longer. Add the spinach; cook 3 minutes longer or until the liquid is evaporated. Transfer spinach mixture to a large bowl; cool.
2. Add feta cheese and eggs to spinach mixture; mix well. Unfold puff pastry. Spread each sheet with half the spinach mixture to within ½ in. of edges. Roll up jelly-roll style. Cut each into twelve ¾-in. slices. Place cut side down on greased baking sheets.
3. Bake at 400° for 18-22 minutes or until golden brown. Serve warm.
1 PINWHEEL: 197 cal., 13g fat (5g sat. fat), 39mg chol., 392mg sod., 14g carb. (1g sugars, 3g fiber), 7g pro.

SPICY EDAMAME

Edamame (pronounced eh-duh-MAH-may) are young soybeans in their pods. In our Test Kitchen, we boiled and seasoned them to create a distinctive finger food.
—Taste of Home *Test Kitchen*

Takes: 20 min. • **Makes:** 6 servings

1 pkg. (16 oz.) frozen edamame pods
2 tsp. kosher salt
¾ tsp. ground ginger
½ tsp. garlic powder
¼ tsp. crushed red pepper flakes

Place edamame in a large saucepan and cover with water. Bring to a boil. Cover and cook until tender, 4-5 minutes; drain. Transfer to a large bowl. Add seasonings; toss to coat.

1 SERVING: 52 cal., 2g fat (0 sat. fat), 0 chol., 642mg sod., 5g carb. (1g sugars, 2g fiber), 4g pro.

BEST DEVILED EGGS

Herbs lend an amazing flavor to these deviled eggs, which truly are the best you'll ever make!
—*Jesse and Anne Foust, Bluefield, WV*

- -

Takes: 25 min. • **Makes:** 2 dozen

- ½ cup mayonnaise
- 2 Tbsp. 2% milk
- 1 tsp. dried parsley flakes
- ½ tsp. dill weed
- ½ tsp. minced chives
- ½ tsp. ground mustard
- ¼ tsp. salt
- ¼ tsp. paprika
- ⅛ tsp. garlic powder
- ⅛ tsp. pepper
- 12 hard-boiled large eggs
  Minced fresh parsley and additional paprika

In a small bowl, combine the first 10 ingredients. Cut eggs lengthwise in half; remove yolks and set whites aside. In another bowl, mash yolks; add to the mayonnaise mixture, mixing well. Spoon or pipe filling into egg whites. Sprinkle with parsley and additional paprika. Refrigerate until serving.

1 STUFFED EGG HALF: 73 cal., 6g fat (1g sat. fat), 108mg chol., 81mg sod., 0 carb. (0 sugars, 0 fiber), 3g pro.

AVOCADO GOAT CHEESE TRUFFLES

Give your guests the VIP treatment with luxurious truffles you can make in your own kitchen. The goat cheese is mild, and red pepper heats up each bite. Crackers are the perfect accompaniment.
—*Roxanne Chan, Albany, CA*

- -

Prep: 45 min. + chilling • **Makes:** 4 dozen

- 1 pkg. (8 oz.) cream cheese, softened
- ½ cup shredded pepper jack cheese
- ¼ cup fresh goat cheese
- 1 garlic clove, minced
- 1 tsp. grated lime zest
- 1 tsp. olive oil
- ½ tsp. chili powder
- ¼ tsp. crushed red pepper flakes
- 1 green onion, minced
- 1 Tbsp. minced fresh cilantro
- 3 medium ripe avocados, peeled
- 1 Tbsp. lime juice
- 2 cups salted pumpkin seeds or pepitas, finely chopped
  Pretzel sticks, optional

1. In a small bowl, beat cheeses, garlic, lime zest, oil, chili powder and pepper flakes until blended. Stir in onion and cilantro. Refrigerate 1 hour or until firm.
2. With a small melon baller, scoop out avocado balls onto a baking sheet; sprinkle with lime juice. Shape 1½ tsp. cheese mixture around each ball, then roll in pumpkin seeds. Place on a waxed paper-lined baking sheet. Refrigerate until serving. If desired, serve with pretzel sticks.

1 TRUFFLE: 65 cal., 6g fat (2g sat. fat), 7mg chol., 43mg sod., 2g carb. (0 sugars, 1g fiber), 2g pro.

CORNMEAL TOWERS WITH
STRAWBERRIES & CREAM
P. 282

Room for Dessert

There's always room for dessert! Sweeten any occasion with one of these fresh, wholesome vegetarian treats.

HONEY-ROASTED PEARS

My family has passed down this recipe for generations. The elegant pears are simple to make and only require a few minutes of easy prep, but the results are sensational.

—*Jan Sokol, Overland Park, KS*

Prep: 10 min. • **Bake:** 45 min.
Makes: 4 servings

- 4   medium pears, peeled
- 2   cardamom pods, crushed
- 1   tsp. sugar
- ¼   tsp. ground cinnamon
- ⅛   tsp. ground cloves
- ⅔   cup water
- ¼   cup honey
-     Whipped cream

1. Preheat oven to 400°. Core pears from bottom, leaving the stems intact. Place in a greased 11x7-in. baking dish. Sprinkle with cardamom, sugar, cinnamon and cloves. In a small saucepan, combine the water and honey; bring to a boil for 3 minutes. Pour over pears.

2. Bake pears, uncovered, until tender, 45-55 minutes, basting every 15 minutes. Serve warm, with whipped cream.

1 PEAR: 166 cal., 0 fat (0 sat. fat), 0 chol., 3mg sod., 44g carb. (35g sugars, 5g fiber), 1g pro.

TEST KITCHEN TIP

We recommend using Bosc or Concorde pears for this recipe. Both varieties have a beautiful tear-drop shape with a tapered neck and rounded bottom, and their firm flesh holds up well to baking.

PUMPKIN CRUMBLE

I created this tasty dessert on a rainy fall afternoon while my son was taking a nap. It filled the house with a wonderful aroma, and I was able to make it with ingredients I already had in my pantry. Stir some chocolate chips into the filling for a change of pace.
—Sarah Graham, Independence, MO

- -

Prep: 15 min. • **Bake:** 35 min.
Makes: 6 servings

1 can (15 oz.) pumpkin
¼ cup 2% milk
¼ cup sour cream
½ cup packed brown sugar
2 Tbsp. all-purpose flour
1 tsp. ground cinnamon

TOPPING

¼ cup packed brown sugar
¼ cup all-purpose flour
¼ cup old-fashioned oats
½ tsp. ground cinnamon
⅛ tsp. each ground ginger, ground nutmeg and ground allspice
3 Tbsp. cold butter
2 Tbsp. finely chopped pecans
Vanilla ice cream, optional

Preheat oven to 375°. In a large bowl, whisk pumpkin, milk and sour cream until smooth. Combine the brown sugar, flour and cinnamon; stir into the pumpkin mixture. Pour into a greased 8-in. square baking dish. For topping, in another bowl, combine the brown sugar, flour, oats and spices. Cut in butter until crumbly. Stir in pecans; sprinkle over pumpkin mixture. Bake until the topping is golden brown, 35-40 minutes. Serve warm, with ice cream if desired.

1 SERVING: 208 cal., 8g fat (4g sat. fat), 16mg chol., 59mg sod., 33g carb. (21g sugars, 3g fiber), 3g pro.

SLOW-COOKED BLUEBERRY GRUNT

If you love blueberries, you'll fall for this easy slow-cooked dessert. For a special treat, serve it warm with ice cream.
—*Cleo Gonske, Redding, CA*

- -

Prep: 20 min. • **Cook:** 2½ hours
Makes: 6 servings

4 cups fresh or frozen blueberries
¾ cup sugar
½ cup water
1 tsp. almond extract
DUMPLINGS
2 cups all-purpose flour
4 tsp. baking powder
1 tsp. sugar
½ tsp. salt
1 Tbsp. cold butter
1 Tbsp. shortening
¾ cup 2% milk
  Vanilla ice cream, optional

1. Place blueberries, sugar, water and extract in a 3-qt. slow cooker; stir to combine. Cook, covered, on high for 2-3 hours or until bubbly.

2. For dumplings, in a small bowl, whisk the flour, baking powder, sugar and salt. Cut in the butter and shortening until crumbly. Add the milk; stir just until a soft dough forms.

3. Drop dough by tablespoonfuls on top of hot blueberry mixture. Cook, covered, 30 minutes longer or until a toothpick inserted in center of dumplings comes out clean. If desired, serve warm, with ice cream.

1 CUP: 360 cal., 5g fat (2g sat. fat), 7mg chol., 494mg sod., 73g carb. (37g sugars, 3g fiber), 6g pro.

MADEIRA CAKE

This classic British cake is often served with Madeira wine, which is how it got its name. Similar to a pound cake, it is commonly flavored with lemon and can also be enjoyed with a cup of tea or sweet liqueurs.
—*Peggy Woodward, Shullsburg, WI*

- -

Prep: 15 min. • **Bake:** 45 min. + cooling
Makes: 12 servings

1 cup unsalted butter, softened
1 cup plus 2 Tbsp. sugar, divided
2 tsp. grated lemon zest
3 large eggs, room temperature
2¼ cups all-purpose flour
2 tsp. baking powder

1. Preheat oven to 325°. Line bottom of a greased 8x4-in. loaf pan with parchment; grease parchment.
2. In a large bowl, cream butter and 1 cup sugar until light and fluffy, 5-7 minutes. Beat in the lemon zest. Add eggs, 1 at a time, beating well after each addition. In another bowl, whisk the flour and baking powder; gradually add to the creamed mixture.
3. Transfer to prepared pan. Sprinkle with remaining 2 Tbsp. sugar. Bake until a toothpick inserted in center comes out clean, 45-50 minutes. Cool in the pan for 10 minutes before removing to a wire rack to cool completely.

1 PIECE: 304 cal., 17g fat (10g sat. fat), 87mg chol., 100mg sod., 35g carb. (17g sugars, 1g fiber), 4g pro.

TEST KITCHEN TIP

Madeira cake is a dense cake, which can make it prone to cracking on top while baking. This is often caused by the top of the cake setting too quickly, which cracks when the cake's center then cooks and expands. This can happen due to too-high temperatures, often caused by an oven out of calibration or a rack that's positioned too high inside the oven. Use an oven thermometer to check your oven's temperature, and make sure your rack is set in the middle or a little lower before you preheat.

RASPBERRY PATCH CRUMB BARS

To give these fresh, fruity bars even more crunch, add a sprinkling of nuts to the yummy crumb topping. Everyone will want to indulge.
—*Leanna Thorne, Lakewood, CO*

Prep: 30 min. • **Bake:** 35 min.
Makes: 3 dozen

- 3 cups all-purpose flour
- 1½ cups sugar, divided
- 1 tsp. baking powder
- ¼ tsp. salt
- ¼ tsp. ground cinnamon
- 1 cup shortening
- 2 large eggs, room temperature, lightly beaten
- 1 tsp. almond extract
- 1 Tbsp. cornstarch
- 4 cups fresh or frozen raspberries

1. In a large bowl, combine the flour, 1 cup sugar, baking powder, salt and cinnamon. Cut in the shortening until mixture resembles coarse crumbs. Stir in eggs and extract. Press two-thirds of the mixture into a greased 13x9-in. baking dish.
2. In a large bowl, combine cornstarch and remaining ½ cup sugar; add berries and gently toss. Spoon over crust. Sprinkle with remaining crumb mixture.
3. Bake at 375° for 35-45 minutes or until bubbly and golden brown. Cool on a wire rack. Cut into bars. Store in the refrigerator.
1 BAR: 131 cal., 6g fat (1g sat. fat), 12mg chol., 31mg sod., 18g carb. (9g sugars, 1g fiber), 2g pro.

LEMON OLIVE OIL CAKE

Olive oil cakes are tender and moist—and stay that way longer than butter-based cakes—so they are wonderful if you need to make dessert ahead of time. Serve this recipe with fresh berries when your favorite are in season.
—*Nicole Gackowski, Antioch, CA*

Prep: 15 min. • **Bake:** 30 min. + cooling
Makes: 8 servings

- 2 large eggs
- ⅔ cup sugar
- ½ cup extra virgin olive oil
- ⅓ cup 2% milk
- 1 Tbsp. grated lemon zest
- 3 Tbsp. lemon juice
- 1 cup all-purpose flour
- 1 tsp. baking powder
- ¼ tsp. salt
  Confectioners' sugar

1. Preheat oven to 350°. Line a greased 8-in. round baking pan with parchment. In a large bowl, beat eggs on high speed 3 minutes. Gradually add sugar, beating until thickened. Gradually beat in oil. Beat in milk, lemon zest and lemon juice.
2. In another bowl, whisk flour, baking powder and salt; fold into egg mixture. Transfer the batter to prepared pan, spreading evenly. Bake until a toothpick inserted near the center comes out clean, 30-35 minutes. Cool in pan for 15 minutes before removing to a wire rack; remove parchment. Cool the cake completely. Lightly dust with confectioners' sugar.
1 PIECE: 266 cal., 15g fat (2g sat. fat), 47mg chol., 157mg sod., 30g carb. (18g sugars, 1g fiber), 4g pro.

TEST KITCHEN TIP

This simple cake lends itself to a simple finish—a dusting of powdered sugar or a dollop of whipped cream, mascarpone cheese or crème fraiche. You can also drizzle it with a homemade lemon glaze.

SLOW-COOKER BAKED APPLES

On a cool fall day, coming home to the lovely scent of this apple dessert cooking and then eating it is a double dose of just plain wonderful.
—*Evangeline Bradford, Covington, KY*

Prep: 25 min. • **Cook:** 4 hours
Makes: 6 servings

- 6 medium tart apples
- ½ cup raisins
- ⅓ cup packed brown sugar
- 1 Tbsp. grated orange zest
- 1 cup water
- 3 Tbsp. thawed orange juice concentrate
- 2 Tbsp. butter

1. Core apples and peel the top third of each if desired. Combine the raisins, brown sugar and orange zest; spoon into apples. Place in a 5-qt. slow cooker.
2. Pour water around apples. Drizzle with orange juice concentrate. Dot with butter. Cover and cook on low for 4-5 hours or until apples are tender.
1 STUFFED APPLE: 203 cal., 4g fat (2g sat. fat), 10mg chol., 35mg sod., 44g carb. (37g sugars, 4g fiber), 1g pro.

MELOMAKARONA

Growing up in Cyprus, we would see this famous cookie everywhere during the holidays. Every year my mother, Thelma, would make batch after batch.
—*Paris Paraskeva, San Francisco, CA*

Prep: 15 min. • **Bake:** 20 min./batch
Makes: 4½ dozen

- 1 cup sugar
- 1 cup water
- ¾ cup honey

COOKIES
- 1 cup confectioners' sugar
- 2 cups olive oil
- ½ cup Cognac
- ½ cup orange juice
- 1 Tbsp. honey
- 7½ cups all-purpose flour
- 4 tsp. grated orange zest
- 3 tsp. baking powder
- 1 tsp. ground cinnamon
- ½ cup ground toasted walnuts

1. Preheat oven to 350°. In a saucepan, combine the sugar, water and honey; bring to a boil. Reduce the heat; simmer, uncovered, 10 minutes. Cool completely.
2. For cookies, beat confectioners' sugar and oil until blended. Beat in Cognac, orange juice and honey. In another bowl, whisk the flour, orange zest, baking powder and cinnamon; gradually beat into the sugar mixture.
3. Shape tablespoons of dough into 1-in.-thick ovals. Place 1 in. apart on parchment-lined baking sheets. Bake until lightly browned, 20-25 minutes. Cool on pans 5 minutes. Remove to wire racks.
4. Float and turn warm cookies in syrup about 10 seconds; allow excess to drip off. Place on waxed paper; sprinkle with walnuts. Let stand until set. Store between pieces of waxed paper in airtight containers.
1 COOKIE: 172 cal., 9g fat (1g sat. fat), 0 chol., 27mg sod., 20g carb. (7g sugars, 1g fiber), 2g pro.

🕐 🔢 SPECIAL STUFFED STRAWBERRIES

These sweet bites can be made ahead of time, and they look colorful on a tray. I sometimes sprinkle the piped filling with finely chopped pistachio nuts.
—*Marcia Orlando, Boyertown, PA*

Takes: 20 min. • **Makes:** 2 dozen

- 24 large fresh strawberries
- ½ cup spreadable strawberry cream cheese
- 3 Tbsp. sour cream
  Graham cracker crumbs

1. Place strawberries on a cutting board and cut off tops; remove bottom tips so they sit flat. Using a small paring knife, hull out the center of each berry.

2. In a small bowl, beat cream cheese and sour cream until smooth. Pipe or spoon filling into each berry. Top with graham cracker crumbs. Refrigerate until serving.

1 STRAWBERRY: 18 cal., 1g fat (1g sat. fat), 4mg chol., 22mg sod., 1g carb. (1g sugars, 0 fiber), 1g pro.

GINGERED APRICOT-APPLE CRUMBLE

This crumble is tasty hot or cold, plain or topped with ice cream. If you're not fond of apricots, leave them out for a traditional apple crisp.

—*Sylvia Rice, Didsbury, AB*

Prep: 15 min. • **Bake:** 50 min.
Makes: 12 servings

- 1 cup apricot nectar
- ¾ cup finely chopped dried apricots
- ⅓ cup honey
- ¼ cup maple syrup
- 2 Tbsp. lemon juice
- 8 cups sliced peeled tart apples (about 8 large)
- 3 Tbsp. all-purpose flour
- 1 tsp. ground cinnamon
- ½ tsp. ground ginger
- ½ tsp. ground cardamom

TOPPING

- ¾ cup all-purpose flour
- ½ cup quick-cooking oats
- ¼ cup canola oil
- ¼ cup maple syrup
- ½ cup chopped pecans, optional

1. In a large bowl, combine the first 5 ingredients; set aside. Arrange apples in an ungreased 13x9-in. baking dish.

2. Combine flour, cinnamon, ginger and cardamom; stir into the apricot mixture. Spoon over apples.

3. Combine topping ingredients, including pecans if desired; sprinkle over the fruit. Bake at 350° for 50-60 minutes or until the topping is golden brown and the fruit is tender.

1 SERVING: 228 cal., 5g fat (1g sat. fat), 0 chol., 8mg sod., 46g carb. (32g sugars, 3g fiber), 2g pro.

QUINOA, FRESH FIG & HONEY-BALSAMIC PARFAITS

This recipe is special to me because of the two main ingredients, quinoa and figs. Quinoa is gluten-free, which is good for those who have food allergies, like my daughter. And I love fresh ripe figs when they are in season. Enjoy these parfaits for breakfast or dessert.
—*Dawn Hutchins, St. Johns, FL*

Takes: 30 min. • **Makes:** 4 servings

- 1 cup water
- ½ cup quinoa, rinsed
- ¼ cup balsamic vinegar
- 1 tsp. vanilla extract
- ¼ tsp. ground cinnamon
- ⅛ tsp. salt
- ¼ cup honey
- 8 fresh figs, quartered
- 1 cup (8 oz.) vanilla yogurt

1. In a small saucepan, bring water to a boil. Add quinoa. Reduce heat; simmer, covered, 12-15 minutes or until liquid is absorbed. Remove from the heat; fluff with a fork.

2. Meanwhile, place the vinegar in a small saucepan. Bring to a boil; cook for 1-2 minutes or until liquid is reduced by half.

3. In a small bowl, mix cooked quinoa, vanilla, cinnamon and salt. Layer half the quinoa mixture, half the honey, the balsamic vinegar, half the figs and half the yogurt into 4 parfait glasses. Top with remaining quinoa mixture, honey, yogurt and figs.

1 PARFAIT: 272 cal., 2g fat (1g sat. fat), 3mg chol., 117mg sod., 59g carb. (43g sugars, 4g fiber), 7g pro.

TEST KITCHEN TIP

Any leftover reduced vinegar can be saved for a later use, such as drizzling over salad with a little goat cheese.

51 CASHEW BUTTER COOKIES

These cashew butter cookies are on a more sophisticated level than standard peanut butter cookies. They are vegan and gluten-free, so you'll be able to share with all your friends.
—Taste of Home *Test Kitchen*

Prep: 15 min. • **Bake:** 20 min./batch
Makes: 20 cookies

- 1 cup creamy cashew butter
- ¼ cup maple syrup
- ¼ cup ground flaxseed
- ¼ tsp. salt

1. In a large bowl, mix all ingredients. Roll level tablespoons into balls. Place on an ungreased baking sheet; flatten with a fork.
2. Bake at 350° until edges are lightly browned, 15-18 minutes. Remove to a wire rack to cool.

1 COOKIE: 98 cal., 8g fat (1g sat. fat), 0 chol., 72mg sod., 7g carb. (4g sugars, 1g fiber), 2g pro.

RHUBARB TART

The rhubarb flavor in this tart balances nicely with the honey and amaretto. The mascarpone cheese makes it rich and creamy. Sometimes I'll double the rhubarb for extra sumptuous tarts.
—*Ellen Riley, Murfreesboro, TN*

- -

Prep: 35 min. • **Bake:** 15 min.
Makes: 2 tarts (8 servings each)

1	pkg. frozen puff pastry (17.30 oz.), thawed
1	large egg
1	Tbsp. water

RHUBARB TOPPING

12	rhubarb ribs (½ in. x 7 in.)
1	cup orange juice
½	cup honey
2	Tbsp. amaretto

FILLING

1	pkg. (8 oz.) mascarpone cheese
2	Tbsp. amaretto
1	Tbsp. honey

1. Preheat oven to 400°. Unfold 1 pastry sheet and place on a parchment-lined baking sheet; repeat with remaining pastry sheet. Whisk egg and water; brush over pastries. Using a sharp knife, score a 1-in. border around edges of pastry sheets (do not cut through). With a fork, prick center of pastries. Bake until golden brown, about 15 minutes. With a spatula, press down center portion of pastries, leaving outer edges intact. Remove to wire racks to cool.

2. Meanwhile, for topping, arrange the rhubarb in a single layer in a 13x9-in. baking dish. Combine the orange juice, honey and amaretto; pour over rhubarb. Bake at 400° until the rhubarb is just tender but still holds its shape, about 10 minutes. Remove with a slotted spoon, reserving the cooking liquid; let rhubarb cool. Transfer reserved cooking liquid to a small saucepan; bring to a boil over medium-high heat. Reduce heat; simmer until reduced to ½ cup, about 20 minutes. Allow cooking liquid to cool.

3. For filling, stir together mascarpone cheese, amaretto and honey until smooth. Spread mascarpone mixture over center of each pastry. Top with rhubarb ribs. Brush rhubarb with cooled cooking liquid. Refrigerate leftovers.

1 PIECE: 259 cal., 15g fat (6g sat. fat), 29mg chol., 115mg sod., 26g carb. (8g sugars, 3g fiber), 4g pro.

TEST KITCHEN TIP

Rhubarb is a perennial plant that grows well in cool climates. The stalks are edible, but it's sometimes planted as an ornamental plant because of its beautiful, vibrant red stalks and wide green leaves. Consumed raw, rhubarb has an intensely tart flavor that is not generally liked by most people. But toss it with sugar and bake it into cake, pie, shortbread or jam, and rhubarb's bitterness fades and becomes delicious.

BERRY BREAKFAST PARFAITS

Expecting brunch company but short on time? Parfaits are the perfect solution. Feel free to mix and match with whatever berries you have on hand.
—*Lisa Speer, Palm Beach, FL*

Takes: 20 min. • **Makes:** 8 servings

- 6½ cups frozen unsweetened raspberries
- ¼ cup packed brown sugar
- ¼ cup orange juice
- 2 Tbsp. cornstarch
- ½ tsp. grated orange zest
- 2 cups fresh blueberries
- 2 cups fresh blackberries
- 2 cups granola without raisins
- 4 cups vanilla Greek yogurt
  Additional brown sugar, optional

1. Place raspberries and brown sugar in a blender; cover and process until pureed. Press through a sieve; discard the seeds.

2. In a small saucepan, combine the raspberry puree, orange juice, cornstarch and orange zest. Cook and stir over medium heat until thickened and bubbly. Reduce heat to low; cook and stir 2 minutes longer. Remove from the heat; cool.

3. In 8 parfait glasses, layer half the raspberry sauce, berries, granola and yogurt. Repeat layers. Sprinkle with additional brown sugar if desired. Serve parfaits immediately.

1 SERVING: 304 cal., 4g fat (0 sat. fat), 0 chol., 64mg sod., 54g carb. (27g sugars, 9g fiber), 17g pro.

ZUCCHINI WALNUT CAKE

When zucchini is abundant in my garden, I shred and freeze plenty so I have it on hand to bake this cake all year long. The cream cheese frosting is yummy, and the big panful always goes fast at a picnic or potluck. I have a friend who started to grow zucchini just to make this cake!
—*Marie Hoyer, Hodgenville, KY*

Prep: 20 min. • **Bake:** 35 min. + cooling
Makes: 24 servings

- 2 cups shredded zucchini
- 2 cups sugar
- 1 cup canola oil
- 4 large eggs
- 2½ cups all-purpose flour
- 1½ tsp. ground cinnamon
- 1 tsp. salt
- ½ tsp. baking powder
- ½ tsp. baking soda
- ½ cup chopped toasted walnuts, optional

FROSTING

- 3 oz. cream cheese, softened
- ¼ cup butter, softened
- 1 Tbsp. 2% milk
- 1 tsp. vanilla extract
- 2 cups confectioners' sugar
  Chopped toasted walnuts, optional

1. Preheat the oven to 350°. Grease a 13x9-in. baking pan; set aside.
2. In a large bowl, beat the zucchini, sugar, oil and eggs until well blended. Combine the flour, cinnamon, salt, baking powder and baking soda; gradually beat into zucchini mixture until blended. Fold in walnuts if desired.
3. Pour into prepared pan. Bake until a toothpick inserted in the center comes out clean, 35-40 minutes. Cool the cake completely on a wire rack.
4. For frosting, in a small bowl, beat the cream cheese, butter, milk and vanilla until smooth. Add the confectioners' sugar and mix well. Frost cake. Sprinkle the cake with walnuts if desired. Store in the refrigerator.

1 PIECE: 275 cal., 13g fat (3g sat. fat), 45mg chol., 174mg sod., 37g carb. (26g sugars, 1g fiber), 3g pro.

TEST KITCHEN TIP

Zucchini contains a lot of water. Each one-cup serving is about 90% water. That water releases as it cooks, which could mean a soggy disaster for your baked goods. So before baking with grated zucchini, squeeze out all the excess moisture. To do this, place the zucchini in a large piece of cheesecloth or a clean kitchen towel. Wring the cloth or towel with your hands to remove as much moisture as possible. You can also squeeze the zucchini in between clean hands, place the zucchini in a sieve and then press it firmly with the back of a spoon.

GRILLED CRANBERRY PEAR CRUMBLE

My husband loves this dessert. Fruit crisps are easy and quick to prepare, so I make them often. I created this fall-flavored grilled version with fresh pears and items I had on hand.
—Ronna Farley, Rockville, MD

Takes: 30 min. • **Makes:** 6 servings

- 3 medium ripe pears, sliced
- ½ cup dried cranberries
- ¼ cup sugar
- 2 Tbsp. all-purpose flour
- ¼ tsp. ground cinnamon
- 1 Tbsp. butter

TOPPING
- 2 Tbsp. butter, melted
- ¼ tsp. ground cinnamon
- 1 cup granola without raisins

1. Toss pears and cranberries with sugar, flour and cinnamon. Place 1 Tbsp. butter in a 9-in. cast-iron skillet. Place on grill rack over medium heat until butter is melted. Stir in fruit; grill, covered, until pears are tender, 15-20 minutes, stirring occasionally.
2. For topping, mix melted butter and cinnamon; toss with granola. Sprinkle over pears. Grill, covered, 5 minutes. Serve warm.
1 SERVING: 258 cal., 9g fat (4g sat. fat), 15mg chol., 54mg sod., 47g carb. (29g sugars, 7g fiber), 4g pro.

OATMEAL CARAMEL APPLE COOKIES

This recipe for caramel apple cookies is a fun twist on traditional oatmeal raisin. These treats are hard to resist!
—Rachel Lewis, Danville, VA

Prep: 10 min. • **Bake:** 15 min./batch
Makes: 4 dozen

- ½ cup butter, softened
- ¾ cup packed brown sugar
- ¼ cup sugar
- 1 pkg. (3.4 oz.) instant caramel pudding mix
- 2 large eggs, room temperature
- ½ cup unsweetened applesauce
- 1¼ cups all-purpose flour
- 1 tsp. baking soda
- 3½ cups old-fashioned oats
- 1 medium apple, peeled and chopped

1. Preheat oven to 350°. In a large bowl, cream butter, sugars and pudding mix until light and fluffy, 5-7 minutes. Add eggs; mix well. Beat in applesauce. In another bowl, whisk flour and baking soda; gradually beat into creamed mixture. Stir in oats and apple.
2. Drop dough by tablespoonfuls 2 in. apart onto greased baking sheets. Bake cookies 15-18 minutes or until golden brown. Cool on pans 3 minutes. Serve warm or remove to wire racks to cool completely. Store in an airtight container.
FREEZE OPTION: Freeze baked cookies in freezer containers, separating layers with waxed paper. To use, thaw before serving.
1 COOKIE: 80 cal., 3g fat (1g sat. fat), 13mg chol., 78mg sod., 13g carb. (7g sugars, 1g fiber), 1g pro.

⏱ 5i GRILLED STONE FRUITS WITH BALSAMIC SYRUP

Get ready to experience another side of stone fruits. Hot off the grill, this late-summer dessert practically melts in your mouth.
—*Sonya Labbe, West Hollywood, CA*

Takes: 20 min. • **Makes:** 4 servings

- ½ cup balsamic vinegar
- 2 Tbsp. brown sugar
- 2 medium peaches, peeled and halved
- 2 medium nectarines, peeled and halved
- 2 medium plums, peeled and halved

1. In a small saucepan, combine vinegar and brown sugar. Bring to a boil; cook until liquid is reduced by half.

2. On a lightly oiled grill rack, grill the peaches, nectarines and plums, covered, over medium heat or broil 4 in. from the heat until they are tender, 3-4 minutes on each side.

3. Slice the fruit; arrange on a serving plate. Drizzle with sauce.

1 SERVING: 114 cal., 1g fat (0 sat. fat), 0 chol., 10mg sod., 28g carb. (24g sugars, 2g fiber), 2g pro. **DIABETIC EXCHANGES:** 1 starch, 1 fruit.

CONTEST-WINNING EASY TIRAMISU

Sweet little servings of tiramisu, dusted with a whisper of cocoa, end any meal on a high note. What a fun use for pudding snack cups!
—*Betty Claycomb, Alverton, PA*

Takes: 10 min. • **Makes:** 2 servings

14 vanilla wafers, divided
1 tsp. instant coffee granules
2 Tbsp. hot water
2 snack-size cups (3½ oz. each) vanilla pudding
¼ cup whipped topping
1 tsp. baking cocoa

1. Set aside 4 vanilla wafers; coarsely crush remaining wafers. Divide wafer crumbs between 2 dessert dishes.

2. In a small bowl, dissolve the coffee granules in hot water. Drizzle over wafer crumbs. Spoon pudding into 2 dessert dishes. Top with the whipped topping; sprinkle with cocoa. Garnish with reserved vanilla wafers.

1 SERVING: 267 cal., 9g fat (4g sat. fat), 4mg chol., 219mg sod., 41g carb. (28g sugars, 1g fiber), 3g pro.

GRILLED BANANA BROWNIE SUNDAES

My niece Amanda Jean and I have a lot of fun in the kitchen creating different dishes. One of us will start with a recipe idea and it just grows from there—and so does the mess! In this case, the happy result was our scrumptious Grilled Banana Brownie Sundae.
—Carol Farnsworth, Greenwood, IN

Takes: 15 min. • **Makes:** 8 servings

2 medium bananas, unpeeled
4 oz. cream cheese, softened
¼ cup packed brown sugar
3 Tbsp. creamy peanut butter
8 prepared brownies (2-in. squares)
4 cups vanilla ice cream
½ cup hot fudge ice cream topping, warmed
½ cup chopped salted peanuts

1. Cut unpeeled bananas crosswise in half, then lengthwise in half. Place quartered bananas on an oiled grill rack, cut side down. Grill, covered, over medium-high heat on each side until lightly browned, 2-3 minutes. Cool bananas slightly.
2. In a bowl, beat cream cheese, brown sugar and peanut butter until smooth.
3. To serve, remove bananas from peel; place over brownies. Top with cream cheese mixture, ice cream, fudge topping and peanuts.

1 SERVING: 505 cal., 28g fat (11g sat. fat), 62mg chol., 277mg sod., 57g carb. (33g sugars, 3g fiber), 10g pro.

TEST KITCHEN TIP

Homemade brownies are amazing, but if you want speed things up, use a boxed mix.

BERRY BROWNIE PIZZA

How could you not love pizza for dessert? A fudgy brownie base gets a whipped topping sauce and is covered with fresh berries, chopped nuts and a drizzle of chocolate syrup.
—*Karen Heleski, Ubly, MI*

Prep: 15 min. + chilling
Bake: 20 min. + cooling
Makes: 12 servings

- 1 pkg. fudge brownie mix (8-in. square pan size)
- 1¼ cups cold 2% milk
- 1 pkg. (3.4 oz.) instant vanilla pudding mix
- 2½ cups whipped topping
- 2 cups mixed fresh berries Chocolate syrup and chopped pecans

1. Prepare brownie batter according to package directions; spread onto a greased 12-in. pizza pan.
2. Bake at 350° until a toothpick inserted in the center comes out almost clean, 18-22 minutes. Cool for 15 minutes on a wire rack.
3. Meanwhile, in a large bowl, whisk milk and pudding mix for 2 minutes. Let stand until soft-set, about 2 minutes. Fold in the whipped topping. Spread over the brownie crust.
4. Top with berries and drizzle with the chocolate syrup. Sprinkle with pecans. Refrigerate until chilled.
1 PIECE: 312 cal., 14g fat (5g sat. fat), 19mg chol., 215mg sod., 44g carb. (31g sugars, 2g fiber), 4g pro.

TEST KITCHEN TIP

Get creative with this brownie-crust version of fruit pizza. Top it with your favorite fruits, candies and syrups.

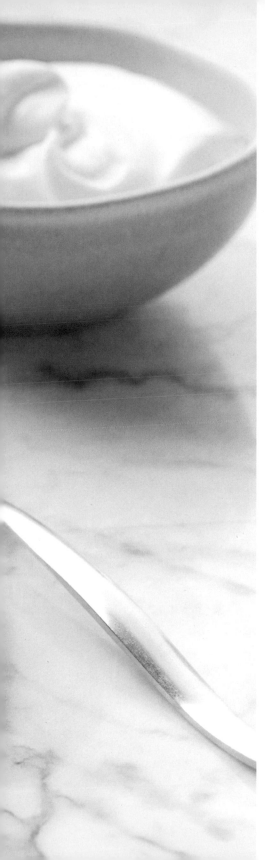

🔟 BLOOD ORANGE UPSIDE-DOWN CUPCAKES

When blood oranges are in season, this is one of my favorite ways to use them. I start with a cake mix and bump up the flavor with essential oil. No one knows these cupcakes are not from scratch.
—*Monica Chadha, Fremont, CA*

Prep: 20 min. • **Bake:** 15 min. + cooling
Makes: 2 dozen

- 4 medium blood oranges
- ¼ cup whole-berry cranberry sauce
- 1 pkg. orange cake mix (regular size)
- 1 cup water
- ⅓ cup olive oil
- 3 large eggs
- 3 to 4 drops orange oil, optional
  Optional: Creme fraiche or sour cream

1. Preheat oven to 350°. Grease or line 24 muffin cups with paper or foil liners. Cut a thin slice from the top and bottom of each orange; stand orange upright on a cutting board. With a knife, remove peel and outer membrane from orange. Thinly slice oranges; trim to fit muffin cups. Place 1 orange slice in each cup; top each with ½ tsp. cranberry sauce. Bake 8 minutes.
2. Meanwhile, in a large bowl, combine cake mix, water, olive oil, eggs and, if desired, orange oil; beat on low speed 30 seconds. Beat on medium speed for 2 minutes. Remove pans from oven; fill with prepared batter.
3. Bake until a toothpick inserted in the center comes out clean, 15-20 minutes. Cool in pans 10 minutes before removing to wire racks to cool completely. Remove liners; serve the cupcakes with creme fraiche if desired.
1 CUPCAKE: 130 cal., 5g fat (1g sat. fat), 23mg chol., 137mg sod., 19g carb. (11g sugars, 0 fiber), 2g pro. **DIABETIC EXCHANGES:** 1½ starch, 1 fat.

VEGAN TROPICAL MAGIC BARS

Magic bars are one of the easiest treats you can make, and I decided to give them a couple of twists. I made them vegan by using a plant-based butter and condensed coconut milk. I also added macadamia nuts and dried pineapple and mango to give them a tropical spin.
—*James Schend, Pleasant Prairie, WI*

Prep: 10 min. • **Bake:** 30 min. + chilling
Makes: 16 bars

- ½ cup vegan butter-style sticks
- 1 cup graham cracker crumbs
- 1 cup sweetened shredded coconut
- 1 cup dairy-free white baking chips
- 1 cup macadamia nuts, chopped
- ½ cup dried pineapple, chopped
- ½ cup dried mangoes, chopped
- 1 can (11.6 oz.) sweetened condensed coconut milk

Preheat oven to 350°. Melt butter in a 9-in. square baking pan. On top of the melted butter, sprinkle crumbs, then coconut, then baking chips, then nuts, then pineapple and then mango. Pour well-stirred coconut milk over all. Do not stir. Bake 30-35 minutes or until a toothpick inserted in center comes out clean. Refrigerate at least 4 hours or overnight. Cut into bars and serve.
1 BAR: 323 cal., 20g fat (9g sat. fat), 2mg chol., 188mg sod., 34g carb. (27g sugars, 2g fiber), 2g pro.

VEGAN CHOCOLATE CUPCAKES

These indulgent cupcakes don't call for butter, eggs or dairy milk, but you'd never know. This recipe is perfect for any gathering that includes guests with food restrictions.
—Taste of Home *Test Kitchen*

Prep: 20 min. • **Bake:** 15 min. + cooling
Makes: 2 dozen

- 2½ cups all-purpose flour
- ⅔ cup baking cocoa
- 2 tsp. baking soda
- 2 cups refrigerated unsweetened coconut milk
- 1½ cups sugar
- ⅓ cup canola oil
- 2 Tbsp. cider vinegar
- 1 tsp. vanilla extract

FROSTING
- 1 cup dairy-free margarine, softened
- 3 cups confectioners' sugar
- ⅓ cup baking cocoa
- 2 tsp. vanilla extract

1. Preheat oven to 350°. In a large bowl, whisk flour, cocoa and baking soda. In a small bowl, whisk coconut milk, sugar, oil, vinegar and vanilla. Stir into the dry ingredients just until moistened.
2. Fill paper-lined muffin cups half full. Bake until a toothpick inserted in the center comes out clean, 15-20 minutes. Cool 10 minutes before removing from pans to wire racks to cool completely.
3. For frosting, in a large bowl, beat margarine until light and fluffy. Beat in confectioners' sugar, cocoa and vanilla. Frost cupcakes.
1 CUPCAKE: 265 cal., 12g fat (2g sat. fat), 0 chol., 194mg sod., 40g carb. (27g sugars, 1g fiber), 2g pro.

🟠 STRAWBERRY SORBET

I first made a raspberry sorbet with an abundance of raspberries I had growing, but this simple recipe is amazing with any kind of berry. Strawberry is another of my go-tos.
—*Karen Bailey, Golden, CO*

Prep: 5 min. + freezing
Makes: 7 servings

- ¼ cup plus 1½ tsp. fresh lemon juice
- 3¾ cups fresh or frozen unsweetened chopped strawberries
- 2¼ cups confectioners' sugar

Place all ingredients in a blender or food processor; cover and process until smooth. Transfer to a freezer-safe container, freeze until firm.
½ CUP: 181 cal., 0 fat (0 sat. fat), 0 chol., 2mg sod., 46g carb. (42g sugars, 2g fiber), 1g pro.

TEST KITCHEN TIP

When making sorbet, always select the best available fruit. Fruits with a lot of pectin, such as stone fruits and berries, as well as fibrous fruits, such as apples bananas, give sorbet a beautiful creamy texture.

EASY ALMOND JOY CHIA PUDDING

I enjoy making this recipe because it's easy and I can find all the ingredients at my local market. No baking is required, and it's served in individual jars for guests. For more flavor, add shredded coconut on top.

—Ashley Altan, Hanover, MD

Prep: 15 min. + chilling
Makes: 2 servings

- 1 cup refrigerated unsweetened coconut milk
- 4 Tbsp. chia seeds
- 3 Tbsp. maple syrup
- 2 Tbsp. baking cocoa
- ¼ cup dairy-free semisweet chocolate chips
- ¼ cup slivered almonds

1. In a small bowl, mix coconut milk, chia seeds and maple syrup. Remove half the mixture to a small bowl; stir in cocoa until blended. Refrigerate both plain and chocolate mixtures, covered, until thickened, at least 6 hours.
2. In each of 2 dessert dishes, layer a fourth of the white pudding, chocolate pudding, chocolate chips and almonds. Repeat layers. Serve immediately or store in the refrigerator up to 3 days.
1 SERVING: 414 cal., 24g fat (8g sat. fat), 0 chol., 7mg sod., 50g carb. (30g sugars, 12g fiber), 9g pro.

CORNMEAL TOWERS WITH STRAWBERRIES & CREAM

My kids love to help make these towers. They measure, mix, whisk and build stacks. It's a family custom and a perfect summer dessert.

—Josie Shapiro, San Francisco, CA

Prep: 40 min. • **Cook:** 5 min./batch
Makes: 12 servings

- 3 large egg whites
- 1 cup heavy whipping cream
- 1 cup cornmeal
- 1 cup all-purpose flour
- 1½ tsp. baking powder
- ½ tsp. ground cardamom
- ¼ tsp. salt
- 1¼ cups 2% milk
- 1 cup whole-milk ricotta cheese
- ¼ cup orange juice
- 2 Tbsp. honey
- 1 tsp. almond extract
- 1 to 2 Tbsp. butter
- 1 lb. fresh strawberries, sliced
- 2 Tbsp. sugar

1. Place egg whites in a small bowl; let stand at room temperature 30 minutes. Meanwhile, in a small bowl, beat cream until soft peaks form; refrigerate, covered, until serving.
2. In a large bowl, whisk cornmeal, flour, baking powder, cardamom and salt. In another bowl, mix milk, ricotta cheese, orange juice, honey and extract until blended. Add to cornmeal mixture; stir just until moistened. With clean beaters, beat egg whites on high speed until stiff but not dry; fold into batter.
3. Heat a griddle or large nonstick skillet over medium heat; grease with butter. Filling a ¼-cup measure halfway with batter, pour batter onto griddle or skillet. Cook until edges begin to dry and bottoms are golden brown. Turn; cook until second side is golden brown. Cool pancakes slightly.
4. In a bowl, toss fresh strawberries with sugar. For each serving, stack 3 pancakes, layering each pancake with strawberries and whipped cream.
3 PANCAKES WITH 3 TBSP. EACH STRAWBERRIES AND WHIPPED CREAM: 245 cal., 11g fat (7g sat. fat), 40mg chol., 167mg sod., 30g carb. (10g sugars, 2g fiber), 7g pro.

VEGAN PECAN PIE

This vegan pecan pie has a flaky crust and an ooey-gooey, delicious filling. It is the perfect way to complete a special holiday meal. You can replace the pecan halves with additional chopped pecans if you prefer.

—Echo Tillman, Freeport, FL

Prep: 50 min. • **Cook:** 35 min. + chilling
Makes: 8 servings

- 1½ cups all-purpose flour
- ¼ tsp. salt
- ½ cup cold butter-flavored coconut oil
- 3 to 4 Tbsp. refrigerated unsweetened coconut milk

FILLING

- 1¼ cups maple syrup
- ⅔ cup water, divided
- 3 Tbsp. cornstarch
- 2 Tbsp. butter-flavored coconut oil
- 1 tsp. vanilla extract
- ½ tsp. salt
- 1½ cups chopped pecans
- ½ cup pecan halves
  Vegan vanilla ice cream, optional

1. In a large bowl, mix flour and salt; cut in coconut oil until crumbly. Gradually stir in enough coconut milk until mixture holds together when pressed. Shape into a disk. Cover and refrigerate 30 minutes or up to 2 hours.

2. On a lightly floured surface, roll dough into a ⅛-in.-thick circle; transfer to 9-in. pie plate. Trim crust to ½ in. beyond rim of plate; flute the edge. Refrigerate for 30 minutes. Preheat oven to 425°.

3. Line crust with a double thickness of foil. Fill with pie weights, dried beans or uncooked rice. Bake on a lower oven rack until crust is set, about 5 minutes. Remove foil and weights; bake until crust just starts to brown, about 10 minutes. Reduce oven temperature to 350°.

4. In a small saucepan, combine maple syrup and ⅓ cup water. Bring to a boil over medium heat. Reduce heat; simmer, uncovered, for 5 minutes. In a small bowl, whisk cornstarch and remaining ⅓ cup water until smooth. Gradually stir into pan. Return to a boil. Cook and stir until slightly thickened, 1-2 minutes. Remove from the heat. Stir in coconut oil, vanilla and salt. Stir in chopped pecans.

5. Pour into crust. Arrange pecan halves over top. Bake until puffed and golden (center will not be set), 30-35 minutes. Cool on a wire rack for 1 hour. Refrigerate overnight or until set. If desired, serve with vegan vanilla ice cream.

1 PIECE: 563 cal., 37g fat (18g sat. fat), 0 chol., 228mg sod., 58g carb. (31g sugars, 3g fiber), 5g pro.

TEST KITCHEN TIP

Serve this vegan pecan pie with a hearty dollop of dairy-free coconut whipped cream or with your favorite flavor of vegan ice cream.

5i RASPBERRY SORBET

When I have an abundant crop of fresh raspberries from my backyard, I rely on this recipe for a tasty frozen dessert that couldn't be simpler.
—*Karen Bailey, Golden, CO*

Prep: 5 min. + freezing
Makes: 6 servings

- ¼ cup plus 1½ tsp. fresh lemon juice
- 3¾ cups fresh or frozen unsweetened raspberries
- 2¼ cups confectioners' sugar

Place all ingredients in a blender or food processor; cover and process until smooth. Transfer to a freezer container; freeze until firm.

1 SERVING: 216 cal., 0 fat (0 sat. fat), 0 chol., 1mg sod., 55g carb. (46g sugars, 5g fiber), 1g pro.

PEANUT BUTTER POPCORN BARS

If you're looking for a fun snack for kids, try these chewy popcorn treats that have a mild peanut butter taste. They are easy to stir up and can be pressed into a pan to form bars or shaped into balls.
—*Kathy Oswald, Wauzeka, WI*

Takes: 30 min. • **Makes:** 2 dozen

- 10 cups popped popcorn
- ½ cup sugar
- ½ cup light corn syrup
- ½ cup creamy peanut butter
- ½ tsp. vanilla extract

1. Place popcorn in a large bowl; set aside. In a saucepan over medium heat, bring sugar and corn syrup to a boil, stirring constantly. Boil for 1 minute. Remove from the heat.
2. Stir in the peanut butter and vanilla; mix well. Pour over popcorn and stir until well coated. Press into a buttered 13x9-in. pan. Cool slightly before cutting.
1 BAR: 90 cal., 4g fat (1g sat. fat), 0 chol., 74mg sod., 13g carb. (8g sugars, 1g fiber), 2g pro.

TEST KITCHEN TIP

For extra fun and color, add some of your favorite candies, like M&M's minis, Reese's Pieces or chopped peanut butter cups, to the popcorn mixture. Or add chopped salted peanuts for a salty-sweet combo.

BLACKBERRY-MANGO CRUMBLE

My husband and I love fresh-picked blackberries at the height of summer, and mango is a favorite combination with the berries in this crumble. A little lime adds just enough zing to balance the sweetness of the filling.
—*Patricia Quinn, Omaha, NE*

Prep: 20 min. • **Bake:** 35 min.
Makes: 8 servings

- 4 cups cubed peeled mangoes (about 4 medium)
- 4 cups fresh blackberries
- 1 Tbsp. lime juice
- ½ cup sugar
- ¼ cup cornstarch
- ¼ tsp. salt

TOPPING
- ½ cup quick-cooking oats
- ¼ cup macadamia nuts, chopped
- ¼ cup packed brown sugar
- 2 Tbsp. sweetened shredded coconut
- 2 Tbsp. all-purpose flour
- 1 Tbsp. grated lime zest
    Dash salt
- ¼ cup cold butter, cubed

1. Preheat oven to 375°. In a large bowl, toss mangoes and blackberries with lime juice. In a small bowl, mix sugar, cornstarch and salt; add to fruit and toss to coat. Transfer to a greased 11x7-in. baking dish.
2. In a small bowl, mix the first 7 topping ingredients; cut in butter until crumbly. Sprinkle over fruit. Bake until filling is bubbly and topping is golden brown, 35-40 minutes. Serve warm.
1 SERVING: 285 cal., 10g fat (5g sat. fat), 15mg chol., 161mg sod., 49g carb. (35g sugars, 6g fiber), 3g pro.

🕐 🉐 LEMON ICE

Pucker up for this sweet-tart treat. This refreshing lemon dessert is a perfect way to end a summer meal—or any meal, for that matter.
—*Concetta Maranto Skenfield, Bakersfield, CA*

- -

Prep: 15 min. + freezing
Makes: 6 servings

- 2 cups sugar
- 1 cup water
- 2 cups lemon juice
  Optional: Lemon slices and fresh mint leaves

1. In a large saucepan over low heat, cook and stir sugar and water until sugar is dissolved. Remove from the heat; stir in lemon juice.
2. Pour into a freezer container. Freeze until mixture becomes slushy, about 8 hours, or overnight. If desired, top servings with lemon slices and mint.
½ CUP: 278 cal., 0 fat (0 sat. fat), 0 chol., 1mg sod., 73g carb. (69g sugars, 0 fiber), 0 pro.

CAST-IRON PEACH CROSTATA

While the crostata, an open-faced fruit tart, is actually Italian, my version's peach filling is American all the way.
—*Lauren McAnelly, Des Moines, IA*

Prep: 45 min. + chilling • **Bake:** 45 min.
Makes: 10 servings

- 1½ cups all-purpose flour
- 2 Tbsp. plus ¾ cup packed brown sugar, divided
- 1¼ tsp. salt, divided
- ½ cup cold unsalted butter, cubed
- 2 Tbsp. shortening
- 3 to 5 Tbsp. ice water
- 8 cups sliced peaches (about 7-8 medium)
- 1 Tbsp. lemon juice
- 3 Tbsp. cornstarch
- ½ tsp. ground cinnamon
- ¼ tsp. ground nutmeg
- 1 large egg, beaten
- 2 Tbsp. sliced almonds
- 1 Tbsp. coarse sugar
- ⅓ cup water
- 1 cup fresh raspberries, optional

1. Mix flour, 2 Tbsp. brown sugar and 1 tsp. salt; cut in butter and shortening until crumbly. Gradually add ice water, tossing with a fork until dough holds together when pressed. Shape into a disk. Cover and refrigerate 1 hour or overnight.
2. Combine peaches and lemon juice. Add the remaining ¾ cup brown sugar, cornstarch, spices and remaining ¼ tsp. salt; toss gently. Let stand 30 minutes.
3. Preheat oven to 400°. On a lightly floured surface, roll the dough into a 13-in. circle; transfer to a 10-in. cast-iron skillet, letting excess hang over edge. Using a slotted spoon, transfer peaches into crust, reserving liquid. Fold crust edge over filling, pleating as you go, leaving center uncovered. Brush folded crust with beaten egg; sprinkle with almonds and coarse sugar. Bake until crust is dark golden brown and filling is bubbly, 45-55 minutes.

4. In a small saucepan, combine the reserved liquid and water; bring to a boil. Simmer until thickened, 1-2 minutes; serve warm, with crostata. If desired, top with fresh raspberries.
1 PIECE: 322 cal., 13g fat (7g sat. fat), 43mg chol., 381mg sod., 49g carb. (30g sugars, 3g fiber), 4g pro.

⏱ 🖐 EASY RHUBARB SAUCE

Celebrate spring with the sweet-tart taste of rhubarb in this simple sauce. I enjoy it on toast, English muffins and pancakes, but it's equally decadent drizzled on pound cake or ice cream.
—*Jackie Hutshing, Sonoma, CA*

Takes: 20 min. • **Makes:** 1¼ cups

- ⅓ cup sugar
- ¼ cup water
- 2¼ cups sliced fresh or frozen rhubarb
- 1 tsp. grated lemon zest
- ⅛ tsp. ground nutmeg
  Pound cake or vanilla ice cream

1. In a small saucepan, bring the sugar and water to a boil. Add rhubarb; cook and stir until the rhubarb is tender and the mixture is slightly thickened, 5-10 minutes. Remove from the heat; stir in lemon zest and nutmeg.
2. Serve warm or chilled over pound cake or ice cream. Refrigerate leftovers.
NOTE: If using frozen rhubarb, measure the rhubarb while still frozen, then thaw completely. Drain in a colander, but do not press liquid out.
¼ CUP: 64 cal., 0 fat (0 sat. fat), 0 chol., 2mg sod., 16g carb. (14g sugars, 1g fiber), 1g pro.

VEGAN VANILLA CUPCAKES

We love using this simple vegan vanilla cupcake recipe as a base to layer on extra flavor. Enjoy them as is, or stir in grated orange zest and chopped pecans, vegan chocolate chips and cinnamon, or your own favorite mix-ins.
—Taste of Home *Test Kitchen*

Prep: 20 min. • **Bake:** 15 min. + cooling
Makes: 2 dozen

2½ cups all-purpose flour
2 tsp. baking powder
½ tsp. baking soda
¼ tsp. salt
1¾ cups refrigerated unsweetened coconut milk
1½ cups sugar
⅓ cup canola oil
2 Tbsp. cider vinegar
1 tsp. vanilla extract

FROSTING
1 cup dairy-free margarine, softened
3 cups confectioners' sugar
2 tsp. vanilla extract

1. Preheat oven to 350°. In a large bowl, whisk flour, baking powder, baking soda and salt. In a small bowl, whisk coconut milk, sugar, oil, vinegar and vanilla. Stir into dry ingredients just until moistened.
2. Fill paper-lined muffin cups half full. Bake until a toothpick inserted in the center comes out clean, 15-20 minutes. Cool 10 minutes before removing from pans to wire racks to cool completely.

3. For frosting, in a large bowl, beat margarine until light and fluffy. Beat in the confectioners' sugar and vanilla. Frost cupcakes.

1 CUPCAKE: 255 cal., 11g fat (2g sat. fat), 0 chol., 180mg sod., 38g carb. (27g sugars, 0 fiber), 1g pro.

TEST KITCHEN TIP

Vegan cupcakes do not need to be refrigerated. You can if you'd like, but you can also store them at room temperature. Either way, these cupcakes will keep for up to 3 days in an airtight container.

CHOCOLATE SQUASH MOUSSE

This recipe is rich and decadent yet made with healthy plant-based ingredients. Even though it's quick to whip up, it's something you'll want to slowly savor. Use canned pumpkin to keep preparation simple, or if you have more time, cook and puree a butternut squash for a delicious variation.
—*Andy Huffman, Reno, NV*

Prep: 15 min. + standing
Makes: 8 servings

- 1½ cups raw cashews
- 1 can (13.66 oz.) unsweetened coconut cream
- 1 cup sweet potato puree or canned pumpkin
- ⅓ cup baking cocoa
- ¼ cup maple syrup
- ½ tsp. salt
  Optional: Cashews, chocolate shavings and flake sea salt

1. Rinse cashews in cold water; drain. Place in a large bowl; add enough water to cover by 3 inches. Cover bowl and let stand overnight.
2. Drain and rinse cashews, discarding the liquid. Place the cashews in a food processor. Add coconut cream, puree, cocoa, syrup and salt; cover and process until pureed, scraping down the side as needed. Transfer to 8 dessert dishes. Refrigerate, covered, until well chilled, at least 4 hours. If desired, top with cashews, chocolate shavings and flake sea salt before serving.
½ CUP: 286 cal., 19g fat (11g sat. fat), 0 chol., 177mg sod., 23g carb. (11g sugars, 2g fiber), 6g pro.

SMOKY VEGAN BACON
P. 306

Bonus: Vegan

If you're exploring vegan possibilities or creating a special menu to accommodate vegan guests, here are some great recipes to get you started. Dips and snacks, salads, soups and mains— even delicious quick bread. It's all on the table!

VEGAN BECHAMEL SAUCE

As one of the original classic "mother sauces," bechamel is a vital part of a wide variety of recipes, including casseroles, white lasagnas, and mac and cheese.
—Taste of Home *Test Kitchen*

Takes: 20 min.
Makes: 4 servings (2 cups)

3   Tbsp. vegan butter-style sticks, such as Earth Balance
2   Tbsp. all-purpose flour
1½ cups unsweetened refrigerated soy milk
2   Tbsp. nutritional yeast
½   tsp. salt
¼   tsp. pepper
    Dash ground nutmeg
    Hot cooked pasta

In a small saucepan, melt vegan butter over medium heat. Stir in flour until smooth; gradually whisk in soy milk. Bring to a boil, stirring constantly. Remove from heat; stir in nutritional yeast, salt, pepper and nutmeg until smooth. Let rest 3 minutes or until thickened. Serve with pasta.

½ CUP: 135 cal., 10g fat (4g sat. fat), 0 chol., 433mg sod., 7g carb. (2g sugars, 1g fiber), 4g pro.

VEGAN RANCH DRESSING

There are so many ways to serve ranch dressing! Use this vegan version for dipping, on salads or in recipes that call for regular ranch dressing. Fresh herbs brighten the flavor, but dried herbs can be used too.

—*Peggy Woodward, Shullsburg, WI*

Prep: 10 min. + chilling • **Makes:** 1¼ cups

1 cup vegan mayonnaise
¼ to ½ cup unsweetened almond milk or soy milk
3 Tbsp. minced fresh parsley or 1 Tbsp. dried parsley flakes
1 Tbsp. minced chives
2 tsp. cider vinegar
1 garlic clove, minced
¾ tsp. onion powder
½ tsp. dill weed
¼ tsp. salt
¼ tsp. pepper
¼ tsp. paprika

In a small bowl, whisk all ingredients. Cover and refrigerate at least 1 hour before serving. If desired, garnish with additional chives.

2 TBSP: 74 cal., 8g fat (1g sat. fat), 0 chol., 96mg sod., 0 carb. (0 sugars, 0 fiber), 0 pro.

TEST KITCHEN TIP

Once you've made the ranch dressing, you can store it in an airtight container in the refrigerator for up to 2 weeks, ready to be used on salads or for dipping.

❄ VEGAN POTPIE

The ultimate comfort food takes a healthy, vegan turn! This savory, heartwarming dish is perfect for family dinners on chilly evenings.
—Taste of Home *Test Kitchen*

- -

Prep: 50 min. + chilling
Bake: 30 min. + standing
Makes: 8 servings

2½ cups all-purpose flour
1 tsp. salt
⅔ cup vegan butter-style sticks, such as Earth Balance
8 to 10 Tbsp. ice water

FILLING

1 cup cubed peeled potato
¾ cup sliced fresh carrot
½ cup vegan butter-style sticks, such as Earth Balance
½ cup chopped celery
⅓ cup chopped onion
2 garlic cloves, minced
½ cup all-purpose flour
½ tsp. salt
1 tsp. minced fresh thyme or ¼ tsp. dried thyme
¼ tsp. pepper
1½ cups vegetable broth
¾ cup unsweetened almond milk
1 pkg. (8 oz.) refrigerated vegan lightly seasoned chicken
½ cup frozen peas
½ cup frozen corn

1. In a large bowl, mix flour and salt; cut in the vegan butter until crumbly. Gradually add ice water, tossing with a fork until dough holds together when pressed. Divide dough in half. Shape each into a disk; wrap and refrigerate 1 hour or overnight.

2. Preheat oven to 425°. For the filling, place the potato and carrot in a small saucepan; add water to cover. Bring to a boil. Reduce heat; cook, covered, until crisp-tender, 8-10 minutes; drain.

3. In a large skillet, heat the vegan butter over medium-high heat. Add celery and onion; cook and stir until tender. Add the garlic; cook and stir 1 minute longer. Stir in the flour, salt, thyme and pepper until blended. Gradually stir in the broth and almond milk. Bring to a boil, stirring constantly; cook and stir until thickened, about 2 minutes. Stir in vegan chicken, peas, corn and potato-carrot mixture; remove from heat.

4. On a lightly floured surface, roll half the dough into a ⅛-in.-thick circle; transfer to a 9-in. pie plate. Trim even with rim. Add filling. Roll the remaining dough to a ⅛-in.-thick circle. Place over top of filling. Trim, seal and flute edge. Cut slits in top crust.

5. Bake until crust is golden brown and filling is bubbly, 30-35 minutes. Let stand 15 minutes before cutting.

FREEZE OPTION: Cover and freeze the unbaked pie. To use, remove from freezer 30 minutes before baking (do not thaw). Preheat oven to 425°. Place pie on a baking sheet; cover the edge loosely with foil. Bake 30 minutes. Reduce oven setting to 350°; bake for 80-90 minutes longer or until the crust is golden brown and a thermometer inserted in center reads 165°.

1 SERVING: 519 cal, 29g fat (11g sat. fat), 0 chol., 1035mg sod., 48g carb. (2g sugars, 3g fiber), 15g pro.

VEGAN STIR-FRY

Quick and easy, fresh and tasty, stir-fries are the answer to the big "What's for dinner?" question on the busiest night! Even better, they're endlessly flexible—you can scale up or down easily to serve a couple or a crowd, and can add anything you like to suit your tastes.
—Taste of Home *Test Kitchen*

- -

Prep: 20 min. • **Cook:** 15 min.
Makes: 6 servings

1   cup vegetable broth
⅓   cup soy sauce
3   Tbsp. packed brown sugar
1   Tbsp. cornstarch

3   garlic cloves, minced
1   Tbsp. minced fresh gingerroot
2   tsp. sesame oil
3   Tbsp. olive oil, divided
4   cups fresh broccoli florets
2   cups fresh sugar snap peas
1½ cups julienned carrots
1   cup julienned onions
2   cups sliced fresh mushrooms
2   cups julienned sweet red pepper
1   cup canned whole baby corn
3   green onions, thinly sliced
1   Tbsp. sesame seeds
    Hot cooked rice, optional

1. In a small bowl, combine the first 7 ingredients until smooth; set aside. In a large skillet or wok, heat 2 Tbsp. olive oil over medium-high heat. Add broccoli, snap peas, carrots and onions. Stir-fry 5 minutes. Add mushrooms, sweet red pepper, corn and remaining 1 Tbsp. olive oil; cook until vegetables are crisp-tender, 4-5 minutes longer.
2. Stir cornstarch mixture and add to pan. Bring to a boil; cook and stir until sauce is thickened, 1-2 minutes. Top with green onions and sesame seeds. If desired, serve with rice.
1 CUP: 215 cal., 10g fat (1g sat. fat), 0 chol., 768mg sod., 26g carb. (16g sugars, 5g fiber), 7g pro.

❄ VEGAN PUMPKIN BREAD

This recipe was given to me by my stepmom shortly after she and my dad got married 40 years ago. It's perfect for potlucks since it makes two loaves and is free of dairy and eggs. Everyone who tries it loves it!
—*Susan Johnson, Payne, OH*

Prep: 10 min. • **Bake:** 50 min. + cooling
Makes: 2 loaves (16 pieces each)

    3½ cups all-purpose flour
     3 cups sugar
    1½ tsp. salt
     1 tsp. baking soda
     1 tsp. ground cinnamon
     ½ tsp. ground nutmeg
     ½ tsp. baking powder
     1 can (15 oz.) pumpkin
     1 cup canola oil
     ⅔ cup water
     2 tsp. vanilla extract

1. Preheat oven to 350°. In a large bowl, whisk flour, sugar, salt, baking soda, cinnamon, nutmeg and baking powder. In another bowl, whisk pumpkin, oil, water and vanilla until blended. Add to flour mixture; stir just until moistened.
2. Transfer batter to 2 greased 9x5-in. loaf pans lined with parchment. Bake until a toothpick inserted in the center comes out clean, about 50 minutes. Cool in pans for 10 minutes before removing to wire racks to cool completely.
FREEZE OPTION: Securely wrap and freeze cooled loaf in foil. To use, thaw at room temperature.
1 PIECE: 190 cal., 7g fat (1g sat. fat), 0 chol., 159mg sod., 31g carb. (19g sugars, 1g fiber), 2g pro.

VEGAN PIZZA

Pizza is the perfect party food, since it can be customized to anyone's taste. Make the recipe as written, or add your favorite toppings to all or part of the pie!
—Taste of Home *Test Kitchen*

Prep: 40 min. • **Bake:** 25 min.
Makes: 8 servings

- 1 medium onion, sliced
- 1½ cups sliced fresh mushrooms
- ½ cup sliced sweet red pepper
- ½ cup sliced green pepper
- 2 garlic cloves, minced
- 2 Tbsp. canola oil
- ¼ tsp. each dried oregano, thyme and rosemary, crushed
- 1 recipe Basic Pizza Crust (right)
  Cornmeal
- ½ cup pizza sauce
- 2 medium tomatoes, thinly sliced
- ½ cup shredded dairy-free Parmesan-flavored cheese
- ¼ cup loosely packed basil leaves, thinly sliced, divided

1. Preheat oven to 425°. Place the first 5 ingredients on a rimmed baking sheet. Drizzle with oil and sprinkle with the seasonings; toss to coat. Roast until crisp-tender, 10-12 minutes.
2. Meanwhile, prepare the pizza dough. Roll dough into a 15-in. circle. Grease a 15- or 16-in. pizza pan and sprinkle with cornmeal. Transfer dough to the pan, building up edge slightly. Do not let the dough rise. Bake until the edge is lightly browned, 12-15 minutes.
3. Coarsely chop the roasted vegetables. Spread crust with pizza sauce; top with roasted vegetables and tomato slices. Sprinkle with Parmesan-flavored cheese and 2 Tbsp. fresh basil. Bake until crust is golden brown, 12-15 minutes longer. Top with remaining 2 Tbsp. basil.
1 PIECE: 261 cal., 10g fat (2g sat. fat), 0 chol., 231mg sod., 38g carb. (3g sugars, 3g fiber), 6g pro.

BASIC PIZZA CRUST

My aunt shared this basic pizza dough recipe quite a few years ago. I like to double the recipe and keep one baked crust in the freezer for a quick snack or meal later.
—*Beverly Anderson, Sinclairville, NY*

Prep: 10 min. + resting
Makes: 1 pizza crust

- 1 package (¼ ounce) active dry yeast
- 1 cup warm water (110° to 115°)
- 2 Tbsp. canola oil
- 1 tsp. sugar
- ¼ tsp. salt
- 2½ to 2¾ cups all-purpose flour

In a large bowl, dissolve yeast in warm water. Add oil, sugar, salt and 1½ cups flour. Beat until smooth. Stir in enough remaining flour to form a firm dough. Turn onto a floured surface; cover and let rest for 10 minutes before rolling out and using as pizza recipe directs.

MEAT LOVER OPTION
P 320

AIR-FRYER VEGAN BUTTER CAULIFLOWER

If you follow a vegetarian diet or simply love Indian butter chicken, I encourage you to try this vegan version made with cauliflower. If you don't follow a plant-based diet, you can substitute cubed chicken for the cauliflower.
—*Mihaela Metaxa-Albu, London, NY*

- -

Prep: 25 min. • **Cook:** 10 min./batch
Makes: 4 servings

1   large head cauliflower,
    cut into florets
2   Tbsp. coconut oil, melted
1   Tbsp. minced fresh gingerroot
2   garlic cloves, minced
1   tsp. garam masala
¼   tsp. salt
¼   tsp. pepper

SAUCE
1   Tbsp. olive oil
½   cup chopped onion
1   Tbsp. minced fresh gingerroot
2   garlic cloves, minced
2   tsp. garam masala
2   tsp. curry powder
1   tsp. cayenne pepper, optional
1   can (15 oz.) crushed tomatoes
1   can (13.66 oz.) coconut milk
¼   tsp. salt
¼   tsp. pepper
¼   cup chopped fresh cilantro
    Optional: Hot cooked rice, naan
    flatbreads and lime wedges

1. Preheat air fryer to 400°. In a large bowl, combine the first 7 ingredients; toss to coat. In batches if necessary, place the cauliflower in a single layer on greased tray in air-fryer basket. Cook until brown and crisp-tender, 8-10 minutes, turning once.

2. Meanwhile, in a large skillet, heat olive oil over medium-high heat. Add onion; cook and stir until tender, 4-5 minutes. Add ginger, garlic, garam masala, curry powder and, if desired, cayenne pepper; cook 1 minute longer. Stir in tomatoes, coconut milk, salt and pepper. Bring to a boil; reduce heat. Simmer, uncovered, until thickened, 10-12 minutes, stirring occasionally.

3. Stir in the cauliflower; sprinkle with cilantro. If desired, serve with rice, naan and lime wedges.

NOTE: In our testing, we find cook times vary dramatically among brands of air fryers. As a result, we give wider than normal ranges on suggested cook times. Begin checking at the first time listed and adjust as needed.

1½ CUPS: 349 cal., 27g fat (23g sat. fat), 0 chol., 584mg sod., 24g carb. (11g sugars, 7g fiber), 8g pro.

🕐 VEGAN PESTO

A jar of pesto is an incredibly handy thing to have in your refrigerator! Use it directly with pasta, lightly spread on sandwiches, tossed with vegetables or baked into bread—the flavor is unmistakable!

—Taste of Home *Test Kitchen*

- -

Takes: 10 min. • **Makes:** ¾ cup

- 2   cups fresh basil leaves
- ¼   cup pine nuts, toasted
- 2   Tbsp. nutritional yeast
- 1   Tbsp. lemon juice
- 2   garlic cloves, peeled and halved
- ½   tsp. sea salt
- ¼   cup olive oil

Pulse the first 6 ingredients in a food processor until chopped. While processing, gradually add the oil in a steady stream until mixture is smooth. Store tightly covered in refrigerator; use within 5 days.

2 TBSP: 127 cal., 13g fat (2g sat. fat), 0 chol., 163mg sod., 2g carb. (0 sugars, 1g fiber), 2g pro.

LENTIL SLOPPY JOES

When I experimented with making more vegetarian-friendly recipes, this was one of my biggest hits—we still eat it weekly! My preschooler will always eat every bite of these tangy lentil sandwiches.
—*Christina Rock, Covington, WA*

Prep: 30 min. • **Cook:** 35 min.
Makes: 14 servings

- 2 Tbsp. olive oil
- 1 large sweet onion, chopped
- 1 medium green pepper, chopped
- ½ medium sweet red pepper, chopped
- 1 medium carrot, shredded
- 6 garlic cloves, minced
- 2½ cups reduced-sodium vegetable broth
- 1 cup dried red lentils, rinsed
- 5 plum tomatoes, chopped
- 1 can (8 oz.) tomato sauce
- 2 Tbsp. chili powder
- 2 Tbsp. yellow mustard
- 4½ tsp. cider vinegar
- 2 tsp. vegan Worcestershire sauce
- 2 tsp. maple syrup
- 1½ tsp. tomato paste
- ¼ tsp. salt
- ⅛ tsp. pepper
- 14 whole wheat hamburger buns, split and toasted
  Vegan coleslaw, optional

1. In a large skillet, heat oil over medium-high heat. Add onion, peppers and carrot; cook and stir until the vegetables are crisp-tender, 6-8 minutes. Add garlic; cook 1 minute longer.
2. Add broth and lentils; bring to a boil. Reduce heat; simmer, uncovered, until lentils are tender, about 15 minutes, stirring occasionally.
3. Stir in chopped tomatoes, tomato sauce, chili powder, mustard, vinegar, Worcestershire sauce, syrup, tomato paste, salt and pepper. Bring to a boil. Reduce heat; simmer until thickened, about 10 minutes.
4. Serve on buns. If desired, top with coleslaw.
1 SANDWICH: 215 cal., 5g fat (1g sat. fat), 0 chol., 438mg sod., 38g carb. (8g sugars, 7g fiber), 8g pro. **DIABETIC EXCHANGES:** 2½ starch, 1 fat.

❄ CREAMY VEGAN CAULIFLOWER SOUP

You will love this cozy, lightened-up version of cauliflower soup. What's our secret ingredient? Coconut milk! Once it is mixed in with the vegetables and broth, the result is a delicious, silky-smooth soup that's completely dairy free.
—*Jenna Urben, McKinney, TX*

Prep: 15 min. • **Cook:** 30 min.
Makes: 7 servings

- 1 Tbsp. olive oil
- 1 small onion, chopped
- 1 medium head cauliflower, broken into florets (about 6 cups)
- 1 small potato, peeled and cubed
- 2 cans (14½ oz. each) vegetable broth
- 1 can (13.66 oz.) coconut milk
- ¾ tsp. salt
- ¼ tsp. pepper
  Nutritional yeast, chopped green onions and fresh herbs

1. In a large saucepan, heat the oil over medium heat. Add onion; cook and stir until softened, 2-3 minutes. Stir in the cauliflower, potato and broth; bring to a boil. Reduce heat; simmer, covered, about 20 minutes.
2. Remove from heat. Stir in the coconut milk, salt and pepper; cool slightly. Puree in batches in a blender or food processor until smooth. Top with nutritional yeast, green onions and fresh herbs.
FREEZE OPTION: Before adding toppings, cool soup. Freeze the soup in freezer containers. To use, thaw in refrigerator overnight. Heat through in a saucepan, stirring occasionally. Re-blend with blender or immersion blender if the coconut milk does not melt fully. Sprinkle with toppings.
1 CUP: 158 cal., 11g fat (9g sat. fat), 0 chol., 566mg sod., 12g carb. (4g sugars, 2g fiber), 3g pro.

❄ VEGAN MEATBALLS

Classic spaghetti and meatballs, meatball sandwiches, casseroles and cocktail appetizers—these savory little bites are delicious eaten one at a time or as part of a larger dish.
—Taste of Home *Test Kitchen*

- -

Prep: 30 min. • **Cook:** 10 min.
Makes: 4 servings

- 1   can (15 oz.) black beans, rinsed and drained
- 6   tsp. olive oil, divided
- 1   large shallot, minced
- 1   garlic clove, minced
- ⅓   cup quick-cooking oats
- 2   Tbsp. tomato paste
- ½   tsp. ground fennel seed
- ½   tsp. dried basil
- ¼   tsp. garlic salt

1. Preheat oven to 350°. Spread beans evenly on a parchment-lined rimmed baking pan. Bake until beans start to split open, 6-8 minutes; cool slightly.
2. Meanwhile, in a large skillet, heat 2 tsp. oil over medium heat. Add the shallot; cook and stir until tender, about 5 minutes. Add garlic; cook 1 minute longer.
3. Transfer beans to a food processor. Add the shallot mixture, oats, tomato paste and seasonings; pulse until mixture is just combined. Shape level tablespoons of dough into balls.
4. In the same skillet, heat the remaining 4 tsp. oil over medium heat. In batches if needed, cook meatballs until browned and cooked through, 6-8 minutes, turning occasionally.
FREEZE OPTION: Cover and freeze uncooked meatballs on waxed paper-lined baking sheets until firm. Transfer to freezer containers; return to freezer. To use, cook meatballs as directed.
ABOUT 4 MEATBALLS: 186 cal., 7g fat (1g sat. fat), 0 chol., 331mg sod., 23g carb. (2g sugars, 5g fiber), 7g pro.
DIABETIC EXCHANGES: 1½ starch, 1½ fat, 1 lean meat.

🕐 SMOKY VEGAN BACON

This recipe is a must for any vegetarian! You won't believe how much this tastes like the real thing.
—Taste of Home *Test Kitchen*

- -

Prep: 15 min. • **Cook:** 5 min./batch
Makes: 12 servings

- 1   large carrot
- 2   Tbsp. maple syrup
- 1   tsp. smoked paprika
- ½   tsp. garlic powder
- ¼   tsp. onion powder
- ⅛   tsp. salt
- ⅛   tsp. liquid smoke
- 2   Tbsp. olive oil

1. With a mandoline or vegetable peeler, cut the carrot into long, thin strips. In a shallow bowl, whisk the maple syrup, paprika, garlic powder, onion powder, salt and liquid smoke. Dip carrot slices into the syrup mixture, allowing excess to drip off.
2. In a large skillet, heat oil over medium heat. Cook carrot slices in batches until browned, 4-6 minutes, turning once.
1 PIECE: 32 cal., 2g fat (0 sat. fat), 0 chol., 29mg sod., 3g carb. (2g sugars, 0 fiber), 0 pro.

DID YOU KNOW?

Real liquid smoke is made from actual smoke—captured, condensed and filtered to remove impurities. Look for "smoke" or "smoke flavor" on the ingredient list. While smoke itself contains carcinogens, liquid smoke is actually safer to eat than food cooked over an open fire, due to the filtering process.

VEGAN MACARONI SALAD

All the classic flavors come through in this vegan macaroni salad, from the pickle relish to the ground mustard. The only thing you'll be missing is leftovers!
—Taste of Home *Test Kitchen*

Takes: 30 min. • **Makes:** 8 servings

- 2 cups uncooked elbow macaroni
- 1 cup vegan mayonnaise
- 2 Tbsp. sweet pickle relish
- ¾ tsp. ground mustard
- ¼ tsp. salt
- ⅛ tsp. pepper
- 1 celery rib, chopped
- 1 small carrot, chopped
- ¼ cup chopped onion
  Dash paprika

1. Cook macaroni according to package directions; drain and rinse with cold water. Cool completely.
2. For dressing, in a small bowl, combine mayonnaise, pickle relish, mustard, salt and pepper. In a large bowl, combine the macaroni, celery, carrot and onion. Add dressing and toss gently to coat.
3. Refrigerate until serving. Garnish with paprika.

¾ CUP: 93 cal., 1g fat (0 sat. fat), 0 chol., 114mg sod., 20g carb. (2g sugars, 1g fiber), 3g pro.

VEGAN CASHEW CREAM OF BROCCOLI SOUP

To me, Sundays are for rest and spending time with family. This soup reminds me of Sunday family dinners because they always request it. I love making this because it's not complicated and I can get dinner on the table in about an hour.
—*Christine King, Vista, CA*

Prep: 20 min. • **Cook:** 30 min.
Makes: 8 servings (2 qt.)

- 1 bunch broccoli, cut into florets
- 5 cups water, divided
- ½ cup raw cashews
- 3 Tbsp. vegan butter-style sticks, such as Earth Balance
- 1 medium onion, chopped
- 1 Tbsp. minced fresh sage
- 1 Tbsp. minced fresh thyme
- 1 tsp. garlic powder
- ½ tsp. onion powder
- 2 medium Yukon Gold potatoes, peeled and cut into 1-in. pieces
- 1 bay leaf
- 4½ tsp. no chicken vegetable base or vegetable base
- 1 Tbsp. nutritional yeast
- ½ tsp. salt
- ¼ tsp. pepper

1. In a large saucepan, place a steamer basket over 1 in. water. Place broccoli in basket. Bring water to a boil. Reduce heat to maintain a simmer; steam, covered, until just tender, 5-6 minutes. Let broccoli cool, then coarsely chop and set aside.

2. Place 1 cup water and the cashews in a blender or food processor; cover and process until smooth. Set aside. In a Dutch oven, melt vegan butter over medium-high heat. Add onion; cook and stir until just tender, 3-4 minutes. Add sage, thyme, garlic powder and onion powder; cook 1 minute longer. Add potatoes, bay leaf, vegetable base and the remaining 4 cups water.

3. Bring to a boil; reduce heat. Simmer, covered, until potatoes are tender, 10-12 minutes. Stir in nutritional yeast, salt, pepper, cashew mixture and the broccoli. Heat through. Discard bay leaf.

1 CUP: 166 cal., 8g fat (2g sat. fat), 0 chol., 224mg sod., 21g carb. (3g sugars, 4g fiber), 5g pro. **DIABETIC EXCHANGES:** 1½ starch, 1½ fat.

VEGAN GRAVY

This vegan gravy is really easy to make. I like to use it for poutine, but it's perfect with mashed potatoes, stuffing and other foods too.

—*Lisa Grant, Kingston, ON*

Takes: 30 min. • **Makes:** 1¾ cups

- 2 Tbsp. vegan butter-style sticks
- 1 medium onion, finely chopped
- 2 Tbsp. all-purpose flour
- 2 Tbsp. cornstarch
- 1½ cups vegetable broth
- 1 to 2 Tbsp. soy sauce
- 1 tsp. yeast extract (such as Vegemite)
- ½ tsp. garlic salt
- ¼ tsp. pepper

1. In a small saucepan, melt vegan butter over medium heat. Add onion; cook and stir until tender, 3-5 minutes. Stir in flour until blended; cook and stir until lightly golden brown, 8-9 minutes (do not burn).
2. Whisk cornstarch and broth. Gradually whisk into flour mixture. Bring to a boil, stirring constantly; cook and stir until thickened, 2-3 minutes. Stir in soy sauce, yeast extract, garlic salt and pepper.
2 TBSP: 28 cal., 2g fat (1g sat. fat), 0 chol., 295mg sod., 3g carb. (0 sugars, 0 fiber), 0 pro.

TEST KITCHEN TIP

You can customize this recipe by adding your favorite herbs. Fresh rosemary, thyme or oregano would be perfect!

VEGAN GREEN GODDESS POTATO SALAD

Don't be fooled by the green color—this salad is delicious! It's perfect for potlucks as it's a crowd-pleaser that even those with dietary restrictions can enjoy!
—*Laura Wilhelm, West Hollywood, CA*

Prep: 30 min. + chilling
Makes: 8 servings

- 2 lbs. baby red potatoes, halved
- 4 green onions
- 2 medium ripe avocados, peeled and pitted
- ½ cup sprigs fresh parsley, stems removed
- ½ cup vegan mayonnaise
- 3 tarragon sprigs, stems removed
- 2 tsp. capers, drained
- 1 tsp. seasoned salt
- 1 celery rib, finely chopped
  Sliced radishes

1. Place potatoes in a large saucepan; add water to cover. Bring to a boil. Reduce heat; cook, uncovered, until tender, 8-10 minutes.

2. Meanwhile, chop the green onions, reserving white portions. Add green portions to a blender. Add the avocados, parsley, mayonnaise, tarragon, capers and seasoned salt. Cover and process until blended, scraping down the side as needed.

3. Drain the potatoes; transfer to a large bowl. Add celery, white portions of green onions, and the dressing; toss to coat. Refrigerate, covered, for at least 1 hour. Before serving, top with radishes and additional parsley.

¾ CUP: 235 cal., 15g fat (2g sat. fat), 0 chol., 295mg sod., 24g carb. (1g sugars, 4g fiber), 3g pro. **DIABETIC EXCHANGES:** 3 fat, 1½ starch.

❄ VEGAN SQUASH SOUP WITH NAAN CROUTONS

This butternut squash soup is full of flavor—you won't miss the meat or dairy! The added can of pumpkin helps to make the soup creamy and smooth, while the coconut milk adds a light sweetness. I love to make this comforting soup as the seasons change!
—*Audrey Fell, Nashville, TN*

Prep: 45 min. • **Cook:** 25 min.
Makes: 8 servings (about 2¾ qt.)

1   large butternut squash, peeled and cut into 1-in. cubes (about 8 cups)
3   Tbsp. olive oil, divided
1   tsp. salt, divided
¼   tsp. pepper
1   medium onion, chopped
1   Tbsp. minced fresh gingerroot
2   garlic cloves, minced
1   tsp. ground turmeric
½   tsp. ground cumin
1   carton (32 oz.) reduced-sodium vegetable broth
1   can (15 oz.) pumpkin
1   can (13.66 oz.) coconut milk
2   naan flatbreads, cut into 1-in. squares
    Optional: Minced fresh cilantro, crushed red pepper flakes and plain soy yogurt

1. Preheat oven to 400°. Place squash in a shallow roasting pan; drizzle with 1 Tbsp. oil. Sprinkle with ½ tsp. salt and the pepper. Roast until tender, 25-30 minutes, turning once.

2. Reduce oven setting to 350°. In a Dutch oven, heat 1 Tbsp. oil over medium-high heat. Add the onion; cook and stir until tender, 5-7 minutes. Add ginger, garlic, turmeric, cumin and remaining ½ tsp. salt; cook 1 minute longer. Stir in broth, pumpkin and roasted squash. Bring to a boil; reduce heat. Simmer, uncovered, 15-20 minutes to allow flavors to blend. Add coconut milk; cook 5 minutes longer. Cool slightly. In a blender, cover and process soup in batches until smooth. Return pureed mixture to pan; cook and stir until heated through.

3. Meanwhile, place naan on a baking sheet. Drizzle with remaining 1 Tbsp. oil; toss to coat. Bake until crispy, 12-15 minutes, stirring once. Serve soup with naan croutons and toppings as desired.

FREEZE OPTION: Freeze cooled soup in freezer containers. To use, partially thaw in refrigerator overnight. Heat through in a saucepan, stirring occasionally; add broth if necessary.

1⅓ CUPS: 249 cal., 14g fat (9g sat. fat), 1mg chol., 506mg sod., 29g carb. (8g sugars, 7g fiber), 4g pro.

CRISPY AIR-FRIED TOFU

These delectable little bites are crispy on the outside, and smooth and creamy on the inside. You will keep coming back. Don't skip the first step—pressing out the liquid. This ensures that your tofu has the right texture and doesn't get gummy.
—*Ralph Jones, San Diego, CA*

Prep: 15 min. + standing • **Cook:** 15 min.
Makes: 4 servings

- 1 pkg. (16 oz.) firm or extra-firm tofu
- 2 Tbsp. soy sauce
- 1 Tbsp. olive oil
- 1 Tbsp. sesame oil
- 2 tsp. cornstarch
- 1 tsp. garlic powder
- ¾ tsp. salt
- ¼ tsp. pepper
  Sliced green onions, optional

1. Blot tofu dry. Cut into ¾-in. cubes. Place on a clean kitchen towel; cover with another towel. Place a cutting board on top; gently place a large cast-iron skillet on top. Let stand 10 minutes.
2. Meanwhile, preheat air fryer to 375°. In a shallow dish, whisk together the soy sauce, olive oil, sesame oil, cornstarch, garlic powder, salt and pepper. Add tofu to soy mixture; turn to coat.
3. Place tofu on greased tray in air fryer basket. Cook until golden brown and crispy, 12-15 minutes. Garnish with green onions if desired.
1 SERVING: 159 cal., 12g fat (2g sat. fat), 0 chol., 911mg sod., 4g carb. (1g sugars, 0 fiber), 10g pro.

VEGAN POTATO SOUP

It can be a challenge to find a great vegan potato soup, as most recipes contain cream. But this delicious version keeps the luxurious texture without the dairy.
—*Jenna Urben, McKinney, TX*

Prep: 15 min. • **Cook:** 35 min.
Makes: 8 servings (2 qt.)

- 6 medium potatoes, peeled and chopped
- 3 celery ribs, chopped
- 2 medium carrots, chopped
- 4 cups vegetable broth
- 2 cups water
- 6 Tbsp. vegan butter-style sticks, such as Earth Balance buttery sticks
- 1 medium onion, chopped
- 6 Tbsp. all-purpose flour
- 1 tsp. salt
- ½ tsp. pepper
- 1½ cups soy milk
  Optional: Minced fresh parsley, shredded vegan cheddar-flavored cheese and nutritional yeast

1. In a Dutch oven, cook potatoes, celery and the carrots in broth and water until tender, 20-25 minutes. Drain, reserving liquid and setting vegetables aside.
2. In the same pan, melt the vegan butter over medium-high heat. Add onion; cook and stir until tender, 3-4 minutes. Stir in flour, salt and pepper; gradually add soy milk. Bring to a boil, cook and stir until thickened, about 2 minutes. Gently stir in cooked vegetables. Add 2½ cups or more of the reserved cooking liquid until soup is the desired consistency. Serve with toppings as desired.
1 CUP: 232 cal., 9g fat (4g sat. fat), 0 chol., 779mg sod., 33g carb. (5g sugars, 3g fiber), 5g pro.

QUICK BEAN & RICE BURRITOS

These hearty and zippy burritos can be whipped up in a jiffy, so you'll have a quick dinner solution on even the busiest days.
—*Kimberly Hardison, Maitland, FL*

Takes: 25 min. • **Makes:** 8 servings

- 1½ cups water
- 1½ cups uncooked instant brown rice
- 1 Tbsp. olive oil
- 1 medium green pepper, diced
- ½ cup chopped onion
- 1 tsp. minced garlic
- 1 Tbsp. chili powder
- 1 tsp. ground cumin
- ⅛ tsp. crushed red pepper flakes
- 1 can (15 oz.) black beans, rinsed and drained
- 1 cup salsa
- 10 flour tortillas (8 in.), warmed
  Optional: Avocado slices, lime wedges, vegan sour cream and salsa

1. In a small saucepan, bring water to a boil. Add rice. Return to a boil. Reduce heat; cover and simmer for 5 minutes. Remove from the heat. Let stand until water is absorbed, about 5 minutes.
2. Meanwhile, in a large skillet, heat oil over medium-high heat. Add the green pepper and onion; cook and stir until tender, 3-4 minutes. Add garlic; cook 1 minute longer. Stir in chili powder, cumin and red pepper flakes until combined. Add beans and the rice; cook and stir until heated through, 4-6 minutes. Stir in the salsa and remove from heat.
3. Spoon about ½ cup filling off-center on each tortilla. Fold the sides and ends over the filling and roll up. Serve with optional toppings as desired.
1 BURRITO: 345 cal., 7g fat (1g sat. fat), 0 chol., 544mg sod., 61g carb. (2g sugars, 6g fiber), 10g pro.

RECIPE INDEX

A

Air-Fryer Chickpea Fritters with
  Sweet-Spicy Sauce...........251
Air-Fryer General Tso's
  Cauliflower...................36
Air-Fryer Italian Bread Salad
  with Olives 156
Air-Fryer Portobello Melts.........81
Air-Fryer Salsa Black Bean
  Burgers......................100
Air-Fryer Spinach Feta
  Turnovers....................10
Air-Fryer Vegan Butter
  Cauliflower...................302
All Veggie Lasagna 58
Appetizer Wreath.................229
Apple-Honey Dutch Baby........198
Arugula & Mushroom
  Breakfast Pizza...............193
Asparagus & Red Pepper
  Frittata 198
Asparagus Soup with Lemon
  Creme Fraiche................131
Avocado & Artichoke Pasta
  Salad........................155
Avocado Goat Cheese Truffles 255

B

Baked Brie with Mushrooms......229
Basic Pizza Crust................300
Basil-Tomato Grilled Cheese.......94
Berry Breakfast Parfaits 270
Berry Brownie Pizza 277
Best Deviled Eggs 255
Black Bean-Pumpkin Soup 151
Black Bean Quinoa Bowls 112
Black Bean Rice Burgers 92
Black Bean Tortilla Casserole......30

Black Bean Veggie Burger
  Salad 158
Blackberry-Mango Crumble 286
Blood Orange Upside-Down
  Cupcakes 279
Blueberry Cornmeal Pancakes....203
Blueberry Crunch Breakfast
  Bake........................207
Broccoli Chowder 134
Broccoli-Mushroom Bubble
  Bake........................195
Brussels Sprouts Salad 163
Buffalo Tofu Wrap 87
Bulgur Chili....................142
Butternut Burrito Bowl..........19
Buttery Radish Baguette 244

C

Caribbean Potato Soup..........133
Carrot Broccoli Soup............145
Cashew Butter Cookies..........268
Cashew Cheese 248
Cast-Iron Peach Crostata........289
Cayenne Pretzels...............242
Cheddar Cauliflower Soup.......133
Cheese Enchiladas 23
Cheese-Stuffed Cherry
  Tomatoes 235
Cheese Tortellini with
  Tomatoes & Corn.............56
Cheesy Quesadillas.............247
Cheesy Vegetable Egg Dish 189
Chickpea & Chipotle Tostadas......19
Chickpea & Potato Curry 31
Chipotle Focaccia with Garlic-Onion
  Topping 244
Chocolate Squash Mousse........291
Cider Cheese Fondue 243

Coconut-Ginger Chickpeas &
  Tomatoes 35
Coconut Lentils with Rice........121
Colorful Brunch Frittata.........190
Contest-Winning Easy Tiramisu ...275
Cool Beans Salad...............172
Corn & Black Bean Salad........163
Corn & Squash Quesadillas.......83
Corn, Rice & Bean Burritos 41
Cornmeal Towers with
  Strawberries & Cream.........282
Couscous Tabbouleh with
  Fresh Mint & Feta 105
Creamy Pasta Primavera.........71
Creamy Vegan Cauliflower
  Soup 304
Crisp Caraway Twists 248
Crispy Air-Fried Tofu............313
Crispy Rice Patties with
  Vegetables & Eggs 42
Crispy Tofu with Black Pepper
  Sauce........................33
Cumin-Spiced Lentil Burgers 91
Curried Coleslaw 165
Curried Egg Salad 92
Curried Tofu with Rice 28
Curry Pomegranate Protein
  Bowl........................16

D

Dilly Chickpea Salad
  Sandwiches 96
Dilly Veggie Pizza...............243

E

Easy Almond Joy Chia Pudding ...282
Easy Moroccan Chickpea Stew.....22
Easy Pesto Pizza 70

Easy Rhubarb Sauce............289
Easy Vegetable Lasagna 48
Edamame Corn Carrot Salad 182
Egg-Free Spiced Pancakes 214
Eggplant Flatbread Pizzas........51
Eggplant Muffuletta.............91
Eggplant Parmesan.............165
Eggplant Roll-Ups 32

F

Farro Salad with Charred Shishito
   Peppers & Corn...............119
Fennel Wild Rice Salad..........121
Festive Fall Falafel..............80
Festive Three-Grain Salad........122
Feta Asparagus Frittata 196
Feta Bruschetta 224
Fiery Stuffed Poblanos...........38
Fire-Roasted Tomato
   Minestrone...................146
Four-Cheese Stuffed Shells.......77
Fresh Fruit Bowl 164
Fresh Herb Vegetable Dip 226

G

Garbanzo-Stuffed Mini Peppers...239
Garbanzo-Vegetable Green Curry...25
Garden Salad with Chickpeas.....180
Garlic-Herb Mini Quiches........234
Garlic Tomato Bruschetta 238
Ginger Butternut Squash
   Bisque......................148
Gingered Apricot-Apple
   Crumble 266
Grandma's Tomato Soup 138
Great Grain Salad 111
Great Granola...................210
Greek Couscous Salad 106
Greek Isle Pizza 57
Greek Spinach Bake 29
Greek Tofu Scramble 196
Green Beans & Radish Salad with
   Tarragon Pesto 185

Green Chile Grilled Cheese Melt....85
Green Chile Quiche Squares 206
Grilled Banana Brownie
   Sundaes 276
Grilled Black Bean & Pineapple
   Burgers.....................96
Grilled Chickpea Salad
   Sandwich 86
Grilled Cranberry Pear Crumble...272
Grilled Eggplant Panini with
   Basil Aioli 98
Grilled Goat Cheese & Arugula
   Sandwiches 88
Grilled Potatoes & Peppers 177
Grilled Romaine Salad 166
Grilled Stone Fruits with
   Balsamic Syrup..............274
Grilled Veggie Sandwiches with
   Cilantro Pesto 95

H

Heirloom Tomato Salad 171
Herbed Artichoke Cheese
   Tortellini 59
Herby Pea Salad 175
Homemade Manicotti 68
Homemade Meatless Spaghetti
   Sauce......................60
Honey-Roasted Pears...........258
Hummus Pasta Salad...........167

I

Italian Garden Frittata...........194
Italian Tomato Cucumber Salad...178

K

Kale Quinoa Salad..............117
Kale Slaw Spring Salad 172
Kimchi Fried Rice...............104

L

Lactose-Free Spinach Lasagna 60
Lemon Ice 288

Lemon Olive Oil Cake 263
Lemon Rice Salad 106
Lemony Chickpeas 15
Lentil Burritos 42
Lentil Sloppy Joes..............304
Lentil Taco Cups...............231
Loaded Mexican Pizza 76

M

Madeira Cake 260
Mama Rachel's Mediterranean
   Pizza 54
Marinated Almond-Stuffed
   Olives......................237
Marinated Broccoli 183
Marinated Cauliflower Salad......169
Marinated Mozzarella & Tomato
   Appetizers 230
Mediterranean Bulgur Salad.....111
Mediterranean Veggie
   Brunch Puff.................212
Melomakarona..................264
Migas Breakfast Tacos 193
Mini Italian Frittatas 209
Mini Mac & Cheese Bites 234
Minted Rice with Garbanzo
   Curry 108
Monterey Artichoke Panini.......100
Moroccan Cauliflower & Almond
   Soup 140
Moroccan Stuffed Mushrooms 232
Mozzarella Mushrooms with
   Garlic Toast 12
Mushroom Broccoli Pizza 36
Mushroom-Gouda Quiche 200

O

Oatmeal Breakfast Bars.........219
Oatmeal Caramel Apple
   Cookies 272
One-Pot Black Bean Enchilada
   Pasta......................15
Onion Brie Appetizers...........225

Onion-Garlic Hash Browns 209
Onion Orange Salad 173
Open-Faced Frico Egg
    Sandwich 218
Orzo-Lentil Rice. 112
Over-the-Top Baked Ziti 64

P

Pasta Fagioli Soup Mix 129
Peanut Butter Popcorn Bars 286
Pear-Stuffed French Toast with
    Brie, Cranberries & Pecans. 215
Pecan Wheat Waffles 212
Penne with Veggies & Black
    Beans .54
Peppered Cilantro Rice. 115
Pesto Bean Soup 130
Pesto Quinoa Salad. 114
Pesto Vegetable Pizza. 63
Philly Cheese Fakes 89
Pinto Bean Zucchini Boats. 13
Pizza Margherita 72
Portobello Polenta Stacks 16
Pressure-Cooker Raisin Nut
    Oatmeal. 199
Pressure-Cooker Vegetable
    Wild Rice Soup. 138
Pull-Apart Herb Bread 232
Pumpkin Crumble 259

Q

Quick Bean & Rice Burritos 314
Quinoa Fresh Fig &
    Honey-Balsamic Parfaits. 267

R

Raspberry Patch Crumb Bars 263
Raspberry Sorbet 285
Ravioli Appetizer Pops 226
Rhubarb Tart. 269
Roasted Buffalo Cauliflower
    Bites. .236
Roasted Pepper Potato Soup 145

Roasted Pumpkin Nachos 237
Roasted Vegetable & Chevre
    Quiche 220
Rustic Tuscan Pepper
    Bruschetta 247

S

Saucy Mac & Cheese. 65
Saucy Tempeh Sloppy Joes. 83
Savory Party Bread. 241
Shaved Fennel Salad 160
Shredded Kale & Brussels
    Sprouts Salad 169
Simple Vegetarian Slow-Cooked
    Beans .159
Slow-Cooked Black Bean Soup. . . .127
Slow-Cooked Blueberry Grunt 260
Slow-Cooker Baked Apples 264
Slow-Cooker Thai Butternut
    Squash Peanut Soup 146
Slow-Cooker Veggie Lasagna 67
Smoky Cauliflower 160
Smoky Tempeh Bacon 216
Smoky Vegan Bacon 306
Southern Okra Bean Stew 35
Southwest Tortilla Pie. 11
Spanakopita Pinwheels 252
Special Stuffed Strawberries 265
Spiced Blueberry Quinoa 205
Spicy Edamame. 254
Spicy Peanut Soup 150
Spicy Roasted Carrot Hummus . . .252
Spinach & Broccoli Enchiladas. 40
Spinach Lasagna Roll-Ups 72
Spinach Pizza. 49
Spinach Quesadillas 85
Stir-Fry Rice Bowl 20
Strawberry Bliss Omelet 203
Strawberry Salsa. 250
Strawberry Sorbet. 281
Stuffed Pasta Shells 62
Stuffed Vegetarian Shells 50
Succulent Strawberry Soup 134

Summer Avocado Salad. 177
Summer Squash Salad 170
Sunflower Strawberry Salad 180
Super Grilled Cheese
    Sandwiches 88
Sweet Potato & Egg Skillet 200
Sweet Potato Curry. 45
Sweet Potato Lentil Stew. 28
Sweet Potato Pancakes with
    Cinnamon Cream 188
Sweet Potato Tortellini with
    Hazelnut Sauce 75
Sweet Potatoes with Cilantro
    Black Beans 184

T

Tabbouleh 109
Tasty Marinated Tomatoes. 179
Tex-Mex Grain Bowl. 220
Tex-Mex Potato Salad 179
The Best Eggplant Parmesan 44
Three-Cheese Quiche 190
Tofu Salad 154
Tomato Basil Tortellini Soup 137
Tomato Mac & Cheese 67
Tortellini with Tomato Spinach
    Cream Sauce 71
Turnip Greens Salad 174

V

Vegan Bechamel Sauce 294
Vegan Cashew Cream of Broccoli
    Soup .309
Vegan Chocolate Cupcakes 281
Vegan Gravy 310
Vegan Green Goddess Potato
    Salad .311
Vegan Macaroni Salad 308
Vegan Meatballs. 306
Vegan Pecan Pie 284
Vegan Pesto 303
Vegan Pizza. 300
Vegan Potato Soup 314

Vegan Potpie. 297
Vegan Pumpkin Bread 299
Vegan Ranch Dressing 295
Vegan Squash Soup with
  Naan Croutons. 312
Vegan Stir-Fry 298
Vegan Tropical Magic Bars 279
Vegan Vanilla Cupcakes 290
Vegetable Barley Bake 116
Vegetarian Bean Tacos. 39
Vegetarian Black Bean Pasta 57
Vegetarian Buffalo Dip 241
Vegetarian Pea Soup. 137
Vegetarian Potatoes au Gratin 21
Vegetarian Red Bean Chili 141
Vegetarian Skillet Enchiladas 25
Vegetarian Split Pea Soup. 126
Vegetarian Tacos 26
Veggie Brown Rice Wraps 99
Veggie Fajitas 26
Veggie Frittata 205
Veggie-Packed Strata 211

W

Watermelon Fruit Pizza 207
White Beans & Bow Ties. 53
Whole Grain Banana Pancakes. . . . 216

Y

Yellow Rice & Black Bean Salad . . . 123

Z

Ziti Bake. 68
Zucchini Crust Pizza 53
Zucchini Patties 156
Zucchini Walnut Cake 271

Need an option for hungry meat lovers? No problem!
We've paired easy-to-prepare, affordable meats with more than 30 recipes.

RECIPE NAME & PAGE NUMBER	SHREDDED ROTISSERIE CHICKEN	DELI TURKEY OR HAM	CUBED COOKED HAM	SLICED SMOKED SAUSAGE	CRUMBLED COOKED ITALIAN SAUSAGE	TACO MEAT	COOKED BEEF STEAK	COOKED GROUND BEEF OR TURKEY
Air Fryer General Tso's Cauliflower, 36	•							
Cheesy Quesadillas, 247		•				•		
Cheesy Vegetable Egg Dish, 189			•	•				
Creamy Pasta Primavera, 71			•					
Fiery Stuffed Poblanos, 38						•		•
Fire-Roasted Tomato Minestrone, 147	•				•			•
Garden Salad with Chickpeas, 180		•					•	
Hummus Pasta Salad, 167			•					
Mini Italian Frittatas, 209					•			
Mini Mac & Cheese Bites, 234			•					
Monterey Artichoke Panini, 100		•						
One-Pot Black Bean Enchilada Pasta, 15	•							
Open-Faced Frico Egg Sandwich, 218		•						
Over-the-Top Baked Ziti, 64					•			•
Pasta Fagioli Soup Mix, 129			•		•			
Penne with Veggies & Black Beans, 54			•	•				
Ravioli Appetizer Pops, 226				•				
Roasted Pumpkin Nachos, 237						•		
Southern Okra Bean Stew, 35				•				
Spinach Quesadillas, 85	•							
Stuffed Vegetarian Shells, 50					•			
Sweet Potato Lentil Stew, 28					•			
Sweet Potatoes with Cilantro Black Beans, 184	•					•		
Tomato Mac & Cheese, 67			•					
Vegan Pizza, 300	•		•		•			
Vegan Stir-Fry, 298	•						•	
Vegetarian Pea Soup, 137			•	•				
Vegetarian Potatoes Au Gratin, 21			•					
Veggie Brown Rice Wraps, 99	•			•				
Veggie Fajitas, 26							•	
Zucchini Crust Pizza, 53					•		•	